THILLAINATHAN PATHMANATHAN
ANNE CHRISTINA RECK

# Also from Veloce

# www.veloce.co.uk

First published in October 2019 by Veloce Publishing Limited, Veloce House, Parkway Farm Business Park, Middle Farm Way, Poundbury, Dorchester DT1 3AR, England. Tel +44 (0)1305 260068 / Fax 01305 250479 / e-mail info@veloce.co.uk / web www.veloce.co.uk or www.velocebooks.com.
ISBN: 978-1-787114-33-3; UPC: 6-36847-01433-9.

KTM X-BOW

**0642**

THILLAINATHAN PATHMANATHAN

ANNE CHRISTINA RECK

# CONTENTS

This book only exists because many people have been hugely generous with their time and their expertise. Foremost amongst these are the people at KISKA, Dallara and, of course, KTM, who told us that we could have access to all their resources and then actually provided what they had promised. Writing this book has been like becoming part of a family. Thank you KISKA, Dallara and KTM for being so welcoming to two almost virginal automotive authors, who have day jobs as eye surgeons. As the writing of this book draws to a close, we already feel a sense of partial bereavement, such has been the close collaboration throughout. From start to finish, KISKA, Dallara and KTM appear to have been as excited about this book as we have been.

In purely chronological order, we first met with Averill Batman who made the visit to KISKA actually possible, and we are hugely grateful to her for her kind and gentle efficiency. Meeting Andrea Bebber was initially daunting, as we knew that we were being carefully appraised by a marketing expert, who was responsible not only for KISKA, but also for the whole KTM conglomerate. Again, her gentle approach soon put us at rest, and her extensive contribution to this book, despite her very busy schedule, genuinely deserves our sincere thanks. Sebastien Stassin, Chief Creative Officer at KISKA, Partner at KISKA, Lead Designer of the X-BOW, and fellow owner of this extraordinary car, just oozed enthusiasm for the book right from the start, and we are hugely indebted to him for his deep involvement with this book. Sebastien, what more can we say other than to thank you, and to ask you to keep on enjoying your own X-BOW. At the start of our meeting at KISKA with Andrea and Sebastien, we were told that the meeting would last precisely fifteen minutes, so when we were still discussing the book after almost two hours, we had reason to feel optimistic. We are sorry that you were both very late for your next meeting.

The lead author has been in intermittent contact with Michael Woelfling, the long-standing Managing Director of KTM Sportcar, since 2010. Soon after our purchase of Chassis 0642, Michael arranged for us to have a full and detailed tour of the Graz factory, and also invited us as KTM's guests to the Pannonia-Ring X-BOW Battle race meeting. Manfred Wolf spent many hours with us at the Graz facility, talking us through each and every assembly station in detail, introducing us to the technician-engineers on the floor, and patiently answering all our questions. Manfred was also a most generous and entertaining host at a truly delicious Styrian lunch that we still talk about. Thank you Michael and Manfred – it is difficult to fully express our appreciation for all your help. Last, but very much not least, our very sincere thanks to Hartwig Breitenbach. What a truly lovely man – so knowledgeable and so generous with his knowledge, and yet so modest. Thank you, Hartwig, this book would not be half what it is without your extensive help.

And finally on to Dallara. To meet the legend that is Giampaolo Dallara is special, and to find a man who is of the same mould as his Lamborghini contemporaries, Paolo Stanzani and Umberto Marchesi of Countach fame, is to meet vintage Italian suaveness and affability of the finest kind. Both authors consider themselves fortunate to have met these three men, a throwback to a bygone era where gentle politeness was taken for granted. Giampaolo Dallara arranged for us to be taken around the whole Dallara Research and Development Facility by Enrico Giuliani. Never have we met so many PhD holders concentrated within such a small area. It was really stimulating to be in such an environment. The lead author got quite excited when he found out that Dallara was soon opening an Academy with one and two-year courses in specialised Automotive Engineering. His dreams of a sabbatical were soon dashed on hearing that the minimum entry requirement for these courses was a PhD in Aerodynamics or a PhD in Mechanical Engineering. Enrico Giuliani who was intimately involved with the development of the KTM X-BOW was impressively prepared for our visit – a powerpoint presentation was ready, and he too patiently answered our many questions. Within a few days of our return to the United Kingdom, a full information pack with many, many photographs arrived in our inbox. All this was done with true graciousness – the above mentioned vintage Italian gentlemanliness clearly lives on in the next generation. Thank you Ing, Dallara and Enrico.

We are also immensely grateful to Rod Grainger, Publisher of Veloce Publishing for having the courage to take on enthusiastic, but almost virginal authors. Jeff 'Jai' Danton was again presented with a jumble of words and a tangle of photos, and his expertise in design, digital art and layout speaks for itself. Jai also wrote most of the captions, although the responsibility for their accuracy remains all ours. It is difficult to overstate Jai's contribution and involvement in this book – we are especially grateful to him.

Thanks to editor Becky Taylor, as well as Kevin Quinn, Kevin Atkins, Emma Shanes and Tim Nevinson, who all stood guard over this book; we are very grateful to you all for your invaluable help.

Aran Pasupathy has helped both authors with computing input throughout the preparation and assembly of this book. He has a detailed understanding of how computer systems work, but more importantly he is patient, and is able to impart his knowledge effectively. These are important skills, and we are grateful to have benefited from them in the course of writing this book. Thank you, Aran.

We are also very lucky in having come across Craig Johnson, a Master Audi Technician-Engineer. He has looked after Chassis 0642 during our ownership tenure. His involvement is detailed in the main text, and we would like to thank him for his contribution to the Expert Opinions chapter. We do not entrust the care of our steeds to others lightly, but in Craig we found expertise married to enthusiasm – always a winning combination. Craig has worked on numerous different supercar marques throughout his career, and recently won an European-wide contest for most accomplished Technician-Engineer. Craig, thank you

ACKNOWLEDGEMENTS

for your involvement with this book. We and Chassis 0642 can rest easy with you around. Your skill and easy manner will always be wanted and appreciated by a wide audience.

Ian Hunt has been a guiding hand throughout the lead author's short career as an automotive writer. Ian is an expert photographer, has a fine eye for scrutinising text and is highly knowledgeable on all things related to cars. He was hugely generous in providing photographs and guidance for the lead author's first book on the Murcielago. With this KTM X-BOW book, he was totally instrumental in getting an additional chapter included. At a time when the authors were feeling weak, Ian firmly espoused the need for a chapter on the X-BOW's rivals, and followed this up by providing almost all the photographs for this chapter. Ian, thank you for your encouragement, guidance and photographs.

Jim Holder and Olivia Pina of *Autocar* magazine, Stuart Gallagher, Nick Trott and Jane Townsend-Emms of *EVO* magazine, and Colin Overland of *Car* magazine have all been most kind and encouraging throughout this enterprise, and we would like to thank them for allowing us to use selected excerpts from *Autocar*, *EVO* and *Car* in this book.

The Beaulieu National Motor Museum in the United Kingdom is the second home for many of our cars, and we are very grateful to Jonathan Day, Tim David Wood, Russel Bowman and Stephen Munn for the use of the wonderful images taken in the Beaulieu photographic studio.

Mark Hosken at Backdraft Motorsport is an acknowledged expert on aftermarket tuning and development of the X-BOW. His company is actively involved in motorsport, and he has extensive experience in servicing, modifying, and upgrading supercars. Thank you, Mark for your contribution to the Expert Opinions chapter.

We were very lucky in meeting many racing drivers, both amateur and professional, at the X-BOW Battle race meeting at the Pannonia-Ring race circuit in Hungary in September 2018. Thank you to everyone who took the time out to talk to us, but we need to highlight the following racers who went out of their way to give us a three-dimensional view of the X-BOW as a racing car: Naomi Schiff, Mads Siljehaug, Eric Paradis, Gabor Herget and Tomas Kwolek. Such an international mix – five different nationalities!

Thank you again, everyone – the truth is that this book would not be what it is, or possibly not in existence at all, without all your enthusiasm, participation and generosity.

The KTM X-BOW has the power to induce automotive lust. It seduces with its dramatic and brutal beauty, tantalises through the sophistication of its carbon fibre monocoque, mesmerises with the potential of its advanced aerodynamics, dazzles because of its motorsport parentage, charms through its muscular build quality, enchants by virtue of its rarity, and quite simply bewitches the weak and the susceptible. It is temptation.

It bears repeating this again here, purely to try and explain my total captivation with the X-BOW, first upon reading its technical specification in 2007, and then upon seeing it in the flesh for the very first time in 2008.

The pertinent and pressing question is whether it is really just a car. Yes, it is a car, but it is also so much more than just a car. It can, and should, be appreciated on many different levels to fully understand and enjoy it. It is a racing car for the road, and a road car that can excel on track. It is a byword for carbon fibre and aerodynamics. It was the world's first production car with a full carbon composite monocoque. It is an aesthetic masterpiece, created by a near genius working in an almost mythical land, where 'Designing Desire' is not only allowed, but positively encouraged. It was brought to life by the virtually unlimited monetary resources of an industrial giant steeped in motorsport, who demanded that it be technologically cutting-edge. It was honed to perfection by, arguably, the finest racing car engineers in the world, for whom 'best in class' was a minimum requirement. It is an objet d'art that can race in anger, or can transport in style: it startles, it fascinates, it wins.

"A MOST UNUSUAL CAR."

Mr Toad, in *The Wind in the Willows.*

**D**r Pathmanathan was born in Malaysia, where his interest in cars was kindled at the age of eight, by the sight of the Lamborghini Marzal concept car at a Motor Show. His interest in Lamborghini cars has never waned since, and his primary interest is in the mid-engined, wedge-shaped, spaceframe-chassised, Lamborghini supercars, with their south-north orientated Bizzarrini engines and their genuinely vertical-opening guillotine doors.

He boarded at Cheltenham College, obtained a degree in Physiology from the University of London, and then his medical degree from Pembroke College, University of Cambridge. He trained as an eye surgeon in London, Southampton and Liverpool before doing a subspeciality fellowship in glaucoma at the University of Toronto. He has been a Consultant Eye Surgeon since 1999.

He feels immensely privileged to have joint temporary custodianship of KTM X-BOW R Chassis 0642, which only presented itself after a wait of ten years. His long-standing fascination with the X-BOW lies in the similarities and close associations that this radical road-racer shares with its current Lamborghini stablemates: Countach Chassis 12399, a Rosso Siviglia 88 1/2 5000 QV, and Murcielago Chassis 1564, an Arancio Atlas 2005 Roadster.

KTM X-BOW Chassis 0642 has been the inspiration behind the writing of this, the first book dedicated to covering in depth, the concept, design, production and development of the road-homologated KTM X-BOW.

**D**r Anne Christina Reck's deep interest in the KTM X-BOW started on a road trip between the United Kingdom and the Pannonia-Ring Race Circuit in Hungary, during which time she helped draw out the skeleton draft of this book. Her dedication to the X-BOW, and to this book, was best exemplified by her precise and accurate note-taking about the X-BOW, during a 5.20am high-speed drive on the Grossglockner High Alpine Road, on the day prior to the KISKA Design Centre visit.

Dr Reck obtained her medical degree from the University of Copenhagen, and then trained as an eye surgeon in London and Southampton. She did a subspeciality fellowship in the retina at Moorfields Eye Hospital and has been a Consultant Eye Surgeon since 1999.

An expert on orchids, her respect for the X-BOW progressively grew, as she witnessed the care, dedication and expertise which KISKA, Dallara and KTM lavished upon this unusual car, in bringing it from the concept phase through to road-going reality.

Dedication:

TO OUR PARENTS, SIVA AND PATH,
AND JOAN AND SVEND, WITHOUT
WHOM NONE OF THIS WOULD HAVE
BEEN POSSIBLE.

**M**y head is split about the X-BOW. Do I talk about it as a designer, an industry expert, or a driver?

Actually, all three.

As a designer, the X-BOW is *the* dream project. Most designers sketch cars since childhood, and the freedom to develop such an extreme concept – from a blank piece of paper to production – is unheard of now. Such deep involvement happened in the '50s and '60s during the golden age of car design. Not today.

The KISKA design and engineering team defined a new space by satisfying a straightforward brief: the X-BOW should have the cornering speed and lateral acceleration of a race car, but the simplicity of a motorcycle. Introduced by Peter Stevens as: "design with a hand grenade," the X-BOW is reduced to the maximum possible. Designed from the driver outwards (or inside-out) the X-BOW layers body works and attaches all mechanical elements around the seat shell moulded to the monocoque.

Using what is only necessary to fulfil homologation requirements, the X-BOW is focussed on extreme performance. Though sometimes misinterpreted by other designers as over-styling, the X-BOW doesn't have added surfaces or components. Nothing that strokes a designer's ego. Every part has a purpose (sometimes three). Working around production limitations, we invented new ways to design with empty spaces. We exploited and exposed carbon fibre, and made it matt black to make a monocoque a design feature. That's something a million-Euro hypercar wouldn't have done 10 years ago. Using our motorcycle expertise, gave KTM's READY TO RACE attitude four wheels. In fact, it's the only car which motorcyclists wave to.

Guiding my team to push the limits was a life-changing experience. The positive reception and the X-BOW's industry influence give me tremendous satisfaction to this day. Time will tell how ahead of its time it was. Actually, *is*!

For an industry expert, the X-BOW is an adventure in business and branding. In 10 years, 1200 X-BOWs have been produced. That isn't impressive performance for many auto execs, but there are other ways to look at the case. For a start, the scale of development for a small series car is unheard of. Usually a few hundred units is all an exotic car manufacturer can hope for. Never mind over 1,000 – this is especially surprising considering the X-BOW's launch year of 2008, the midst of the great recession.

The X-BOW also defined a new category of vehicle. Lighter than a supercar, safer and more sophisticated than a track-day toy. Modular and engineered up to FIA open standards, it's the only car that could join the GT4 series without a roll cage added. So, what is the X-BOW?

It's a class of its own – but it's the X-BOW's brand-building effect that makes it a powerful asset. With it, KTM expanded its reach to an all-new, car-obsessed fan base. An audience that only increased with the addition of popular X-BOW spin-offs: the windshield-equipped GT and the track-ready GT4.

As a driver, I can tell you that the X-BOW is the ultimate g-force machine. Putting on my *Alipnestars* shoes and *Sparco* carbon fibre helmet are rituals that prepare me for an adrenaline rush. The X-BOW is for release, not for the grocery store.

I drive my X-BOW pure stock, with the suspension and acceleration tuned to my skills and style. Plus, I'm lucky enough to open it up on the street where it was developed. The Rossfeldstraße is the natural habitat of the X-BOW, with its curving mountain roads and elevation changes. Shifts in altitude and temperature are instantly felt in the open cockpit. I can anticipate a humid tarmac on a shaded corner immediately. The experience is pure sensation, because it's the last modern car that is totally mechanical. There are no electronics or power steering, yet it is high-tech. The Turbo Wastegate "Tshitt" sound, high revs and 180° pillarless view give me goose bumps. With sharp steering, I'm connected directly to the wheels and road. The chassis is rock solid and the rally car suspension copes with every bump. I don't feel like I'm in a car. I 'wear' my X-BOW like a backpack.

The X-BOW is surreal. In it, I'll never get overtaken by a Porsche, but I might hunt for some motorcycles to conquer.

Sebastien Stassin

CHIEF CREATIVE OFFICER AND PARTNER,
KISKA. LEAD DESIGNER AND FELLOW OWNER OF THE KTM X-BOW.

The KTM X-BOW is the quintessential 21st-century road-racer. Dramatic in appearance and technology-packed through advanced aerodynamics and extensive use of weight-saving carbon fibre, the X-BOW was conceived, designed and engineered – right from the very beginning – to excel on both road and track.

Although the X-BOW was, at its introduction in 2008, the first car from a brand new automotive company, it boasted an impeccable pedigree in the form of its three main backers: KTM is Europe's largest motorcycle manufacturer, KISKA is one of Europe's biggest and most respected design studios, and Dallara is a world-class race car and engineering consultancy.

Unusually, the X-BOW was a concept-led (rather than engineering-led) vehicle. Two men – Stefan Pierer and Gerald KISKA – neither of them engineers, decided that a niche market for the X-BOW existed, or could be created, and pushed the project through adversity to a successful conclusion.

The concept was for a minimalist vehicle that eschewed electronic intervention in favour of driver involvement. Spartan but technology-laden, lightweight, exposed to the elements, and aesthetically astounding would all become the key elements under-pinning the X-BOW vision.

KTM has a very rich history in participating in and winning a wide range of 2-wheeled motorsport events, and it was natural that KTM would want its first 4-wheeled vehicle to have the same race-winning capability. Happily, KTM recognised that many enthusiasts would both value and want a high quality, bespoke, technically-advanced, race-capable vehicle that could be used, maybe exclusively, on the road, and they designed the X-BOW to cater for this market: the KTM X-BOW is a true road-racer.

## ROAD-RACERS

Nature demands competition for survival: since the beginning of time, man has had a lust for speed, be it on his own two feet or with help from fellow fauna. Competition and speed are the foundation stones of the KTM X-BOW's genesis, as they are to all road-racers.

KTM, in its own literature, says: "Ultimately, KTM pursues a great goal: to compete and win in motorsports. The racing gene of KTM's DNA – the sporting competition – is both a challenge and what drives us. The goal is always to win and to take the title. The KTM X-BOW is a purebred racing car. It is licensed for the road, but the racetrack is its natural habitat. KTM offers an exceptionally wide range of possibilities with which every KTM X-BOW owner or prospective customer can get into motorsports, or just on the racing circuit, in their own individual way – always 'Ready To Race!'"

Vehicular racing as a sport, in its various guises, almost certainly started as soon as new vehicles were invented: Chariot (a vehicle according to the accepted Oxford English Dictionary definition: "an object for transporting people or goods, especially by land") racing being one of the earliest examples of such sport.

Homer (c750 BC), writing about the Funeral Games in honour of Patroclus in The Iliad: Book XXIII, describes how Achilles says that the first and most important event of these games will be chariot racing, and that it will carry the most precious of the games' prizes. Honour within sport is shown by Achilles, who declines to enter the competition as he says that his horses are immortal and so carry an unfair advantage.

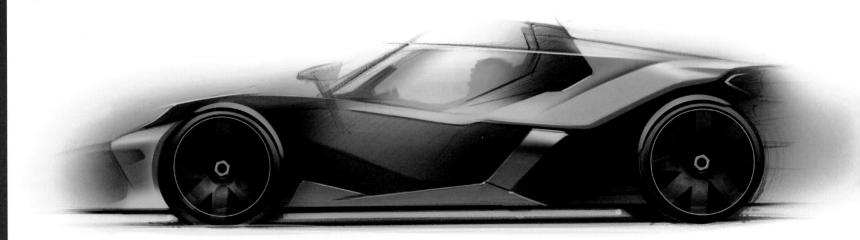

'THE DUALITY OF ROAD-RACERS'

This page and overleaf: The KTM X-BOW GT4 represents an evolution of the X-BOW; design-led engineering and practical thinking about the actual usage of the X-BOW culminates with a thoroughbred race machine that wouldn't look out of place on the Virage Du Tertre Rouge or the Mulsanne straight.

Dishonesty and controversy in sport (as is still sometimes seen in modern motor-racing) makes an appearance when the goddess Athena unfairly helps Diomedes to win; and later, when Achilles attempts to right this wrong by reallocating the second place prize to the rightful winner, heated argument breaks out.

The French-derived word 'automobile' originates from the late 19th century, but powered vehicles predate this, as does self-powered racing, even if only against the clock rather than against another competitor.

Karl Benz's 1886 three-wheeled Benz Patent-Motorwagen Number 1 is generally regarded as the world's first production automobile, and was timed to reach a maximum speed of about 16 kilometres an hour. Prior to this, however, there were notable steam-powered motorised vehicles.

In 1672, Flemish missionary and astronomer Ferdinand Verbiest developed a steam-powered, ball-shaped boiler vehicle for the Kangxi Emperor of China, and by 1769, Nicolas-Joseph Cugnot had made a three-wheeled, steam-powered vehicle. The latter was raced against the clock, and timed at a top speed of about 6 kilometres an hour. Unfortunately, its handling was not commensurate with its prodigious top speed and Cugnot lost control of the vehicle. He crashed into a wall, thereby spilling glowing embers and hot water all around, for which he was promptly arrested and imprisoned. KTM studied this lesson from history very carefully, and the X-BOW is renowned for its handling, roadholding and agility rather than its maximum straight-line speed.

### THE DUALITY OF ROAD-RACERS

The very first recorded race between two autonomously powered road vehicles took place when two steam-fired carriages competed against each other at 4.30am on the August 30, 1867. This competition took place

in England, over an 8-mile route between the towns of Ashton-under-Lyne and Old Trafford; the carriage owned by Mr Issac Watt Boulton won against that owned by Mr Daniel Adamson, with the actual drivers being unknown.

In this contest, both these vehicles had been used as racers, but they were also perfectly road legal. The only traffic law that both violated during the course of this road race was the Red Flag Law, and their violation of it is probably the reason why the identities of both drivers remains a mystery to this day.

In the United Kingdom, the Red Flag Law (more formally known as the Locomotive Act), was enacted in 1865, and it required all self-propelled vehicles to be preceded (at a distance of at least 60 yards) by a pedestrian waving a red flag or carrying a lit lantern. In addition, these vehicles were limited to a top speed of 4mph, which was further reduced to 2mph when in town. The Boulton and Adamson carriages

violated both these requirements during the race, but were otherwise totally street-legal.

At least the United Kingdom's Red Flag Law was not as demanding as its equivalent passed by the Pennsylvania legislature in 1896 which required all motorists happening upon cattle or livestock to "immediately stop their vehicles, immediately disassemble the vehicle, and immediately conceal the various components out of sight behind bushes until the livestock was sufficiently pacified."

Mr Boulton and Mr Adamson's steam carriages are the first recorded and authenticated road-racers, usable both in competition and, arguably, as every day transport – and the KTM X-BOW follows in this tradition. As automotive technology developed, and as motorsport became more established, cars unavoidably became increasingly more specialised, and fell into one of two camps.

"We took Colin Chapman's idea of a spartan, lightweight sports car reduced to the bare essentials, and transferred it into the new millennium — with as many technological innovations as possible."

Stefan Pierer.

Firstly, there were road cars in which purchase cost, comfort, safety, fuel economy, reliability, ease of servicing, and, more recently, low-carbon and particulate emissions took priority. The second camp consisted of pure race cars, and here the priorities were low-weight, agility, cornering prowess, roadhandling, a low centre of gravity, power, acceleration, top speed, braking, a low drag-coefficient, and a small frontal area.

Inevitably, some enthusiasts wanted the benefits of a race car within a road car. *The Times* newspaper of Wednesday, November 12, 1919 was apparently the first publication to use the term 'sports car' in an article titled 'The Development of the Sporting Car' (page 6 of issue 42255). There is no standard definition of a sports car, and the term encompasses a genuinely wide variety of cars. Cars as diverse as the 1903 Mercedes Simplex 60hp, the 1910 Prince Henry Austro Daimler, the 1920 Bugatti Type 13, the 1938 Alfa Romeo 2900, the 1948 Ferrari 166S Barchetta, the 1963 Mercedes 300Sl Gullwing, the 1964 Porsche 911, the 1973 Lamborghini Countach, the 1990 Honda NSX, and the 2001 Lamborghini Murcielago have all rightly been described as sports cars. But equally, smaller cars like the MGB, the Triumph Spitfire, the Mazda MX5, the Lotus Elise, the

A smile is all that's needed to complete the X-BOW set up, and that's what spreads over owners' faces when they get behind the wheel ...

Porsche Boxster, and, in the context of this book, most notably the Lotus Seven all fit into this category too, trading some everyday usability for a more sporting driving experience and a more attractive body.

KTM itself refers to the X-BOW as "a revolutionary sports car concept – Revolutionary. Puristic. Radical." The factory regards the X-BOW as KTM's interpretation of a super sports car for the 21st century.

Stefan Pierer, the CEO of KTM, talking of the X-BOW (the first four-wheeled model in KTM's prize-laden motorsport history) at its launch said: "We took Colin Chapman's idea of a spartan, lightweight sports car reduced to the bare essentials, and transferred it into the new millennium – with as many technological innovations as possible."

Within this category of sports cars, there are further divisions depending on how track- or race-focused each of these road-legal cars is. Towards the more extreme end of this spectrum lies the KTM X-BOW: a car that is totally road legal, yet as a pure-bred race car can be picked up from the factory in Graz, Austria, driven on its street tyres to the nearest track, and raced there with success, all without needing any modifications at all. A true road-racer.

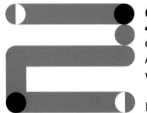

**S**tefan Pierer of KTM, Gerald Kiska of his eponymous design company, and a convivial meeting lubricated by the finest Austrian wine: surely something spectacular would come out of such a conclave.

At the time of writing, in 2018, the Economist Intelligence Unit had just ranked the Austrian capital, Vienna, as the best city to live in, anywhere in the world. It is uncertain if wine played any part in Vienna securing this accolade, but it appears that Austrian wine had much to do with the KTM X-BOW's conception.

Graz, the home of the KTM X-BOW factory, is Austria's second largest city after Vienna, and is also the capital of the state (or Bundesland) of Styria. The automotive industry is one of the fastest growing sectors in Styria. The state has a strong manufacturing base, with primary industries including electronics, iron, steel and paper, and it boasts more than 140 clean technology companies – one of the largest concentrations of such companies in Europe.

Notable Styrians include Jochen Rindt, who won the 1970 Formula One World Drivers' Championship posthumously, Dr Helmut Marko of Red Bull Formula One fame, and Elfriede Jelinek, who won the 2004 Nobel Prize in Literature. The industrialist Johann Puch, who established his first bicycle company in Graz in 1899 (which later became a subsidiary of the giant Steyr-Daimler-Puch conglomerate), was also born in Ptuj, Styria, although this town now belongs to Slovenia. An interesting aside: both Puch and President Josip Tito, who was born in nearby Northern Croatia, were of farming stock, each had at least eight siblings, and both were apprenticed as locksmiths at the ages of twelve and fifteen respectively.

Styria is also known as the land of Kürbiskernöl, due to its production of strong, dark pumpkin seed oil, used almost everywhere in Styrian cooking. But Styria is even more famous for its wine. Renowned Austrian vintners like Manfred and Armin Tement, whose estate is in Ehrenhausen, attribute the excellent quality of the wine to a happy combination of factors: warm days and cool nights and an altitude of 300-600 metres above sea-level make for particularly aromatic grapes, and the varied soil consisting of weathered primordial coral reef, clay and sand allow red and white vine varieties to flourish.

In the autumn of 2005, KTM CEO Stefan Pierer, and Gerald KISKA, the CEO and founder of the KISKA design studio, met for a routine meeting in Salzburg over a bottle of such wine. KTM and KISKA had by that time already established a close and long-standing relationship, which will be detailed later on.

This book is being written shortly after the 10th anniversary of the X-BOW's debut, and immediately after the author's visits to the KTM factory in Graz, the KISKA design studio in Anif, Salzburg, and the Dallara Research and Development centre in Varano de 'Melegari, Parma .

At each venue, the author asked multiple people for the exact date of the Pierer-Kiska meeting that begat the X-BOW. This same question had been posed at the recent anniversary celebrations, but, almost to a

Hans Trunkenpolz and Ernst Kronreif (right), pose next to the KTM R100, circa 1954. Available to the public from 1953 and powered by a 98cc, two-stroke Rotax engine, it was the result of a collaboration combining Trunkenpolz's great engineering mind, and some substantial investment from Kronreif. The KTM R100 is a serious collector's piece now.

Stefan Pierer, left, and Gerard Kiska. (Source: blog.ktm.com)

man, the answer was that no one was able to ascertain the date with any greater precision than "sometime in the autumn of 2005." The Austrian people are known for their attention to detail, precision, accuracy and excellent record keeping – virtues that come to life on the finished X-BOW car – so the lack of clarity on this important date is unexpected. The almost unanimous reason given for this oversight is the excellent wine that flowed freely at that meeting; not for nothing is the wine country south of Graz called 'the Styrian Tuscany.'

If autumn 2005 was the date of conception and Salzburg the site of consummation – and if you subscribe to the gender-biased myth that men are from Mars, and women are from Venus – then Stefan Pierer is the undoubted father of the KTM X-BOW.

Pierer carries a reputation as a highly focused, very determined, straight-talking industrialist, whose bold single-minded decision-making, is tempered by pragmatism. These are all attributes that he has needed to call upon during the KTM X-BOW's life to date, which has not been entirely without event.

Pierer was born on November 25, 1956 in the Styrian town of Bruck an der Mur, one of the oldest in Austria and an important transport hub even in the Middle Ages. He passed out as a graduate engineer from the Montan University in Leoban, Austria in 1982, with a degree in Business and Energy Management. His early career was spent as a sales assistant at the heating and ventilation manufacturer HOVAL GmbH, but he was soon promoted to sales manager for the whole of Upper Austria. In 1987 he founded CROSS Industries, which later evolved into KTM Industries AG. Pierer is the majority shareholder of the KTM Industries Group and is also its CEO.

Danish engineer Jorgen Skafte Rasmusen, founder of DKW Motorcylces, pictured with his wife, Johanna Clementine Therese Liebe in 1904. (Wikimedia Commons)

Above: An overview of how KTM's corporate identities have changed over the years. The first 'tiger' logo, from the R100, originally appeared in outline form on the tank of the bike (see inset picture on next page).

KTM stands for Kraftfahrzeug Trunkenpolz Mattighofen. In 1934, Johann Hans Trunkenpolz, an engineer, set up a car repair business in Mattighofen. (Mattighofen is a town in Innviertel, one of the four traditional quarters that form Upper Austria, and today it has a population of just over 6000 people.) In 1937, Trunkenpolz diversified into selling Opel cars, but also, more pertinently for this book, DKW motorcycles.

DKW, Dampf-Kraft-Wagen ('steam-powered car'), was founded by a Danish engineer called Jorgen Skafte Rasmussen in 1916. His initial intention was to produce a steam-powered car, but when this failed he made a two-stroke toy engine, which he later put a modified version of into a motorcycle: the Das Kleine Wunder ('the little wonder') retained the same company initials.

DKW was highly successful as a motorcycle manufacturer and by 1928 it was the largest in the world.

In 1932, DKW merged with Horch, Audi and Wanderer to form Auto Union AG; the famous four overlapping rings, which was once the trademark symbol of Auto Union, represents these four constituent marques. After various acquisitions and mergers, Auto Union became today's Audi, and those same four rings can be found on its cars. Audi was once a potential co-manufacturer of the KTM X-BOW, and is now the long-standing engine, gearbox and ancillary supplier for the X-BOW. It is fascinating just how closely intertwined, both in terms of geographical and historical links, the various European car companies are.

After the Second World War, Trunkenpolz started building his own motorcycles: the first being the R100, which debuted as a prototype in 1951 and started serial production in 1953. Also in 1953, Ernst Kronreif, a businessman, acquired a substantial shareholding of the KTM company, and it was renamed Kronreif & Trunkenpolz Mattighofen, so again managing to retain the original company initials: KTM.

Racing success soon followed, with the company winning the 1954 Austrian National Championship in the 125cc class; and in 1956, a KTM motorbike won the International Six Days Trials – the oldest 'off-road'

1953 saw the first production models of the R100 actively going into service. (Original picture courtesy John Steam, Flickr)

motorcycle event in the calendar of the Fédération Internationale de Motocyclisme (the global governing body of motorcycle racing): a portend of things to come.

Kronreif died in 1960 and Truckenpolz in 1962, but KTM went from strength to strength, producing over 40 different models by the mid-1970s. It also diversified into motor car radiator production. A North American subsidiary based in Lorain, Ohio was formed in 1978, and in 1980 the company was renamed KTM Motor-Fahrzeugbau. This was to represent a high-point for the company, with an employee total of about 700 people and a turnover of about €60 million in 2018 terms.

Thereafter, things got worse. Erich Trukenpolz, who had taken over from his father Johann in 1962, passed away in 1989. A year prior to this, scooter and moped production had already been halted because of a sudden and marked downturn in demand. KTM went into debt, and in 1989 it was taken over by an investment trust called GIT Trust Holdings, and then in 1991 by a group of creditor banks.

In 1992, KTM was split into four separate divisions: a motorcycle division called KTM Sportmotorcycle GmbH; a bicycle division; a radiator division; and a tooling division.

KTM Sportmotorcycle GmbH now went into the ownership of KTM Motorradholding, itself a subsidiary of CROSS Industries, which was owned and overseen by Stefan Pierer. With these changes came significant new investment, and KTM started developing new product lines; aggressively re-entered the motorsport arena; and in 1996 adopted its now-classic signature orange colour.

Further acquisitions quickly followed in the shape of the Swedish motorcycle manufacturer Husaberg AB in 1995, and later the Dutch White Power (WP) Suspension. Bajaj Auto, an Indian motorcycle manufacturer, bought a stake in KTM in 2007, and KTM, in turn, bought the Swedish motorcycle manufacturer Husqvarna in 2013.

KTM Motorradholding GmbH became KTM AG in 2012, with 51.3 per cent owned by CROSS Industries and 48 per cent by Bajaj Auto.

CROSS Industries itself is owned by KTM Industries AG, which in turn is owned by Pierer Industrie AG (75 per cent stake).

As of 2018, KTM is Europe's largest motorcycle manufacturer, with a 9.6 per cent motorcycle market share in Europe, a six per cent market share in the USA, 3245 employees, and a €1 billion turnover.

KTM has a rich history of participating in motorsport. KTM's statement, "Nothing hurts quite like second place," and Stefan Pierer's answer, "We are in this to win," when asked about the company's ambitions in MotoGP, are backed up by a hugely impressive trophy cabinet. To date (2018) KTM has 281 Motorcycle World Championship titles, 64 wins in MOTO3-Brand, and has had 17 Dakar Rally wins in a row.

KTM may have made its initial mark as a manufacturer of off-road motorbikes, but it now offers a truly extensive range of bikes: high-performance street bikes, adventure-orientated touring bikes, and, of course, off-road dirt bikes. The many motorbikes within each of the MX series, Enduro, Freeride, E-Ride, Adventure Travel series, Duke series, and Supersport bike ranges, illustrate just how wide and varied the offerings from KTM are.

Having achieved commercial and motorsport success with KTM on two wheels, Pierer must have recalled those immortal words in Macbeth: "I have no spur to prick the sides of my intent, but only vaulting ambition, which o'erleaps itself and falls on the other." Clearly the next port of call for Pierer and KTM now needed to be motorsport and commercial success on four wheels.

Pierer was lucky in that the prevailing economic climate, and the perceived customer demand in 2005, were both favourable to just such a four-wheeled venture. He was even more lucky to have Gerald Kiska as a fellow parent for the KTM X-BOW, and that the acclaimed Giampaolo Dallara was waiting in the wings as its godparent.

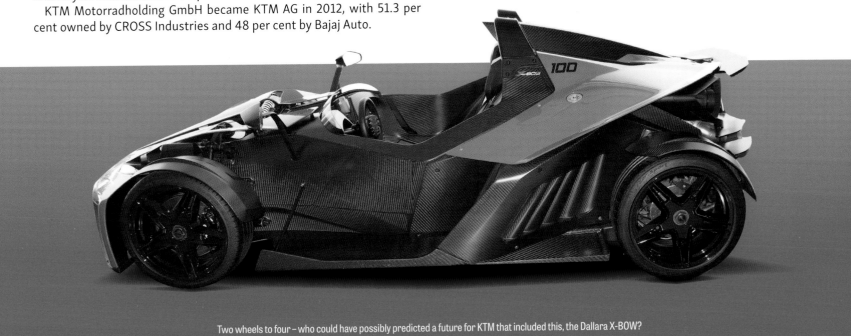

Two wheels to four – who could have possibly predicted a future for KTM that included this, the Dallara X-BOW?

**KISKA & DESIGNING DESIRE**

In Gerald Kiska, the KTM X-BOW found the perfect mother to complement Stefan Pierer's paternal input. This Pierer-Kiska alliance was a critical element to the X-BOW being the covetable car and objet d'art that it instantly was upon its presentation to the public .

'Designing Desire.' What a succinct way to encapsulate any designer's ambition, and capture any premium brand's marketing aspirations.

And this is KISKA's motto: 'Designing Desire.'

And we know that with the KTM X-BOW they succeeded: the press and the people's reaction was unanimously positive, in fact, staggeringly so. Speaking for myself, the first press images of this car released an overwhelming aspiration to own, a yearning to have, that bordered on lust.

Gerald Kiska founded KISKA in 1990. Currently one of Europe's largest design studios, it is also commonly acknowledged as one of the world's best. Since 2009, KISKA's home has been in a 5000-square-metre purpose-built studio – white, modern, very clean-cut and angular, flat-surfaced and glass-fronted – in Anif, on the outskirts of the gorgeous city of Salzburg. This building, which in itself murmurs, "Designing Desire," sits at the foot of the 2000-metre high Untersberg mountain, and is reminiscent of the famous glass-fronted Lamborghini factory in Sant'Agata.

Gerald Kiska, writing in KISKA's 25th anniversary celebration books (there are two of them), says that the last quarter-century has seen KISKA involved with over 1000 projects for more than 200 different clients, which would have meant over one million sketches being produced.

KISKA, which currently employs about 140 people, is almost unique in being one of the world's major design studios to remain independent. Most design studios working on big projects for large companies get bought up or somehow integrated into their clients' companies, but KISKA has successfully avoided this fate.

Gerald Kiska is very clear that a major reason why KISKA has preserved its independence is because of KTM. KTM has been KISKA's largest client for a quarter of a century, and Stefan Pierer was convinced of two things, both of which demanded an independent design studio. Firstly, Pierer had found that he always achieved better results when dealing with an independent entrepreneur, and secondly he felt that dealing with an independent design studio would achieve greater continuity. Kiska says that time has proven the latter assumption to be true; if KTM had established an in-house design studio, history suggests that they would have been on their fourth or fifth Chief Designer by now, but by sticking with an independent KISKA, they still have the continuity of care provided by their very first Chief Designer.

While KTM remains KISKA's largest and most long-standing client, its list of clients and range of design products is genuinely extensive: mineral water bottles for Gasteiner, Kastle snow skis, the lightweight RAKe concept car for Opel, street lighting for OSRAM Siteco, stereo headphones for AKG, lawn mowers for Altoz, binoculars for Carl Zeiss, construction site tools for Hilti, and motor yachts for Frauscher.

But KTM was there from almost the very beginning, and just as KTM nurtured the independent KISKA, Kiska not only designed motorcycles for KTM, but actually redesigned the KTM brand itself! So what do we mean by this, and what is the story behind this extraordinary relationship?

In 1990, KTM was a bankrupt company with an unconvincing and limited product line, poor quality control, and little aesthetic appeal. Additionally, there was no theme underlying the brand, no siren call that would appeal to the faithful and convince them to choose KTM motorcycles over its Far Eastern rivals.

This was the daunting spectacle that faced Pierer when he bought KTM, and it was either inspired decision-making or plain luck, or a combination of both, that he involved Gerald Kiska in his attempt to resurrect this once famous and successful motorcycle company.

One reason that they succeeded was that they not only rejuvenated KTM's product line, but they also redesigned and re-branded the entire company. And this was a novel thing for a design company to do.

While KTM redesigned the mechanical products of the new KTM company, KISKA simultaneously started on what Gerald Kiska calls 'Phase 3 Design Development': "successfully applying design as a strategic tool for building up a brand." Kiska had long been convinced that to be a successful brand, a company needed more than just successful products: "the idea is to convey the message of a brand to the outside world not only through the product, but across all other communication channels as well." KISKA put Phase 3 into practice by designing a new logo for KTM, introducing a new and distinctive colour to the brand, and adding a slogan that captured KTM's core values. In short, KISKA provided KTM with a 'cradle to the grave' design service.

Gerald Kiska's very first independent design project was for a Salzburg-based automated ticketing manufacturer called Skidata, who wanted a design for an electronic access ticket in the form of a watch. Kiska, who already had experience working on watches for Porsche Design, went freelance at this point: "I started working on this project from home at my kitchen table, day and night, until my wife told me I had to find somewhere else to go. Fortunately, she only meant for my work."

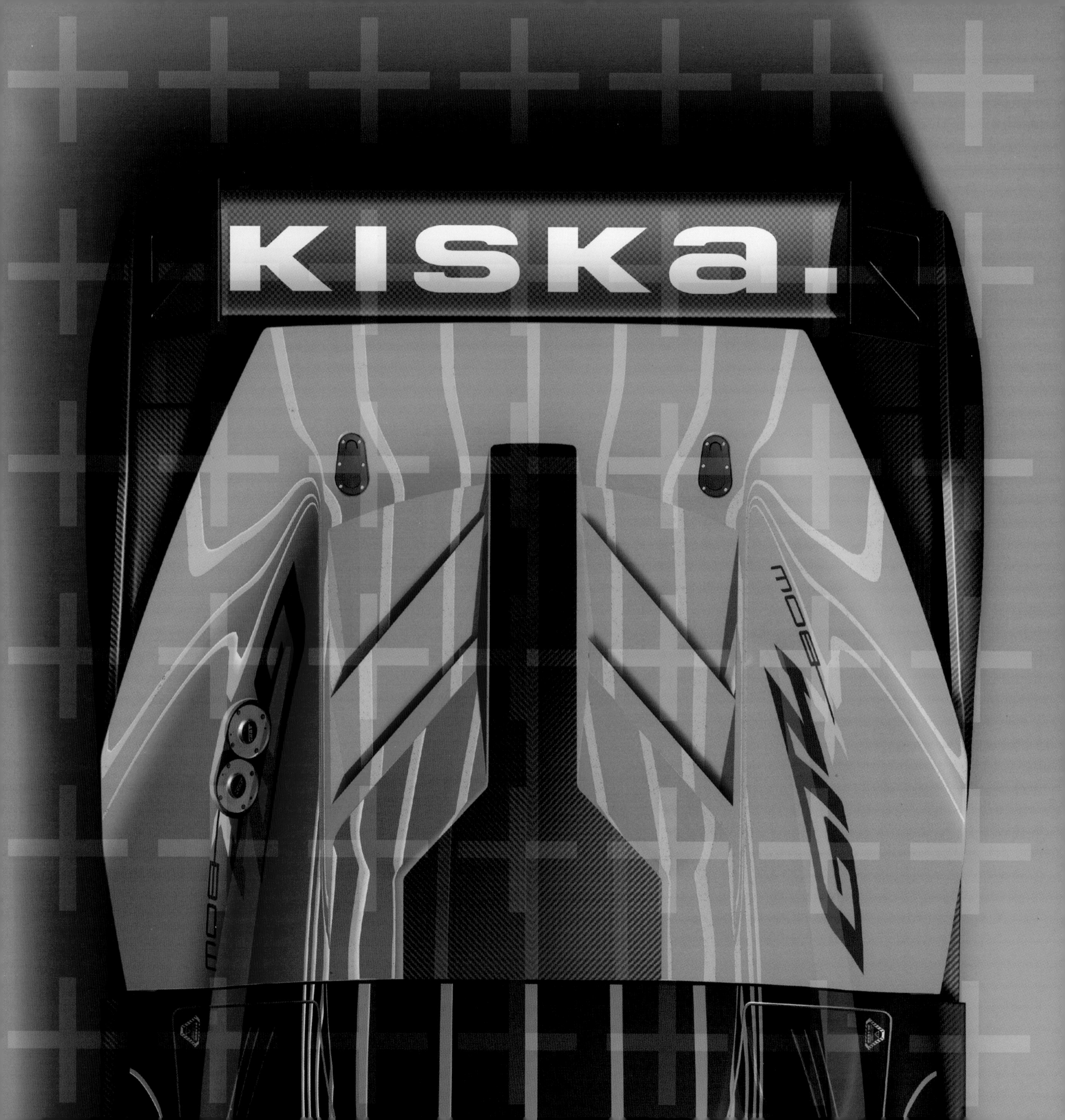
KISKA.

# DE
# SIGN
# ING
# DE
# SIRE

Mean Machine: What could have been? An early rendering, looking more futuristic than the X-BOW we all know and love, and there's something rather appealing about that front end; blade like, mean and purposeful.

Almost as fortunate, the tie up with KTM was to follow very shortly thereafter. The owner of KTM prior to Stefan Pierer had set up a motorcycle design competition that Kiska won; he put this down to his deep knowledge of motorcycles, which was a result of riding them ever since he was old enough to get a motorcycle license.

When Pierer took over, he and Kiska quickly established a bond, and by 1992 KISKA was the official design agency for KTM. In marketing the KTM brand, Gerald Kiska saw a common thread in that Pierer was recognisably

tough, as was off-road motorcycling. He took this theme and established it as a marketing tool for the KTM brand.

KISKA repositioned KTM, emphasising purity, extremeness, adventure, and performance as core brand values.

KISKA's integrated approach to design for KTM obviously included the design of the motorcycles, but also involved redesigning three other things that identify the company to the general public.

Firstly, what is now commonly known as KTM ORANGE became the (continued on page 31)

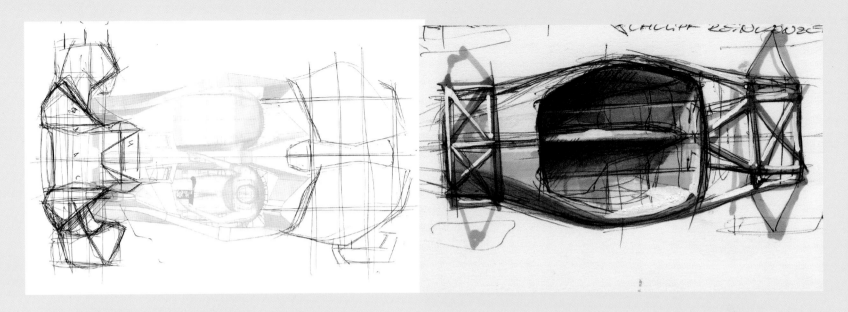

The X-BOW name was only adopted late in the design phase of this car. Manfred Wolf explains that one of the previous leading contenders was the name 'KTM Hawk.' The name 'KTM X-BOW' was finally adopted for two reasons: firstly, when viewed from the top, the X-BOW looks like a drawn crossbow with a bolt in place; secondly, because the X-BOW is a formidable weapon in war, and the X-BOW is a formidable weapon on track.

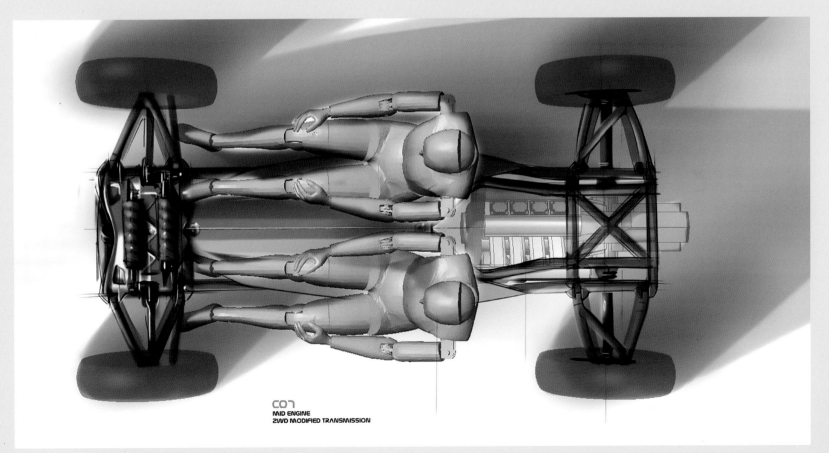

C07
MID ENGINE
2WD MODIFIED TRANSMISSION

This 'Hawk' concept drawing shows the general stance of the X-BOW; it's obvious presence already there. The stacked tailpipes and rear diffuser are both great pieces of design, exuding functionality. The production version, however, sees the exhausts separated and a wider diffuser with more ground clearance.

A production X-BOW with a huge rear wing is as much at home on the race track as it is on an open road. The styling has evolved very slightly since the launch, and although beautifully designed, everything on the X-BOW is practical and purposeful, not for vanity.

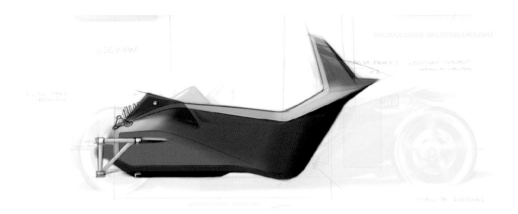

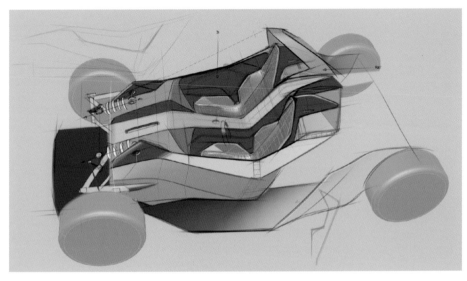

Left and above: The layout of the cockpit is fundamental to the eventual occupants of the X-BOW.

Below: Proportion and air flow is all-important, and KTM expects the driver to be wearing either a helmet, or at the least some form of eye protection.

Getting there: Now named "Crossbow," (due to its shape as seen in an aerial view) the eventual X-BOW shape and style can definitely be seen here. The snorkel, however is considerably higher in the production car.

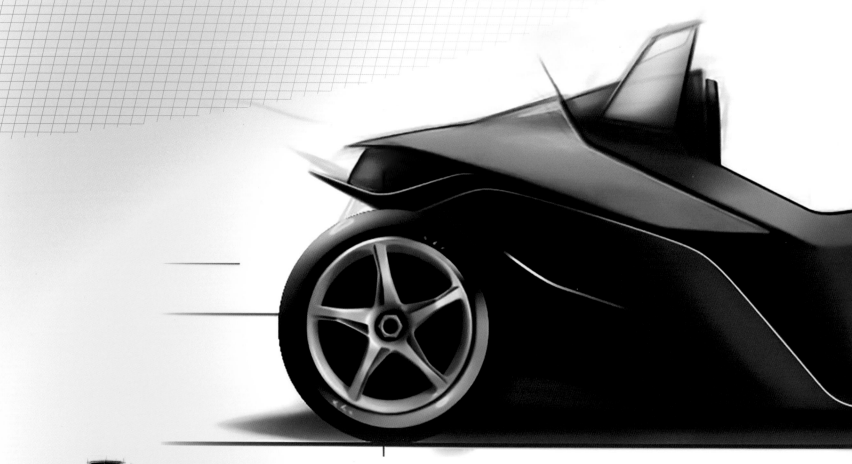

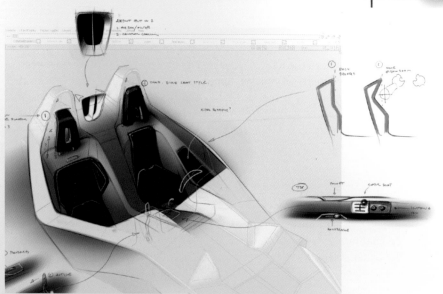

Left and below: Space in the cabin of such a conceptual, driver-oriented car as the X-BOW is at a premium, so attention to details such as room for 'elbows' is as essential as where the engine will sit. Cut-outs for the handbrake, as with other aspects of the cabin, are painstakingly considered parts of the design process.

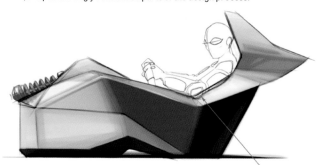

MONOCOQUE SHAPED LOWER IN
THIS AREA - ELLBOWS OUT

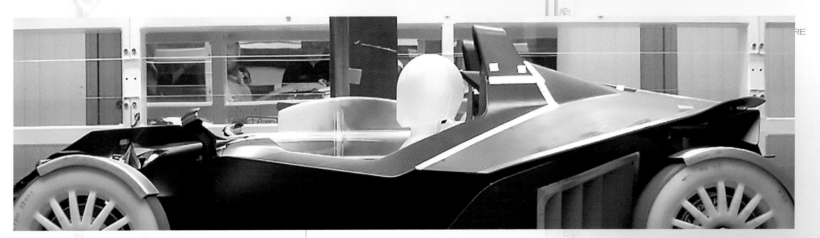

Aerodynamic model testing includes the driver, sat in exactly the right spot to disrupt an aerodynamicist's day ... The angles of the bodywork panels, beautifully executed though they are, do not exist purely for aesthetic reasons, performing specific aerodynamic functions such as producing downforce or directing the air toward specific areas or ducts. Nothing on the X-BOW is superflous.

official brand colour in 1994. This was a brave move at that time, as orange was still associated with the 1970s, and none of KTM's competitors were using this hue, all opting for more sombre reds, blues and blacks.

Secondly, at the same time, KISKA redesigned the KTM logo, and the only change since then was in 2003: a reversal of the orange lettering on its black background, with the font and style both remaining unchanged. This has stood the test of time; another example of the continuity that Pierer was seeking from an independent KISKA design studio.

Finally, in 1995, KISKA designed the KTM slogan that has come to define the brand: 'Ready To Race.' This slogan encapsulates the core KTM values of purity, performance, adventure, and extreme. It also pays homage to KTM's roots on the racetrack: traditionally the last question asked of a competitor just before the start of a race was "race ready?", and KTM's slogan, which is now synonymous with the company, confirms that this brand is always race ready.

With regards to the KTM X-BOW and its design by KISKA, we now need to introduce Sebastien Stassin. Sebastien is the Chief Creative Officer at KISKA. He is also a Partner at KISKA, and KISKA's Transportation Design Director. Sebastien led the KISKA design team that was responsible for the KTM X-BOW's spectacular appearance, and he was kind enough to meet the authors at the KISKA design studio outside Salzburg in August 2018.

Sebastien says that his fellow Belgian designer Luc Donkerwolke, who was responsible for the Lamborghini Murcielago, inspired him to enter the field of car design. With his parents apparently despairing of him ever entering a serious profession, they not only agreed but urged him to enter a design competition. Luc Donkerwolke, who had himself won this particular competition a few years previously, was one of the judges, and when Sebastien won it was a further boost in his pursuit for a career in design.

Another similarity between these two Belgian car designers, both of whom have produced truly startling yet beautiful designs, is that they

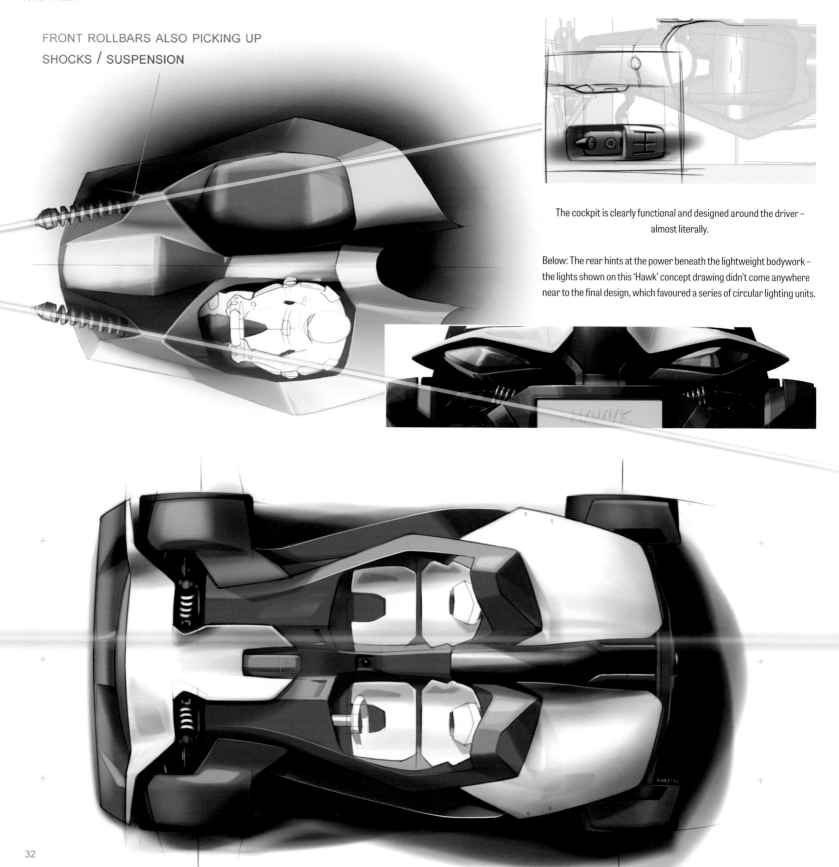

FRONT ROLLBARS ALSO PICKING UP
SHOCKS / SUSPENSION

The cockpit is clearly functional and designed around the driver –
almost literally.

Below: The rear hints at the power beneath the lightweight bodywork –
the lights shown on this 'Hawk' concept drawing didn't come anywhere
near to the final design, which favoured a series of circular lighting units.

are seriously multi-lingual: Donckerwolke speaks ten languages, and Sebastien speaks four languages fluently.

Sebastien was born in Montignies-sur-Sambae in Belgium on February 29, 1972, and, after a four-year course, graduated from the Art Centre College of Design with a Transportation Design degree in 1996. He then worked as a Designer with Piaggio Veicoli SpA (Vespa) until 1998, during which time the transportation projects that he was working on involved collaborating with partners like Stola, Guigiaro and Bertone. He joined Honda R&D Europe as a Transportation Designer and worked there until 2002; he was responsible for the design development of the CBR 600RR during this period. He joined KISKA in 2002 and later led the KTM X-BOW project as its Design Director.

Strikingly friendly and approachable, Sebastien was also extremely modest, and was at pains to point out (on numerous occasions throughout our meeting) that the hugely well-received KTM X-BOW design was the end-product of a lot of hard work done by a KISKA team, and not by an individual. Yet, you could tell almost immediately – from his evident enthusiasm when talking about the KTM X-BOW, or from the regular late night drives from the Salzburg design studio to the Dallara factory in Parma, or from his intense ambition that the X-BOW should be a showcase for 'Designing Desire' – that Sebastien had invested some of his soul into this car.

# READY TO » RACE

Left: KTM's X-BOW statement. The car is. Are you?

Below: KTM X-BOW next to a BAC Mono – another lightweight road-racer weighing in at 580kg and costing from £136,000. Although not as direct a comparison, the McLaren on the track behind is a 570S; at 1356kg, over one and a half times the weight of the X-BOW.

# DALLARA & THE PURSUIT OF EXCELLENCE

**D**allara brought the X-BOW to life by marrying the vision of KTM and the design of KISKA. The X-BOW was concept-led by an entrepreneur and a designer, and the next step demanded hard engineering knowledge and specialist manufacturing skills and facilities in order to develop a credible prototype.

Dallara, with an established track record of engineering race cars and very high-performance road cars, was supremely well positioned to bring to life the X-BOW road-racer idea.

Dallara was founded by Giampaolo Dallara in 1972, and it ranks as one of the most prolific and successful race car manufacturers ever. But Dallara also has a deep understanding of road cars, and it provides engineering consultancy services for some of the world's most prestigious car companies, including: Bugatti, Ferrari, Lamborghini, Maserati, Alfa Romeo and Audi.

Audi was a potential co-manufacturer of the X-BOW at the very beginning of the project. However, its involvement was short-lived, and there are two different reasons commonly cited for why Audi decided to terminate its participation in this enterprise.

The first reason was due to the extreme nature of the X-BOW. It soon became clear that the vision that Pierer and KISKA had for their brain-child was a very lightweight car with few, if any, driver aids, and none of the safety features – like air-bags, ABS brakes, traction control and stability control – that all major manufacturers now take for granted. The legal ramifications of making a car without any of these safety devices would have weighed heavily on a manufacturer like Audi, which had built its reputation on safety and advanced technology; Audi is inseparable from its advertising strapline 'Vorsprung Durch Technik,' which translates as 'Advancement Through Technology.'

Volkswagen, and through it Audi, has recently taken a real dent to its reputation through the Dieselgate Scandal. A study commissioned by the California Air Resources Board in 2014 concluded, in September 2015, that Volkswagen had deliberately designed illegal software inside their turbocharged direct injection diesel engines, so that their

*(continued on page 40)*

Into the light – Dallara Stradale waits patiently with nowhere to hide for its close quality control inspection. It's highly unlikely that anything will be found, but, as one would expect, Dallara has very exacting standards.

Poetry in still life ... every deliberate line meets in perfect proportions, and the use of material is applied to the design in a practical way, producing, some say, one of the most beautiful cars, and certainly one of the best designed, in the world. Italian pride at its best.

Sheer beauty – the practicalities of the Stradale are surprising, inventive and modular in their execution, from aesthetic and pragmatic viewpoints – an automotive statement from a company with form/function at the centre of its soul.

emissions control systems would only be activated when the vehicles recognised that they were being put through laboratory testing for emissions. This allowed the cars to pass the United States' threshold tests for nitric oxide and nitrogen dioxide emissions during laboratory testing, but in real-world driving these same engines produced up to forty times more of these nitrogen-based pollutants than legislation allowed for.

But Audi's reputation had also taken another direct hit in 1998, and this earlier scandal might have been a major reason for Audi abandoning their initial plan to be a co-manufacturer of the X-BOW.

The Mark 1 Audi TT made its debut in 1998, and this Bauhaus-inspired model was commonly accepted as a highly novel, and very attractive, even sexy, design. Tragedy struck soon after its launch, however, with a number of high-speed accidents, including some fatalities, being reported. All these accidents happened due to aerodynamic instability during high-speed lane changes, which caused the cars to spin.

With this instability issue (which was regularly reported by the contemporary press worldwide as one of the most dangerous car scandals of recent times) still fresh in Audi's memory, a stripped-down road-racer was a contentious project to take on, and Audi soon bowed out.

Still, Audi left its mark on the X-BOW in two other ways. It is very well known that the X-BOW carries within it an Audi TFSI engine and an Audi gearbox. Less well known is the fact that it was Audi (which had already benefited from Dallara's engineering consultancy expertise on a number of previous projects) that recommended that Dallara engineer the early concept into a working prototype.

Giampaolo Dallara has a simply stellar curriculum vitae as an engineer. He was born on the November 16, 1936 in the small town of Varano de' Melegari, outside Parma, Italy. He had a privileged childhood, and his father (who, for a time, was mayor of Varano) built his own private race track, which was later used for testing Lamborghinis. Giampaolo graduated from the Politecnico di Milano in 1959 with a degree in Aeronautical Engineering; his thesis was on the supersonic ramjet engine.

Almost immediately after graduation he joined Ferrari as an assistant to the legendary Carlo Chiti, the Technical Director of the Scuderia. Chiti, a Tuscan from Pistoia, also had an Aeronautical Engineering degree but from the University of Pisa. He was responsible for the acclaimed Ferrari 156 Sharknose with which Phil Hill won the 1961 Formula 1 Drivers' Championship, and which secured the Manufacturer's Championship for Ferrari. Dallara gained invaluable experience in engineering single-seater Formula 1 cars, as well as closed-wheel sport prototypes and Touring cars, during his two years at Ferrari.

Dallara then moved on as an understudy to the even more legendary (especially if you are a Countach 5000 QV owner) Giulio Alfieri. Alfieri was Dallara's cousin and was responsible for two genuinely brilliant race cars: the 1960 Maserati Tipo 61 'Birdcage,' and the exquisite Maserati 250F. It was also Alfieri who, as Engineering Director at Lamborghini in the 1980s, enlarged the legendary Bizzarrini-Lamborghini 60-degree V12 engine to 5.2 litres, and added downdraught carburettors to create the 455bhp/369lb/ft Countach 5000 QV of 1985 – which fairly easily kept the then-new 385bhp/361lb/ft flat-12-engined Ferrari Testarossa at bay and at heel.

In 1963, barely out of his mid-twenties, he joined Lamborghini as its first Technical Director. He will always be remembered within Lamborghini circles as the father of the ground-breaking Miura, but he was also responsible for the 350 GT and the Espada.

Dallara then moved on to De Tomaso, where he designed an innovative, aeronautical-inspired F2 car, which performed extremely well in the European Championship.

With all this experience under his belt, Dallara started his own company in 1972: Dallara Automobili da Competizione. In 1973, the Marlboro Williams F1 team recruited Dallara to modify the Iso-Marlboro IR's rear suspension geometry, and with this came bountiful race car participation and success.

Today, every weekend sees 300 Dallara-chassised cars race on tracks all around the world in many different formulas. Dallara is currently the sole supplier of cars for the IndyCar Championship, which really tells you almost everything that you need to know about the status of Dallara within the motor-racing world. Dallara-designed race cars participate in all Formula 3 Championships, Indy Light, GP2, GP3, Formula 3.5 V8, Super Formula, Formula E, Formulino, and the Renault Sport Trophy. Dallara designed the Haas Formula One car for the 2017 season: the VF-17.

Giampaolo Dallara says of the Dallara company: "Our mission is to make race cars faster and safer, with the highest standards of quality and customer support."

On the road car side of the equation, very high-performance cars like the Bugatti Veryon, Bugatti Chiron, Maserati MC12, Alfa Romeo 8C and 4C, and the Ferrari Enzo, all feature within Dallara's portfolio. At the time of writing, Dallara has produced its first very own road car: the Dallara Stradale.

Giampaolo Dallara says that his company's culture can be summed up by its motto: 'The Pursuit of Excellence.'

Stefan Pierer had always wanted the KTM X-BOW to be a premium quality, technologically advanced, lightweight, open-cockpit, street-legal race car – a difficult target, which could only realistically be achieved by a company prepared to strive for perfection.

The Dallara company motto fitted this requirement, but what of the knowledge base and manufacturing facilities needed?

Dallara is renowned for having three key competencies: world-class design and prototyping staff; a highly skilled workforce and the most up-to-date tooling for quick-turnaround manufacturing; and highly trained staff able to develop and evolve a race chassis.

Dallara is particularly skilled in the design and prototyping of carbon fibre materials, aerodynamic development using the wind tunnel and Computational Fluid Dynamics (CFD), and evaluation and continuous development of vehicle dynamics through computer simulations and physical testing.

Within the design sphere, Dallara has expertise in 3D modelling, structural analysis, and rapid prototyping of carbon composite components.

Within the aerodynamics sphere, Dallara has two wind tunnels covering an area of 8600 square metres, one of which can test 40 to 50 per cent test-scale models, and another totally state-of-the-art tunnel that can test 60 per cent models. Dallara has also invested heavily in staff and computer systems that make it a world-leader in CFD – the branch of aerodynamics that simulates tests in a virtual wind tunnel on a supercomputer. CFD is more time and cost efficient than traditional wind tunnel testing, and also

The authors with the wonderful Giampaolo Dallara, centre. A whole history of great models from great marques, both on the racetrack and on-road, exist because of this gentleman's wealth of expertise and knowledge.

Nearly there – the junction sign for Varano De' Melegari, Dallara's birthplace just outside Parma.

allows for thermal analysis, which is not possible in a classic wind tunnel. Dallara also has expertise in stereolithography, or 3D printing, for making models for conventional wind tunnel testing. This in turn requires expertise in computer-aided design (CAD).

Within the vehicle dynamics sphere, Dallara is able to first develop a virtual model of a car, before putting it through simulated acceleration, braking and cornering. Data gathered through simulation is then always verified by testing on track or on the road. Dallara also has a driver training simulator that allows a driver to learn various tracks (over 30 tracks available) using a monocoque of their choice (all Dallara-produced cars are available for simulation, from F3 to IndyCar), while getting real-time feedback that accurately replicates real car behaviour.

Dallara's roll-call of previous race and road cars, and its expert staff and world-class development and test facilities made it the perfect midwife for the X-BOW.

An interesting aside is the story of how the author got to meet and interview Giampaolo Dallara. Sig Dallara is now (in 2018), 81 years old. I initially rang through to ask for a meeting, and his charming receptionist was unsure that he would have the time to meet me, but was kind enough to give me his email address. I wrote to him with a photo of my KTM X-BOW R and its fellow garage residents, and received an almost immediate (but non-committal) reply saying: "Congratulations on your collection."

A week later, I tried again, but this time included a photograph of me with Sig Paolo Stanzani, taken in September 2001 at the Lamborghini Murcielago Launch at Sant'Agata. Sig Stanzani had worked under Giampaolo Dallara in the 1960s at Lamborghini, and succeeded Dallara as Chief Engineer in 1968. Stanzani devised the ingenious south-north engine gearbox orientation, which was first used in the 1971 Countach prototype and is still used in a modified form in the Aventador today.

Again, the reply was almost instantaneous, and so warm in its tone. I had asked for technical help for this X-BOW book and Sig Dallara now replied: "I will ask Ing Enrico Giuliani to give you all the help you need."

When my wife and I turned up at the Dallara Research and Development Centre in Varano a couple of months later, this 81-year-old gentleman was gracious enough to come down the stairs to greet us. He had organised a full tour of the R&D centre, interviews with various engineers related to the X-BOW project, and a test-drive of the Dallara Stradale.

His staff told me that he works a 12-hour day, 6 days a week. The morning following my visit, I wrote to thank him. The time stamp on our email was 7:59am; the time stamp on his was 8:02am, with the lovely words: "I will be happy to meet you every time you come to Italy."

A gracious genius from a bygone era, whom we were truly honoured to meet.

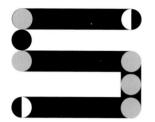

**P**ersonal meetings in Graz and at the Pannonia-Ring race track with Michael Woelfling and Manfred Wolf of KTM; in Salzburg with Sebastien Stassin and Andrea Bebber of KISKA; and in Varano de' Melegari with Giampaolo Dallara and Enrico Giuliani, all informed the authors of how the KTM X-BOW came to be production-ready.

The story is of a clear concept, begat by two non-engineers, that was handed over to arguably the world's most famous and accomplished race and road car consultancy, and tells of the finished prototype making its way through to production and beyond, in the most trying of economic climates.

In 2004, after 13 years of Stefan Pierer's insightful stewardship, KTM had moved from bankruptcy in 1991 to annual worldwide sales of 76,815 motorcycles and revenues of €402.4 million. Accompanying this business success was success on the racetrack: in 2005 alone KTM won a further 16 world championship titles in various categories, taking its total number of world championship motorcycle racing titles to 120.

However, there were clouds on the horizon for KTM, as the long-term outlook for the European motorcycle market was worrying: there had been a year-on-year fall in the number of European motorcycle licenses issued. With KTM already represented in just about every possible segment of the motorcycle industry, further diversification had its attractions.

Economists promote specialisation as a way of creating economies of scale, which in turn, maximises profits and minimises costs. In the farming industry, extreme specialisation is seen in monoculture. Monoculture allows the farmer to choose the crop best suited to local soil and climate conditions, and also develop a level of knowledge and experience that would not be possible if he or she was dealing with many different plant species.

However, monoculture almost defines danger: the Phylloxera-induced Great French Wine Blight, and the Phytophthora-induced Irish Potato Famine are probably the two best-known recent examples of this.

The Romans brought their vines with them when they invaded France, Spain and Portugal, and the Europeans did the same when they colonised the Americas. These European vine species were attacked by indigenous American pests and pathogens, and the settlers overcame this by grafting and hybridising the European Vinifera vines onto local Riparia and Rotundifolia roots with great success. These hybrids were re-imported back to Europe, and in the mid-1860s the Blight began. Within a few seasons, entire vineyards had collapsed, and the entire French wine industry was in danger of extinction. Finally, a French pharmicist Jules-Emile Planchon, and an American entomologist C V Riley established that Phylloxera – tiny parasitic insects – were the cause. The French government offered a 300,000 franc prize to anyone who could invent a suitable insecticide, but no such chemical was ever made. Eventually a genetic solution by way of further hybridisation and grafting was found, but not before what is now a 40-billion-bottle a year industry was almost totally obliterated.

The risks of depending on one product had already been well demonstrated by the Great Hunger, which began in 1845, when an oomycete, or water mould organism, called Phytophora Infestans devastated the potato crop in Ireland. This lasted until 1852, during which time a million people died from starvation, and even more fled Ireland as refugees.

KTM's motorcycle monoculture, its huge recent sales success, its very positive balance sheet and the declining European motorcycle riding population all coincided with a growth in the 'pure' sports car market.

Four-wheeled track-day motorsport is more accessible, both financially and skill-wise, to the average person than racing. Therefore, a track-day car has a larger potential market than a pure racing car. This market widens if the same car can also be used on the road, and extends further still if the car can also be easily and cheaply modified into a pure racing car.

KTM, with established motorsport pre-eminence and a reputation for designing and manufacturing solid and reliable premium motorbikes, was ideally placed to exploit this growing niche market with a small, lightweight, high-quality, four-wheeled vehicle that could give all the excitement and exposure to the elements of a motorcycle, while also providing a level of safety that no motorbike could ever aspire to.

Safety, be it of pedestrian, passenger or driver, has been an ever more important theme within the car industry for the last half century. Ralph Nader is probably the best-known public face of automobile safety legislation. The son of Lebanese immigrants, this Princeton and Harvard educated lawyer (he got his LLB from Harvard at the age of 24 despite skipping classes to hitchhike across the country to investigate Native American issues and migrant worker rights), published his influential book, *Unsafe at Any Speed* in 1965. This book was critical to bringing automobile safety into the international spotlight, and was also instrumental in getting the United States Congress to enact the National Traffic and Motor Vehicle Safety Act.

The 2013 US National Highway Traffic Safety Administration Report found that motorcyclist fatalities occurred 26 times more frequently than passenger car fatalities, per vehicle mile travelled. Motorbikes do not have the structural protection of a car, nor do they carry multiple airbags or seatbelts, so they are inherently more dangerous than cars from a passive safety viewpoint. From an active viewpoint, they can often have excellent power and torque-to-weight ratios, with the safety that this brings, but they do lose out in braking and roadholding – largely because they only have two narrow tyres rather than four wide ones.

Mothers and wives have also had a major role in the declining number of people riding motorcycles in Europe. I can personally vouch for this.

The routine meeting between Stefan Pierer and Gerald Kiska in the autumn of 2005 became seminal when they found that the three pressing problems facing KTM could all be addressed by developing a four-wheeled vehicle: the KTM motorcycle monoculture, the declining European motorcycle market, and the safety issues posed by motorbikes.

Pierer and Kiska decided that this vehicle should be a super sports car – one that would be equally at home on the street, the recreational track or on a formal racing circuit. The car would need to reflect KTM's philosophy and be a true 'Ready To Race' product. It would need to stand out from the already existing road-racers by reflecting KTM's motorcycle heritage: minimal bodywork to expose the KTM X-BOW's driver and passenger to the elements, and in particular to the airstream. The design of the car should also reflect KTM's motorcycles with an aggressive look, its major mechanical components open to view. It should be a car that would advertise the advanced technology available to KTM and KISKA and its development partners.

For its first car, KTM would aim to set a new benchmark within the small super sports car sector, and would try to achieve this goal through the following: a radical design, using only the finest materials and advanced technology, and employing the skills and the know-how of only the most established and respected development partners.

As a street-legal road-racer, entering this small and elite but already crowded market, the new KTM car needed one or more 'unique selling points' to make an impact. This, KTM achieved through advanced aerodynamic efficiency and extreme weight-saving through the extensive use of carbon fibre.

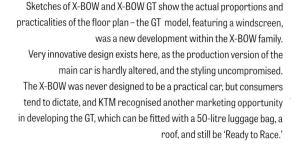

Sketches of X-BOW and X-BOW GT show the actual proportions and practicalities of the floor plan – the GT model, featuring a windscreen, was a new development within the X-BOW family. Very innovative design exists here, as the production version of the main car is hardly altered, and the styling uncompromised. The X-BOW was never designed to be a practical car, but consumers tend to dictate, and KTM recognised another marketing opportunity in developing the GT, which can be fitted with a 50-litre luggage bag, a roof, and still be 'Ready to Race.'

" ... the KTM team had put the test mule and early X-BOW prototypes through more than 100,000km of testing, and only after Dallara had carried out more than 200 wind tunnel test sessions using a 40% scale prototype ..."

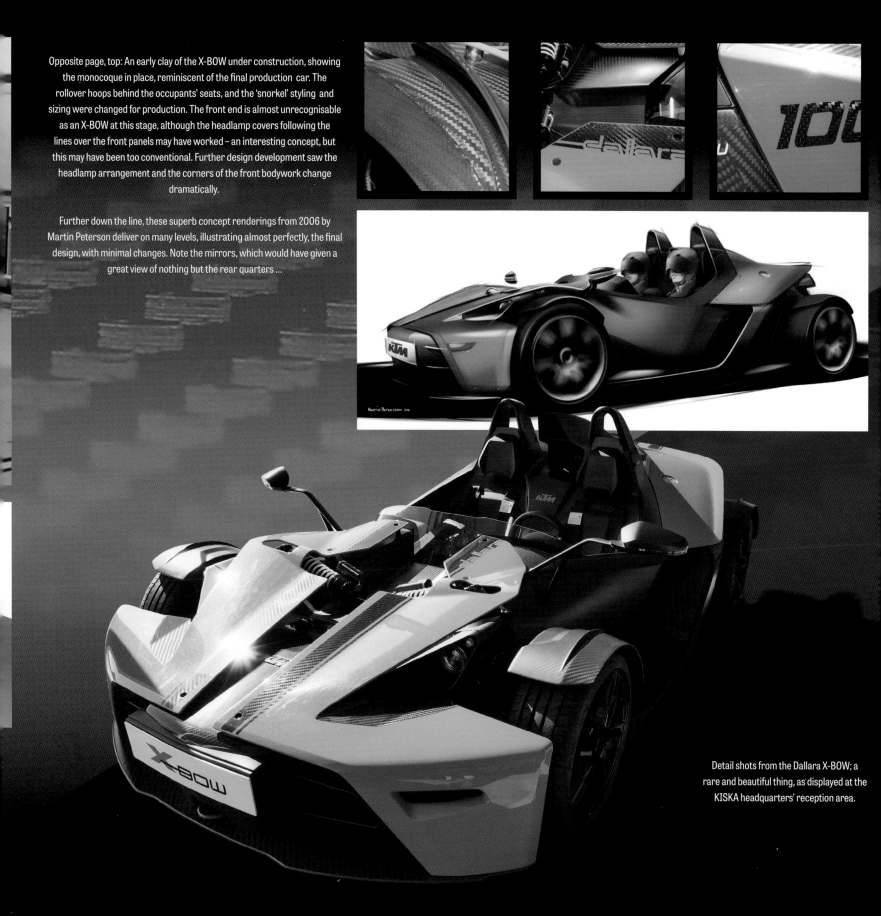

Opposite page, top: An early clay of the X-BOW under construction, showing the monocoque in place, reminiscent of the final production car. The rollover hoops behind the occupants' seats, and the 'snorkel' styling and sizing were changed for production. The front end is almost unrecognisable as an X-BOW at this stage, although the headlamp covers following the lines over the front panels may have worked – an interesting concept, but this may have been too conventional. Further design development saw the headlamp arrangement and the corners of the front bodywork change dramatically.

Further down the line, these superb concept renderings from 2006 by Martin Peterson deliver on many levels, illustrating almost perfectly, the final design, with minimal changes. Note the mirrors, which would have given a great view of nothing but the rear quarters ...

Detail shots from the Dallara X-BOW; a rare and beautiful thing, as displayed at the KISKA headquarters' reception area.

The KTM X-BOW would gain its aerodynamic efficiency through the design skills of KISKA, which would then be further refined and developed by the racing colossus that is Dallara Engineering.

The use of carbon fibre – an expensive and exotic material employed in aerospace and Formula 1 – allowed the X-BOW to be extremely lightweight while readily meeting the stringent demands of the FIA (Federation Internationale de l'Automobile – the governing body of motorsport, founded in 1904) crash tests right from the very beginning.

The typical KTM X-BOW customer was profiled to be male, aged between 35 and 50, with a relatively high disposable income, enjoying access to several cars, and having an interest in motorsport. This original target customer was most likely to have been a previous motorcycle rider, who now wanted (through his choice or family pressure) a safer, four-wheeled vehicle with which to experience open-air recreational street and racing activities.

In 2005, the original business model was for the X-BOW to be sold in 2008 as a €35,000 car. However, by the time the car reached production in 2008, a reasonably well-specified but not extravagantly over-optioned X-BOW would cost almost double this original target price, which, sadly, immediately excluded a large proportion of motorbikers.

Stefan Pierer and Gerald Kiska each carry a reputation as clear-thinking and determined businessmen. Having decided that KTM would diversify into manufacturing a four-wheeled super sports car in the autumn of 2005, things moved ahead at truly remarkable speed.

They were starting with only an idea – no design, no staff, no engineering expertise to support and build on their idea, and no factory.

Not even a name for this new, first-for-KTM, four-wheeled vehicle. This was a truly clean-sheet start up.

There was a very brief period, right at the very beginning, when the KTM X-BOW was a joint corporate project between Audi and KTM. Herr Ronolo Liebchen, a senior Audi Manager involved with GT3 racing, was a keen motorcyclist, and had got to know Stefan Pierer through the German KTM motorcycle dealership. A close and personal relationship therefore already existed at the most senior management level between Audi and KTM. Furthermore, Pierer's insistence that only the best components would be used in the X-BOW fitted in beautifully, as Audi was a recognised premium brand with a solid reputation for quality and involvement in motorsport. The original business plan was for the X-BOW to be sold through Audi dealerships, as one of the most difficult aspects of setting up a new car company is the establishing and maintenance of sales and servicing centres. It was a major set back for the whole X-BOW project when Audi decided, early on, that its corporate structure and its legal liabilities would not allow it to be so closely involved with such an extreme street-legal car. Audi's decision may or may not have been influenced by the trials and tribulations that it suffered with their Mark 1 Audi TT car, which has been detailed elsewhere in this book. Either way, Audi departed from KTM on the very best of terms, and to this day it has been the sole supplier of the X-BOW's drive-train and also supplies many of its ancillary parts.

With Audi now, mostly, out of the picture, KTM and Kiska moved quickly and commissioned an in-house 'test mule' to prove the validity

Evolving the concept: The GT starts its journey from the drawing board.

of their concept. Immediately following this, another critical point was reached in January 2006, when KTM approached the Italian race and road car specialist Dallara, first to assist in testing the feasibility of the X-BOW concept, and then to engineer and develop prototypes of the car. Audi had already worked on a number of projects with Dallara, and held it in high regard. It was Audi that recommended Dallara to KTM, saying it was the best placed engineering consultancy to bring the X-BOW concept to production reality. Again, Dallara's stellar reputation could only work in the X-BOW's favour as a marketing tool, and Dallara also fitted in beautifully with Pierer's requirement that the X-BOW would only be built in conjunction with the most respected development partners. Certainly Dallara's engineering pedigree, in both supercar and race car technology, was beyond question.

KTM and Dallara defined their key performance targets as a minimum lateral acceleration of 1.5G and a minimum downforce of 200kg at 200km/h. The objective of these targets was to allow the X-BOW to set new performance records for street-legal production cars.

Both these objectives were met, but only after the KTM team had put the test mule and early X-BOW prototypes through more than 100,000km of testing, and only after Dallara had carried out more than 200 wind tunnel test sessions using a 40 per cent scale prototype, as well as countless computational fluid dynamic runs.

The 2007 Geneva Motor Show, hosted at the Palexpo in early March, was the world premiere of KTM's first-ever car. The X-BOW's spectacular appearance, with its open construction structure exposing the major mechanical components, its almost unique carbon

fibre monocoque, its aerodynamic-led design, its minimum of purist fittings, and the quality of its drive-train and ancillary fittings, meant it was guaranteed to get some attention.

However, the depth of response – from car enthusiasts and the motoring media alike – to the X-BOW's debut was much, *much* more than could have reasonably been hoped for, and all of it was overwhelmingly positive.

Extensive market research was carried out at this time, and with such positive evidence now in hand, KTM took the momentous decision to put the X-BOW into series production.

The setting up of the Graz factory and the design and engineering development at KISKA and Dallara is covered elsewhere, but the next major time point for the X-BOW was the 2008 Geneva Motor Show, where KTM premiered the production-ready version. The first 100 units were called X-BOW Dallara in acknowledgement of Dallara's key role in engineering the prototype and developing the production-ready car. All 100 of these Dallara-edition cars were pre-sold before the first car even left the factory.

In May 2008, the first unofficial presentation of a running X-BOW took place at the Melk Racetrack in Lower Austria, on a circuit designed by the renowned Hermann Tilke that is now mainly used for motorsport testing purposes. Only KTM, KISKA and Dallara board members and personnel were present, as well as a few selected customers.

In June 2008, a second presentation of the X-BOW took place in Eskira, for both journalists and customers.

In August 2008, the very first car was delivered to a customer.

Chassis 0642 remains absolutely factory standard, with no post-production line modifications at all.

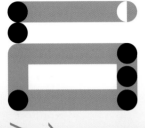

The KTM X-BOW is built by hand in Graz, Austria, in one of the world's most modern car factories, by a small, select, highly skilled and hugely experienced family of specialist technicians.

We are talking about truly bespoke car manufacturing, but with the most advanced tools, components, logistics and planning all pre-integrated into the system.

This is not 'one man in a shed' or 'ten enthusiasts in a converted barn' type small-scale production, so commonly seen with other road-racers.

To my eyes, the manufacturing facilities available in Graz are of a quite different quality to that seen with almost all its direct rivals. The only comparable small-scale production lines are those of Pagani and the Dallara Stradale: cars that cost multiples of the X-BOW's purchase price, and are therefore not really competitors. Incidentally, to use the term 'production line' in reference to the manufacturing process of any of these three marques demeans the care and time that is lavished on each individual car.

Stefan Pierer's CROSS Industries AG and KTM Industries AG issued a 2017 half-year company report showing record sales of 110,000 motorcycles, and revenue of €758.8 million.

The quality and set-up of the X-BOW factory reflects the solid financial foundation that it is built on. The highly logical and hyper-efficient production line of the X-BOW factory also testifies that it is one part of a hugely successful industrial giant, from which it has learnt many lessons.

While the KTM motorcycle division has annual production numbers going into six figures, and further strengthened its position as Europe's largest motorcycle producer in 2017 with an 11 per cent increase in production over 2016 figures, the X-BOW is produced at a rather more leisurely rate.

An average of just 2.8 X-BOWs are hand-built each week, and each and every car is built to the exact specification of a pre-existing customer who has already paid a deposit. This throughput time is, of course, highly variable, as the closed cockpit KTM X-BOW GT4 is more complex, and takes much longer to build than, for example, the open cockpit, windscreen-less R variant.

Every production X-BOW ever built has been built at the KTM X-BOW factory in Graz. The three prototype cars were all built at the Dallara Research and Development Centre in Varano de' Melegari just outside Parma, Italy. It is important to emphasise this point again, as many people are misled into believing that the first 100 Dallara edition cars were built by Dallara in Varano – this is not the case – all the production cars, including every Dallara edition car was built in Graz, Austria.

The decision to proceed to full scale production of the KTM X-BOW was taken at the end of the 2007 Geneva Motor Show, following the tumultuous welcome that the car received. But there was no factory in which to build the X-BOW, and no staff to do the building.

With Audi no longer participating in the project as a corporate partner, the obvious choice for KTM was to sub-contract the build-work out to Dallara. Dallara had expertise in working with carbon fibre, had the

necessary highly skilled personnel to do the car assembly, and was well-versed in the construction of low production volume supercars and race cars. Most importantly, Dallara already had the experience of building the three prototype X-BOWs.

The warm reception that the X-BOW received at, and following, the 2007 Geneva Show, led KTM's management to believe that an annual production of 1000 units was not over-ambitious. When this was put to Dallara, Giampaolo and his team had to admit that their company was not geared to dealing with such large volumes, especially over an extended time-frame.

Another of Dallara's strengths is in reacting quickly to new regulations in the motorsport arena, and adapting race cars to either exploit these regulations, or to be in compliance with them. Dallara is also skilled at engineering and developing very low volume, very expensive supercars, and taking these cars to, and beyond, the prototype stage.

Dallara wasn't, and still isn't, a series car manufacturer. As of 2018, Dallara has started producing its very own road-racer, the street-legal Dallara Stradale, but this car is being produced in much lower volumes and at a much higher price than was originally projected for the X-BOW.

With Dallara unable to build the production X-BOW car, KTM approached Magna Steyr AG to do the manufacturing instead. Magna Steyr engineers, develops and assembles cars for outside manufacturers, and is also based in Graz, Austria. It was previously part of the Steyr-Daimler-Puch empire, and with the capacity to assemble up to 200,000 cars a year, it is the largest contract manufacturer for vehicles anywhere in the world. At the time of writing, Magna produces the Mercedes G-Wagen at one end of the environment-consciousness spectrum, and the battery-powered Jaguar I-Pace at the other, more sensitive, end. Magna is also famous for having developed a new hydrogen fuel cell and electric-battery hybrid platform.

AVL List, another Austria-based automotive consulting company was also approached to build the X-BOW. Again, in keeping with Pierer's desire to only collaborate with the highest quality partners, AVL List is the largest privately owned company in the world designing and engineering powertrain systems utilising the internal combustion engine.

When both Magna and AVL were unable to build the X-BOW, Pierer was faced with the prospect of giving up on the KTM X-BOW dream. Instead, however, he took the bold and very expensive decision to build the X-BOW in a brand new car factory that would be wholly owned by KTM.

KTM Public Relations Manager, Manfred Wolf, pictured here with Path. What this gentleman doesn't know about the X-BOW assembly process is not worth knowing. He also knows where to take his guests for a great lunch, too. Thank you, Manfred.

The choice of Graz as the location of the new manufacturing base for the X-BOW was very deliberate. Most people do not think of Austria as an automotive powerhouse, but it is – not only in terms of research and development, but also as an important vehicle production centre.

The very first hybrid vehicle in the world was the Lohner-Porsche Semper Vivus (Always Alive) Mixte, which was developed in Vienna, Austria. In 1898, Ludwig Lohner, an established Viennese carriage maker, decided that the self-powered carriage was the transport choice of the future, and that electrical power was the best energy source for it. That same year, Lohner employed 18-year-old Ferdinand Porsche, who had no formal engineering education, to develop an electric powertrain for his carriages. A Lohner-Porsche electrically powered carriage was developed with two wheel-hub-mounted electric motors, and promptly exhibited at the 1900 Paris World Fair. It functioned very well but had a poor battery range, so Porsche came up with the ingenious idea of using an internal combustion engine to spin a generator, which would produce electricity to power the wheel-hub-mounted electric motors. With this, Ferdinand Porsche, working in Austria, created the world's first hybrid automobile, and as it had an estimated range of 200km, Porsche felt fully justified in calling it the Semper Vivus. It was first exhibited at the 1901 Paris Motor Show.

Austria, and again, more specifically, Vienna, was also the birthplace of the world's first four-wheel-drive electric vehicle, when Porsche used a hub-mounted electric motor at each corner of a modified carriage in 1899.

Austrian automotive technology, albeit dating back more than six decades, was also instrumental in the Apollo program's Lunar Roving Vehicle. Both NASA and Boeing studied the Lohner-Porsche's design very closely, and many of its principles were adopted for the 'Moon Buggy.' The Lunar Rover mirrored the Lohner-Porsche in that each wheel had its own 190W (0.25HP) direct current motor made by Delco, but differed from its Austrian counterpart in that it was powered by two 36-volt silver-zinc potassium hydroxide non-rechargeable batteries, yielding a range of 57 miles. The Lunar Rover was used in each of the last three Moon missions (Apollo 15, 16 and 17), which took place between July 1971 and December 1972.

Austria is also home to car manufacturing factories for Audi, General Motors, Jaguar and BMW. AVL and Magna both have a major presence in Austria and are world-class players in the automotive sector, as has already been alluded to above.

But within this small country, the Styrian region is Austria's automobile manufacturing hub, and Graz is its automotive crown jewel. Graz is Austria's second largest city (with a 2018 population count of 325,000), is listed as a UNESCO World Heritage Site, and, importantly, has six universities with almost 60,000 students. Magna-Steyr, Mercedes, Tata Motors, BMW, Toyota and Jaguar all have a direct or indirect presence in Graz. Numerous smaller automotive component manufacturers and suppliers are also based in or around Graz. And critically, many of these major and minor companies have been in Graz for a long time, meaning that the infrastructure and the highly-skilled people (and don't forget the talent pool those six universities and 60,000 students bring with them) have both been long present, waiting to be employed.

In March 2008, Stefan Pierer's decision to have the new KTM X-BOW factory in Graz was based on Graz's infrastructure, on Graz's access to

The thrill of the race – let X-BOW Battle commence …

an educated and mechanically proficient workforce, and on the fact that in choosing Graz, the new factory would be surrounded by many other companies with automotive expertise.

This new manufacturing facility was conceived and built in an astonishingly short time – the first car was delivered to a paying customer in August 2008.

Immediately upon making the decision for KTM to go it alone in manufacturing the X-BOW, Pierer rented an abandoned warehouse on a brownfield site that had previously been a storage site for a wholesale company. He also rented an adjacent building for logistics.

Right from the start, KTM wanted the X-BOW to be a world-class car, and it also wanted the factory that the X-BOW was built in to be class-leading. Both the car and the factory would serve as a showcase for KTM Industries and CROSS Industries.

There is a parallel here with Ferruccio Lamborghini wanting his first car, the 350 GT, to be 'the perfect car,' and his 1963 glass-fronted, two-storey Sant'Agata supercar factory to be the most advanced car plant of its type anywhere.

Another parallel between the X-BOW and the Lamborghini supercars was that both had the potential to be superb advertising tools for their parent companies –industrial colossi that shared the same name. Supercars and super sports cars catch the average person's attention like very few other products do.

The oft-touted story is that Ferruccio Lamborghini set up his supercar factory in direct response to repeated insults and slights from Enzo Ferrari. My personal take on this is that Ferruccio Lamborghini was far too astute a businessman to be led down the potentially ruinous path of supercar manufacturing by the odd insult or two.

By the early 1960s, Ferruccio Lamborghini, who was a jovial and approachable man (when asked during an interview, "What sort of man are you?" Ferruccio replied: "A normal person who likes creating things. A good worker in the morning, and a man who likes enjoying himself in the afternoon. Because I'm not interested in ending up like my collegues with heart problems), was already a very successful industrialist in the tractor building, air-conditioning and industrial heating sectors. He employed almost 4500 people, produced up to 5000 tractors annually, had had honorific titles bestowed upon him by the Italian government, and was amongst Italy's wealthiest citizens.

Ferruccio was a genuine petrolhead, and even in his later years could often be found, spanner in hand, working underneath a tractor or a supercar alongside a junior mechanic. He adored cars, and had a varied collection that included Ferraris. But there was one recurrent issue that bothered Ferruccio about his Ferraris: the clutches constantly slipping under acceleration or breaking up. According to his son, Tonino Lamborghini, Ferruccio, together with one of his own tractor mechanics, stripped down one of these broken down Ferraris and found that the clutch Ferrari was using was too small in diameter to cope with the torque output of the engine. He replaced this clutch with a larger diameter clutch from one of his tractors and this absolutely sorted out the problem. In his typically open and straightforward manner, Ferruccio thought that it was worth both their time to explain to Enzo Ferrari that he had diagnosed the cause of the recurrent clutch problem, and that he had also come up with a solution to the problem.

Tonino explained that this was offered up politely and in good faith to Enzo Ferrari.

Enzo Ferrari was of a very different temperament, character and attitude to Ferruccio Lamborghini, and a man whose personal motto could well have been 'divide et imperare' or 'divide and rule.' He was not straightforward in the way that Ferruccio was. Enzo had at his disposal the power to grant or withhold an audience with himself, and he was known to use this power mercilessly, keeping even invited guests waiting for hours. This was not something that the inherently down-to-earth and plain-speaking Ferruccio could relate to:

"Every time I went to Modena, everyone seemed to take a malicious pleasure in making me hang around waiting. Ferrari's answer to my complaint on this score was that one day he had kept the King of Belgium waiting for four hours, so a builder of tractors and boilers really had no cause to object."

The final insult that Ferruccio had to suffer is best recounted by him: "So I decided to talk to Enzo Ferrari. I had to wait for him for a very long time. 'Ferrari,' I said. 'Your cars are rubbish.' Il Commendatore was furious: 'Lamborghini, you may be able to drive a tractor, but you will never be able to handle a Ferrari properly.' This was the point when I finally decided to make a perfect car."

Well, that's the story, but Ferruccio was a shrewd businessman, and it is unlikely that a few unpleasant encounters with Enzo would have been the sole reason for setting up a new car company, with the inherent risk of losing a fortune on a start-up that might well fail. Rather, Lamborghini probably also saw a successful supercar company as a publicity vehicle for his other businesses – what better way to gain recognition in car-mad Italy than to build cars that rivalled, and even exceeded, the best available?

Some of this same thinking was also probably at work with regards to the X-BOW car concept and KTM and CROSS Industries.

What is certain, however, was that Pierer and KTM moved very decisively following the March 2008 declaration that KTM would build the X-BOW itself, and in a brand-new factory of its own design. The choice of the brownfield site warehouse and the adjacent building was finalised within that same month, as was the rental contract.

Setting up a production line for the X-BOW manufacture involved 50 different companies, and the whole factory was fully functional in just three months. The very first Graz-production X-BOW was completed in June 2008.

It is worth repeating this point, to emphasise KTM's determination and financial firepower in getting the X-BOW built: one of the world's most modern, purpose-built car manufacturing factories went from the concept phase to completion in just three months with the help of 50 different companies. The whole factory was certified to ISO standards. Setting up the factory also involved developing imaginative new assembly procedures, innovative transport logistics (especially for the expensive and easily damaged carbon fibre parts, which required specially designed and manufactured transport containers), and resourceful warehousing and logistics for 'just in time' production. All this, too, was done within that same twelve-week time frame. Later, in 2009, Stefan Pierer bought the previously rented warehouse, and at the same time relinquished the rental of the adjacent building.

With such resolute determination, inventive thinking and resourceful deployment of financial muscle, the first KTM four-wheeled vehicle, the X-BOW, was delivered to a customer in August 2008.

## THE STAFF

The KTM X-BOW is a truly bespoke hand-built objet d'art that also masquerades as a car. It is assembled by a tiny group of specialist engineer-technicians, who form the core of the workforce at the Graz factory.

The workforce is one medium-sized family, which currently stands at 26 people. A 'family' in that this group is a very long-standing, stable and loyal band of individuals who have stood by the company through the good times and the less good times. KTM in turn has been a very loyal employer, and this mutual respect has also contributed to the clearly evident family atmosphere that pervades the factory.

At the start of the production, the factory had 120 employees. It was always the plan, right from the very beginning, that this head count would be reduced down to 80 employees once the factory was up and running, as setting up a new factory is always more labour intensive.

A large proportion of the workforce was recruited as fully trained specialist engineers from Magna and other neighbouring engineering firms. In the early days, Dallara sent specialist technicians to the Graz factory to educate and train the new X-BOW labour pool in the advanced techniques needed to assemble this carbon fibre rich car.

The rapturous welcome that the X-BOW received at its debut informed the KTM management board of the expected demand for the car, and also guided them as to the size of the factory and its anticipated workforce. There was a time when production was envisaged to be up to 1000 units a year, with an 80 strong workforce,

This angle of the X-BOW really shows off the floating panel bodywork sections, especially the front panels. The eye-catching graphics are 'standard' for an X-BOW R of this vintage (2012).

but both these targets were vanquished by the 2007/2008 global financial crisis.

In the face of this challenge, which is described in more detail below, the total workforce at the end of 2009 was down to 25 people. 20 of these still work at the Graz X-BOW facility at the time of writing, in the winter of 2018. A very stable workforce indeed. Herr Michael Woelfling, the current Managing Director of KTM Sportcar GmbH, has been in post since the inception of the X-BOW project. Manfred Wolf and Hartwig Breitenbach, who were both instrumental in providing information for this book, are in charge of Public Relations and Customer Services respectively, and have both been with the company since 2008.

Just six of the current 26 X-BOW factory staff actually build the cars. One point that was repeatedly made to me, by many different people during my visits to the factory in Graz, and to the X-BOW Battle race meeting at the Pannonia Ring in Hungary, was that everyone in the company multitasks. One staff member said to me that each and every person, including the Managing Director, has three to five jobs within the company. This was so very evident the day before the Pannonia Ring event, when almost everyone at the factory was packing and preparing for the forthcoming race weekend. The same people who had been involved with logistics and marketing and warehouse duties in Graz, were busy servicing the cars, changing wheels and tyres, and manning the pit-lane at the race circuit the very next day.

For the sake of completion, the tasks besides building the cars include: warehousing, logistics, legislation compliance, sales and marketing, customer sales, after-sales servicing, finance management, customer relations, press briefings, events and customer racing management.

The 2007/2008 global financial crisis started in the United States of America – a market that the X-BOW was not destined for – but it had a massive impact on both the X-BOW and KTM. The precipitating factors to the crisis had their roots firmly implanted before 2007, but this was when the first tangible signs of trouble emerged. In a nut-shell, low interest rates encouraged excessive mortgage borrowing, and lax federal government regulations meant that predatory lenders were able to sell mortgages to home buyers who were clearly not in a position to service these mortgages. This risk was further amplified by two very large, American, quasi-government home-loan associations (Fannie Mae and Freddie Mac) that gave the illusion that the US federal government stood behind these mortgage loans, thereby creating 'moral hazard.'

A glut of risky lending led to excessive liquidity, and all this easy money, together with a limited supply of houses, drove up the prices of homes. When some borrowers who had been lent more than they should have been failed to service their mortgages, the bubble began to burst. The banks that had loaned out the money in the first place were highly exposed to the rapid devaluation of their assets (the mortgaged houses), as house prices went into free fall. The banks therefore tightened liquidity, which in turn led to a smaller pool of potential home buyers, which caused house prices to plummet further. This truly vicious circle led to long-established and previously respected major financial institutions, like Lehman Brothers, filing for bankruptcy, while others, like Merrill Lynch, HBOS, Royal Bank of Scotland and AIG, had to suffer merger or acquisition. The beginning of October 2008 saw

massive falls in the stock market worldwide, and there were serious worries about the stability of the whole global banking system, although the worst affected banks appeared to fall along an Anglo-American axis. Governments around the world responded by setting up bank rescue packages, but it was too little too late. The Dow Jone Industrial Average fell from 14,000 points in October 2007 to 6600 in March 2009, the S&P 500 US stock market index suffered a 45 per cent loss between early 2007 and late 2008, and in the eighteen months after June 2007 Americans lost an estimated 30 per cent of their collective net worth.

In a globalised banking system, the contagion spread to Europe and the rest of the world very rapidly. South America, Asia and Africa all saw significant economic downturns. The oil-producing Middle Eastern countries were the only ones to avoid being immediately affected by this global crisis, courtesy of their vast financial reserves, but even they were affected later on as the price of crude oil fell, and they too had to cut back on investments abroad, domestic public services and the employment of foreign workers.

It was this fiscal backdrop, which many economists consider the harshest financial crisis since the Great Depression of the 1930s, that KTM's original business plan for the X-BOW now had to contend with. The projected annual sales of 1000 cars was clearly not achievable.

Sales faltered, and in August 2009, at which stage fewer than 500 X-BOWs had been made, KTM brought production to a temporary stop. There were already 80 cars unsold, and it would have been financially irresponsible, as well as unsustainable, to continue making cars at a rate

Up the hill - Path demonstrates the acceleration and the stopping power that exists in the X-BOW R; much to the delight of a packed Beaulieu National Motor Museum Supercar Day crowd in 2018.

that the market couldn't absorb, especially part way through a severe worldwide recession.

Foreign currency exchange rates were another unexpected challenge. While the Euro remained relatively strong, the local currency in other markets proved less resilient. The United Kingdom, for example, had been identified as one of the X-BOW's largest markets, but after a year, only 28 cars had been sold, and the exchange rate was partly to blame. At the 2007 Geneva Motor Show, the projected price for the X-BOW was €40,000, which equated to £37,000. In the following 18 months, the pound sterling fell relentlessly against the Euro, and this, combined with rising production costs, meant that by the time the X-BOW arrived on UK shores, the most basic possible car, with no options, cost just a whisker under £50,000. Choosing desirable options with care could add another £20,000, and choosing all options with gay abandon could easily double this latter figure further.

There was worry, too, about how much damage had been done to KTM itself by the X-BOW project. In 2007, the company shares were trading as high as €59.50 per share, but by the autumn of 2009 they'd fallen to just €18 per share. KTM released a financial report in August 2009 that showed that the company had incurred a loss of €66.8 million in the preceding nine months, which contrasted starkly with a profit of €1.4 million over the same period the previous year. Most troubling was a statement within the report that read: "A sale of the entire sports car division will also have to be considered." Such was the X-BOW's rapid fall from grace – so much so that it almost amounted to a stillbirth.

Faced with the termination of X-BOW production, Stefan Pierer and the KTM board took the courageous, but potentially expensive decision, to keep going. They tempered this risk by downsizing the company, and revising down their projected annual sales. The workforce number was reduced to the mid-twenties, where it remains today.

Crucially, the company continued to invest in research and development, which allowed KTM to bring out the much revised and improved 'R' variant in 2011.

Speaking of the X-BOW surviving this trying period, Stefan Pierer said: "Of course it was not easy to achieve at the time of a financial crisis, and it was also a steep learning curve. But the reputation of KTM, in the car industry, in the environment, has thus achieved a whole new level. And with KTM Technologies we created a new, highly successful company that specialises in lightweight construction. We have succeeded where only very few companies who enter the car industry do so: namely to enter this segment and construct a super sports car, to produce it in series, to achieve the small series homologation, and above all to sell it up to date more than 500 times."

More than ten years after the first X-BOW was delivered, the marque now features four model variants within the range: two are road biased, and two are designed for the track. The fact that X-BOWs continue to be produced at a rate averaging 2.8 cars per week (despite carrying the additional burden of being exclusively 'made to order') vindicates Pierer's and KTM's faith in the concept, engineering and execution of this bespoke and spectacular road-racer.

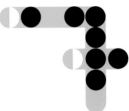

The KTM X-BOW factory carries the placard 'KTM Sportcar GmbH,' and is located at Maggstrabe 20, 8042, Graz, Austria. It sits within a typical industrial estate, although the number of automotive companies surrounding the factory is noteworthy. As an example, a Magna Powertrain factory is only 200 metres away.

The X-BOW factory is a two-storey, rather non-descript, block-like building. Three things make it stand apart. Firstly, the upper storey is painted in signature KTM orange, which is in striking contrast to the grey and white of the neighbouring buildings. Secondly, there are four huge up-and-over garage doors, through which transporters can unload components directly onto the shop floor or collect completed X-BOW cars for the first stage of their delivery to customers located all around the world. On my visit, a couple of days before the 2018 Pannonia-Ring X-BOW race meeting, there was a large lorry backed up to one of these openings, collecting race cars and spare parts for delivery to the Hungarian track. It carried a beautiful image of a black X-BOW RR on its side. Finally, on the other side of the factory, there is a glass-fronted showroom type area that is visible from the adjacent main road. If you were to drive past unsuspectingly, you would be suddenly astonished when your peripheral vision catches sight of a few small multi-coloured spacecraft that have taken temporary refuge (don't tell Pierer or the young Sebastien Kurz) in Graz on their interstellar voyage.

As I have already said, to call the X-BOW's manufacturing process a production line is to demean the care and attention that is lavished on each car during its time-consuming and labour-intensive assembly process. Equally, to call the building in which the X-BOW is made a 'factory' is to give the wrong impression of what actually takes place within. Yes, cars are created here, but not in the conventional manner.

The inside of the building is pristine and largely painted white, which forms a good background for the many brightly hued X-BOW posters that adorn the walls. The upper floor carries a series of offices and conference rooms, and large floor-to-ceiling glass windows overlook the car assembly area. There is a small display area, with completed cars at the very front of the factory floor, and this is visible from the conference rooms on the first floor – which must be very distracting during business meetings.

Manfred Wolf, the long-standing Public Relations Manager, first talked us through the X-BOW's assembly process from the high vantage point of one of these conference rooms, which gave us an overview of the whole factory floor. Then, over the course of a whole day, he walked us around the assembly stations, explaining in detail how the various components were put together, and introduced us to some of the specialist engineer-technicians working on the cars.

This intense, day-long tour was interrupted for a couple of hours when Manfred treated us to a lovely three-course lunch at

Above: Neighbour Magna Powertrain is close to the factory. Below: Truck to track: Outside the factory, a KTM Racing transporter prepares to load up X-BOW contenders, ready for race action.

a typical Styrian restaurant not far from the factory. Manfred did very well in recommending the beef fillet in gravy laced with pumpkin oil, and even now, months later, we still speak about this southern Austrian delicacy. None of us indulged in the famous Austrian wine that had been so instrumental in the X-BOW's conception at that critical Pierer-Kiska meeting in the autumn of 2005, but that was only because we were all working – although for us it seemed more like a visit to Disneyland.

Manfred explained that traditionally the X-BOW's production line has been made up of a pre-assembly area and ten assembly stations. Since early 2018, however, an additional sub-station has had to be added for engine assembly and preparation.

The factory is essentially an assembly area, as none of the components are actually made here. All the component parts arrive fully constructed – cleaned, pre-drilled, pre-painted. There is therefore very little noise, and no smoke or debris polluting the factory's atmosphere. Everyone works, moves and talks in hushed tones, and in this manner, it is more like a library than a car factory.

## WAREHOUSING

To one side of the factory floor, there is the warehousing area. The standard X-BOW R is made up of about 860 different components. The more elaborate GT needs more, and the much more complex GT4 requires the most parts of all. To one side are racks holding gearbox casings and other mechanical components, while on the other side there is a stack of X-BOW carbon fibre monocoques. The monocoques are highly susceptible to damage, and KTM has developed specially designed housings for their transportation and storage. These carbon fibre works-of-art arrive at the factory pre-drilled, and their transport containers have bespoke fittings that very securely clamp and hold them in place. Immediately adjacent are more racks, holding soft grey oblong plastic-like containers with white smooth and pliable inner linings made by Boomerang Systems to KTM's own specification. These are for the smaller, equally delicate carbon fibre parts. Stacks of the large carbon underfloors and rear diffusers are also carefully arranged in one area, standing vertically on special rests.

KTM is used to visitors admiring its work, and what better way to show off than with a trio of KTM X-BOWS, seen here from the first floor conference rooms, proudly displayed on the factory floor. Seeing double? – From left to right, two slightly differently-specced (note the canards and red twelve o'clock marking on the race steering wheel of the middle car) KTM X-BOW Rs. The 'Ten Years' anniversary model was released in 2018. This model shows off its carbon fibre beautifully, with simple splashes of orange, huge black 'X' styling across the front and rear, and a specially-designed 'X YEARS' logo.

## PRE-ASSEMBLY AREA

As you walk further into the factory from the warehousing area, and also bear slightly right, you arrive at the pre-assembly area. On the day we visited, Daniel Slunsky was working in this section. Daniel has been with KTM for the last ten years, and works on the full assembly stations as well as on pre-assembling components. In addition to this he is also the in-house IT technician – another example of the multi-tasking that all KTM staff in Graz do. Daniel was working on assembling the front brake system of an X-BOW as we arrived.

Every safety-critical part and operation is recorded and logged electronically. The torque value of every single tightened bolt is automatically archived through a very expensive electronic system that is hardly ever seen in low-volume car factories. Stefan Pierer apparently insisted that the X-BOW factory should have the most modern and most safety-conscious car assembly systems available, irrespective of cost.

On another workbench within the pre-assembly area, components for the steering wheel system were neatly laid out, waiting to be put together. The craftsmanship of the reach-and-rake steering column adjustment lever was a joy to behold, and the infra-red transmitter that is normally hidden from view within the steering column was intriguing.

Still within the same section, there was an area for putting together the rear light cluster and the rear wing assembly. There were similar pre-assembly areas for the centre console, the rear brake assembly, the mounting of the water-to-air intercooler and the fuel pump to the firewall, and the front crashbox structure carrying its striking red tow eye, and its alien looking headlights. In a corner, there was also a test station for checking that the newly assembled steering wheel and all its infra-red

Above, top: Multi-tasker Daniel composes Brembo brake calipers onto the semi-completed front disc brake assemblies, painstakingly measuring torque settings as he goes. Centre right: The assembled multi-function steering wheel, ready for fitting. Centre: Luvid Harazim does the final assembly of the Audi TFSI engine destined for the X-BOW. Right: Another view of the Audi TFSI engine, which awaits marriage to its chassis.
Far right: Crated complete gearboxes, soon with amazing racing stories to tell.

Overview of the KTM X-BOW factory floor in Graz, Austria.

electronics for controlling the signals and the instrument pod were fully operational.

An optional sequential shift gear-stick assembly as well as a traditional standard manual assembly were being put together on yet another bench.

At the junction between the pre-assembly area and Station One of the assembly line, there were neatly laid out boxes, which Manfred kindly unpacked to reveal front and rear roll bar assemblies. Alongside these boxes were crates containing complete gearboxes.

## ASSEMBLY STATION ONE

There is now a new assembly line sub-station that did not exist prior to early 2018. From the time that the very first production X-BOW was built until 2018, Audi supplied fully built engines for the cars. Since the start of 2018, Audi has supplied the basic crate engine, just as before, but KTM now have to attach the turbocharger, injectors, airflow measuring components and various sensors to the engine block.

All this is done by one KTM specialist engine technician called Luvid

Harazim, who took time out to talk to us about his work. Luvid explained that KTM was now like Aston Martin, Mercedes AMG and Cosworth (in the case of my Brooke 260 RR) in that each engine was assembled by just one engine builder – something that is very rare. He was actually working on a GT4 engine at the time we interrupted him, but he and Manfred took us further along the production line to show us an 'R' variant engine that he had just completed. Luvid explained that adding on all these extra components was meticulous and time-consuming work, and this in turn made the 2018 and onwards cars more expensive to produce.

The completed engine is then moved by crane to further along Station One, where the gearbox, clutch and flywheel are attached.

Meanwhile, the naked carbon fibre monocoque is lowered by an overhead lift onto a pre-placed assembly jig at Station Three.

## ASSEMBLY STATION TWO

At Station Two, the rear aluminium subframe is readied for the driveshafts, the rear suspension assembly, the rear brake discs and the handbrake cables. The rear wheelarches are also attached at this station, and a fire extinguisher system is attached to all the 'Rookie' models.

### ASSEMBLY STATION THREE

The aluminium rear subframe is joined to the rear of the monocoque at

this station. This horizontal marriage of two of the major components of the X-BOW is a key stage in the whole assembly process. The completed rear aluminium subframe from Station Two is now rolled on a trolley to meet the rear of the monocoque, which is already waiting on its jig, to consummate the marriage. The third station is also where the firewall holding the turbo intercooler and the water pump is bolted to the monocoque, and the fuel inlet with its connections plumbed in. The Audi 2.0-litre TFSI engine and gearbox is now lifted up towards the ceiling using an air-hoist before being carefully lowered into the empty cavity formed by the rear of the monocoque and the back of the rear subframe. The Audi engine is transversely mounted in the X-BOW. There are two radiators on each side: one for the engine and one for the

intercooler. These, together with their associated radiator cooling fans, are fitted to the car here.

### ASSEMBLY STATION FOUR

The front suspension assembly takes place at this station. As well as the front shock absorbers and springs, the front suspension consists of aerodynamically profiled double triangular wishbones which are bolted directly to the twin-walled monocoque and the pushrod system

Next, the movable pedal assembly is installed. The accelerator, brake and clutch pedals are all made of lightweight aluminium.

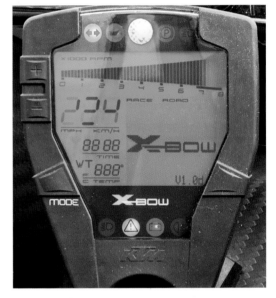

The optional lightweight racing battery and the switch for the optional fire extinguisher system as well as the extinguisher canister itself are all attached at this assembly station if specified by the customer. The standard roll-over bars (which can withstand loads of up to 2.5 times the car's weight) or the racing roll bars (which can withstand up to ten times the car's weight) are bolted into position here. The windscreen for the GT variant is fitted at Station Four, and once aligned and attached it has to be held in place for 24 hours by a special aluminium jig system to ensure that the windscreen frame is tightly affixed to the monocoque. The pre-assembled central console assembly, which covers the gearstick lever and contains the Keyless-Go system and the hazard warning lights button, is connected up to the car's wiring loom. Finally, the single pod, multi-function instrument display (which sits in the centre of the cockpit and is angled towards the driver) is also wired up and screwed into position.

### ASSEMBLY STATION FIVE

At Station Five, the pre-assembled steering column is attached to the car.

The engine torque brace is also fitted at this point. The vehicle identification number is etched onto the monocoque here, and the large white cubic fusebox is wired in. The catalytic converter, the rear silencer (standard, sports or racing) and the main ECU are all also attached at this station. The customer-specified wheels and tyres are fitted on here so that the part-built X-BOW is ready to roll after Station Five.

Above, from top: A recognisable face? The Front crashbox, complete with headlights and splitter is ready for fitting and electrical connections. Seeing the light: Manfred Wolf unveils a delicate carbon fibre component from its specialist transport packaging. The quality of the carbon fibre, and the precision of the prefabricated holes for the components can be seen here in the gearbox tunnel, complete with fire extinguisher system, essential for racing, and a standard fitment on 'Rookie' models.
Right: Rear underfloor diffusers (see page 61).

### ASSEMBLY STATION SIX

Station Six is where the GT4 roll cage, as well as the window glass, is fitted to this circuit-exclusive racer.

### ASSEMBLY STATION SEVEN

The X-BOW finds itself at an automatic fluid input station when it arrives at Assembly Station Seven. Exactly ten litres of 98 octane fuel is added to the car, while engine and gearbox oils, as well as coolant and brake fluids, are filled to capacity. In the case of the GT variants, the windscreen wiper fluid bottle is also topped up. The car's weight distribution is then measured and adjusted.

Laser wheel alignment using a Hunter HawkEye system is carried out next. The car's ECUs are now wired up to Audi's central database through a reserve computer system connected to Audi's headquarters. Once the correct computations are downloaded and activated within any given car, the engine can finally be started.

### ASSEMBLY STATION EIGHT

Station Eight is essentially a rolling road. The X-BOW is started up within the confines of this enclosed space, and basic functional checks and tests are carried out. Each X-BOW is tested on this rolling road first, as a prelude to the final open road test that every car undergoes before it is signed off. While on the dynamometer, the car's power and torque outputs are measured and recorded at various engine speeds and in various gears.

### ASSEMBLY STATION NINE

A four-post lifting system, which sits flush with the factory

Below: Tucked away at the side of one of the factory's wings, is an impromptu display of X-BOWs in various guises, from R to GT4.

floor when retracted, rises out of the floor when activated, in order to lift an X-BOW into the air. This allows for easy and safe fitment of the flat underfloor panels and the main rear diffuser.

## ASSEMBLY STATION TEN

At this final station, the lighting and electrical systems are wired up and tested. The pre-assembled front crashbox, the front splitter, and the four carbon fibre body panels go through a careful final alignment before being fully tightened down. The safety-critical crashbox is attached to the monocoque with impact drivers. If a problem develops during these final tests, there is a side assembly area to hold the car in question while the issue is resolved.

It is inspirational to see how a small and expert team of dedicated engineer-technicians can slowly and carefully hand-assemble top quality components on a bespoke production line, such that one car can survive and triumph within the harsh environment of a race circuit, while the next car is equally at home as a form of garage art.

# READY TO RAISE ⌃⌃

Up and away ... at this late stage in production, the X-BOW is almost complete; with just lighting to connect, body panels to be tightened after final alignment and underfloor panels to be fitted once the car is lifted.

The flat underfloor is designed to give as much 'ground effect' as possible.

Right: Closer views of the underfloor vanes.

The finished X-BOW. Ready to race – now where's that track?

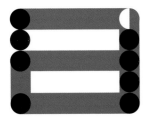
The two outstanding things about the KTM X-BOW are its aerodynamics and its chassis.

The X-BOW's carbon fibre monocoque is one of its unique selling points. At the time of its 2007 Geneva Motor Show debut, the X-BOW was one of a very small and highly select group of cars that boasted this feature. KTM Sportcar GmbH's own promotional literature read: "The world's first production car with a full carbon composite monocoque."

Composite materials have a long history of use within the automotive sector. Kevlar for instance, which was developed by Stephanie Kwolek at DuPont in 1965, was very strong, so was used in the racing tyres of the early 1970s instead of steel. It was also relatively lightweight, and because of this it was used for the front bonnet and the rear engine cover of the 1985 Lamborghini Countach 5000 QV.

The first Formula 1 car with a complete carbon fibre composite monocoque was the McLaren MP4/1, which raced during the 1981 season. Road car uptake of this new technology was slow, largely due to the high cost, the labour intensity, and the specialist facilities and staff needed to manufacture such a monocoque.

Those road cars that did have a complete carbon fibre monocoque at the time of the X-BOW's introduction were all supercars, but not just any old supercars: this technology was reserved for only the most exclusive; those at the very apex of the supercar pyramid. The first production road car with a full carbon fibre monocoque was the Bugatti EB110 of 1991, which was closely followed by the McLaren F1 of 1992.

In featuring a carbon monocoque at its 2007 debut, the X-BOW was keeping the company of hypercars like the Bugatti Veyron of 2005, the Koenigsegg CCR of 2004, the McLaren SLR of 2003, the Ferrari Enzo of 2002 and the Pagani Zonda of 1999. Other such cars included the Jaguar XJR-15 of 1990, the Mercedes CLK-GTR of 1998, the Ascari KZ1 of 2003, and the Porsche Carrera GT of 2004 – exclusive company by any measure.

The KTM X-BOW's carbon monocoque weighs just 81kg, and is a crucial element in allowing the X-BOW to achieve a dry weight of just 790kg. The monocoque not only surrounds the two-seater cockpit, thereby forming its survival cell, but also forms the very stiff central element of the X-BOW, onto which many other critical elements are mounted.

The front suspension is attached directly to this carbon tub. The rear aluminium subframe, which carries the engine, gearbox and parts of the rear suspension, is bolted onto the rear of the carbon fibre monocoque.

This safety critical tub, the low weight of which is directly responsible for the X-BOW's spectacular straight-line performance, can also take credit for the X-BOW's handling, cornering and roadholding, courtesy of its remarkable levels of rigidity – this carbon fibre monocoque boasts 35,000Nm per degree of torsional stiffness.

Stable mates – McLaren's 1992 F1, and the 1991 EB110 from the then reinvented Bugatti with Romano Artiolli at the helm, were both forward thinking enough to sport carbon fibre monocoques. However, these were both low-volume, high retail supercars. KTM has exploited carbon fibre monocoques to the X-BOW's advantage – marrying formidable rigidity with low mass.

81 kilos of carbon fibre heaven! Immaculately finished carbon fibre is an art form in its own right. With additions like seat forms (note the Velcro fastenings) and the multi-function steering wheel to add at this stage, KTM's work to construct the X-BOW is really just beginning. The monocoques are transported in tailor-made carriers, to minimise the possibility of damage during their journey from Wethje in southern Germany (pre-2018) or Mubea Carbo Tech, based in Salzburg, Austria, (post 2018).

Below: Arriving in specially-fabricated transport crates, the monocoques are stored in the pre-assembly area, ready for components to be added. The KTM X-BOW is very much a hand-built car; something that only a handful of car manufacturers worldwide, many with more longevity in the business than KTM, can lay claim to.

Bottom: Manfred Wolf with one of the specially designed transport crates – note the felted edges of the crossmembers – no chances are taken when it comes to damage risk of these precious cargoes.

Dallara, in its Research and Development centre-cum-factory in Varano de' Melegari outside Parma in Italy, built the three X-BOW prototypes. Dallara is an internationally recognised expert in carbon composite technology for automotive use. KTM's technical brief to Dallara was to develop a carbon fibre monocoque that combined KISKA's spectacular design with the lowest possible weight, while delivering FIA compliant safety standards. This was a brief that was ideally suited to Dallara – an engineering company whose back and present catalogues include every chassis currently used in Indycar, the 2018 Haas Formula 1 chassis, and the chassis for many of Audi's legendary Le Mans prototypes.

The three prototype X-BOW monocoques were made by Dallara and produced as one complete unit, so these prototype monocoques have no joins in them.

Every other X-BOW carbon fibre monocoque, including those of the 100 Dallara-edition cars, was produced by Wethje, in southern Germany, as a two-piece unit with a single join that was later bonded together. Or at least this was the case until 2018.

Wethje has huge experience in manufacturing carbon composite components for premium road car manufacturers, touring car race teams, Formula 1, various industrial applications and aerospace. The company was founded by two brothers, Reinhard and Reimer Wethje in Grafing near Munich in 1979, and began series production of the KTM X-BOW at its Pleinting factory in 2008. Sometime after this, Stefan Pierer bought a majority share in Wethje GmbH. In 2014, Mitsubishi Rayon, which is currently the world's largest carbon fibre manufacturer, took a 51 per cent share in Wethje GmbH, and further increased this to 82 per cent in 2016. Mitsubishi Rayon either could not or would not allow Wethje GmbH to produce and sell the X-BOW monocoques to KTM at the previous price. Therefore, in 2018, KTM entered into a contract with Mubea Carbo Tech GmbH to produce the carbon tubs instead. Carbo Tech is a Tier 1 supplier of carbon composite products for the Austrian aeronautics industry, and also has extensive experience with supercar and race car carbon fibre component production.

It is important to stress that both KTM and KISKA went into the concept phase of the X-BOW with open minds, and did not carry the pre-conceived notion that the car should have a carbon fibre monocoque. Other ideas that were floated around during the early discussions of the X-BOW concept included it having a spaceframe chassis made of chromium-molybdenum steel or a steel tub. The former option had the advantage of being cheaper, and while not as light as aluminium alloy, it had high tensile strength and better malleability. However, after due consideration, the carbon fibre tub option won because it offered much better safety, much lower weight and much higher rigidity, all of which Stefan Pierer and KTM prized highly for their showcase 21st-century super sports car.

A full carbon tub also fitted in beautifully with KTM being an established motorsport company whose motto was 'Ready To Race.' And, in 2007, KTM could market the X-BOW as the world's first mass-produced – as well as the world's most affordable (everything in life being relative) – wholly carbon composite monocoque road car.

Carbon fibre was first produced in 1860 by Joseph Swan, a British chemist and physicist, for use in incandescent light bulbs. Sadly, this was commercially impractical at that time, and the venture was a failure. Thomas Edison, a prolific inventor, produced the first practical and commercially successful, all-carbon fibre incandescent light bulb filament in 1879. Over the next 70 years, various companies, particularly in the United States and Japan, attempted to discover a way of producing industrial quantities of carbon fibre while achieving the high tensile strength and stiffness that carbon fibre is theoretically capable of.

Carbon fibre is made up of long, thin strands, which themselves are almost exclusively composed of carbon atoms. The carbon atoms are bonded together into microscopic crystals, which in turn are aligned along the long axis of the fibre to form filaments. Each carbon filament is a continuous cylinder of about 5 to 10 micrometres. Thousands of these filaments are twisted together to form a yarn, which can then be used by itself or woven into a fabric. Once the carbon fibre yarn or fabric is impregnated with a plastic polymer resin and baked, it forms a carbon fibre-reinforced-polymer (commonly abbreviated to carbon fibre), which has an exceptionally high strength-to-weight ratio, and is also very rigid.

There are a number of different autoclaving techniques available for curing carbon fibre, but all essentially attempt to achieve a given desired fibre-to-resin ratio, with the elimination of resin voids; resin voids weaken the carbon fibre's structure. The carbon fibre fabric is laid up in an almost surgically sterile environment, impregnated with the resin, placed under a vacuum, and then pressurised in an autoclave while going through a heat cure cycle. The high pressure and temperature within the autoclave (typically a nitrogen atmosphere set at about 7 bar, and running between 120°C and 230°C, with curing times that can range from 90 minutes to 12 hours) can achieve a resin void of less than 2 per cent – which is acceptable for aerospace structures and the KTM X-BOW.

In the case of the KTM X-BOW, first Wethje and now CarboTech lay carbon fibre mats onto a mould. Specific mats are chosen for each location and application, based on the strength and the torsional stiffness required at that location or for that function. The X-BOW monocoque is made up of a bottom section and a top section. Each is made up of four layers of fibre mats infused with epoxy resin. This laying up of the carbon fibre mats and the associated infusion takes place in a 'clean room,' which resembles an operating theatre and features four large ceiling-mounted humidifiers. These humidifiers produce a high grade mist that provides the ideal environment in which to lay up pre-cut sheets of woven carbon fibre smeared with epoxy resin into moulds. This process laminates the single carbon fibre layers together. Putty knives are used to conform the layers into the corners of the mould, and to remove any air pockets. The technicians now put a thick plastic protective covering, like big carrier bags, over each mould, completely enclosing it. These plastic bags have metal couplings to which air suction hoses are attached, with air thereby removed from inside. This causes a partial vacuum to form within the plastic bags, which forces the four layers of carbon fibre to compress together as well as encouraging them to closely conform to the mould. Next, the carbon fibre monocoque is cured in a pressurised autoclave at 248°C, which forces the carbon fibre mats to release the epoxy resin.

The top half of the monocoque is then put on an automatic trolley system that moves it into an enclosed finishing chamber, where it is cleaned
(continued on p74)

Below, top to bottom: Racing headrests, although an option, are a must-have for track use, when the X-BOW throws itself into corners the G-force can be immense. Even the front towing eye has an air of engineering efficiency about it; owners all hope that it never gets used, of course! Powerful but simple headlights are mounted within plastic surrounds. The transmission tunnel is part of the monocoque, and here, the wiring loom for the centrally-mounted switch panel can be seen, as well as the gear selection lever.

Left: Monocoque no more, as the hundreds of components, such as those that make up the rear light assembly (right) required to hand-build an X-BOW are now fitted, and the car is ready for its first road-test.

The workmanship that goes into the monocoque is nothing short of miraculous. Fixings for the mirrors and the floating body panels all have to be precisely placed; this is after all, a hand-built, precision-engineered piece of performance machinery, the likes of which can really only be paralelled by Lamborghini, Ferrari and a handful of other supercar manufacturers.

Fresh out of the box! The moncoque as it arrives at the factory in Graz, perfectly engineered. This one is for a GT, as it's complete with a windscreen mount.

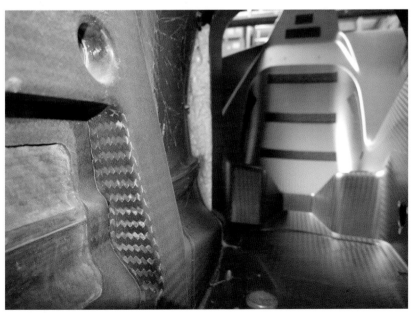

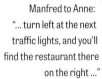

A driver's big toe's view of the cockpit.

Manfred to Anne: "... turn left at the next traffic lights, and you'll find the restaurant there on the right ..."

The carbon fibre monocoque crash-test results were very favourable, and with only minor damage (inset) being sustained, it takes pride of place, high up on the factory wall, as testament to the engineering excellence that went into its design and conception.

Above and main picture: 'X' marks the spot – the fact that the X-BOW has been in production since 2008 is worthy of celebration, and in 2018, KTM launched its ten-year anniversary model, complete with Roman numeral-inspired decals and a distinctly dark nature to the overall look, with the inevitable 'KTM orange' splashes of colour on the panelwork. The fabulous design features a huge black 'X' when viewd from above, seen here as diagonal sections of exposed carbon fibre running from the top of the front headlamps, and behind the rollover bars.

No bull, it's the same monocoque – the GT4 track car is an incredible achievement, bearing in mind the minimal changes required during production, engine-tuning aside. The lifting front canopy is an inspired solution to the age-old problem of how to allow access without the added weight gain that conventional doors would bring. The canopy is unique to the GT4, with an extended hinge at the front central position, between the shock absorbers. Like the coventional X-BOW, the body panels are minimal in number, and modular for ease of replacement, should the need arise during a race.

Beautifully turned out: This pair of GT4s pose for a pre-race photoshoot. No prizes for guessing which company puts the boots on the X-BOW!

before a robot very accurately drills holes in pre-defined locations of the monocoque. The top and bottom sections of the carbon fibre monocoque are later joined together with a high-strength epoxy resin.

Carbon fibres are classified according to the tensile modulus of the fibre, which is measured in pounds of force per square inch of cross-sectional area. The strongest carbon fibres are ten times stronger than steel, while being five times lighter. Carbon fibre also has excellent fatigue and corrosion-resistant properties. The main drawback of carbon fibre has traditionally been its high production cost, but recently it has become more widely known that carbon fibre is wasteful to produce and difficult to recycle.

Industry loves the exceptionally high strength-to weight ratio and the rigidity of carbon fibre, and its use has been increasing globally at a rate of about 10 per cent year-on-

year. Carbon fibre is particularly used in aerospace applications, military engineering, wind turbine blades and, of course, high-performance road cars and race cars.

Specialist car companies in particular have taken a special interest in carbon fibre technology, both as a way of meeting increasingly stringent emissions legislation, and also as a way to increase a car's performance. Lamborghini, for example, currently an Audi subsidiary, has become something of an expert on composite technology within the Volkswagen Group. It established an Advanced Composite Research Centre at the Sant'Agata factory in 2007, together with an engineering division and a manufacturing

division. Lamborghini also set up a collaboration with Boeing in 2007, focussing on material crashworthiness, modular construction processes and the repair of damaged composite structures. This cooperation in material sciences between Lamborghini, Boeing and various universities and research institutes from around the world was further cemented by the establishment of the Advanced Composites Structures Laboratory in Seattle in 2014. The Sesto Elemento prototype is an example of this technology in action – not only with regards to the monocoque, but also due to the shock absorbers, wheels, and transmission shaft in the Sesto being made of carbon fibre. Another example is a material developed by

Lamborghini's composite division called Carbonskin – a flexible carbon fibre matrix suitable for use in a car's interior. It is pleasing to the eye and touch, durable, and weighs 65 per cent less than leather and 28 per cent less than Alcantara. It would not be surprising (considering the long-standing and close relationship that exists between KTM and Audi) to find that some of this Lamborghini-derived carbon composite technology filters its way into the next generation X-BOW.

At any rate, the KTM X-BOW has already made its presence known in the carbon composite world by being the world's first production car with a full carbon composite monocoque. The X-BOW is doubly significant in this arena, because unlike some hypercars, it can genuinely be used on both road and track, and is also relatively affordable.

The monocoque in place and fitted out with every component, body panel, sensor, pipe, wheel and customer-ordered extra now on board, the X-BOW is ready for its first actual test drive, carried out by KTM Engineer-Technicians.

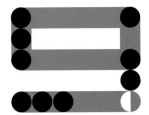

The complex and meticulously engineered aerodynamics of the KTM X-BOW are, together with its wholly carbon fibre chassis, one of the two unique selling points of this revolutionary car. The pedigree of the team responsible for the X-BOW's aerodynamics is unsurpassed in the automotive world, and Dallara Engineering has also invested heavily to procure state-of-the-art manufacturing machinery and test facilities.

KTM's intention, that its first four-wheeled vehicle should incorporate as many technological innovations as possible, found material expression in the way that the X-BOW was designed to not only pass through air efficiently, but also to exploit this passage to generate downforce. To master the dark art of aerodynamics is to find the holy grail of race car engineering.

### THE ETYMOLOGY

The first part of the word aerodynamics 'aer' has both an ancient Greek and a Latin etymology and means 'air.' 'Aer' itself derives from the Greek word 'aemi,' which means 'to breathe unconsciously.' Much, much later in time, around the 14th century, the Italians transmuted the word 'aer,' and coined the word 'aria,' in relation to singing. By the 17th century, 'aria' was an everyday word in Italy and France, in relation to the opera. The many descendants of the word 'aer' (and there are many others, stretching from Portuguese and old Irish through to Albanian and Sardinian) remain in common usage today. Fundamentally though, the word 'aer' means 'air.'

The second half of the word again has its origin in ancient Greek. The word 'dunamis' translates into English as 'strength' or 'power,' and is used 120 times in the New Testament. The term 'dunamis' itself derives from the word 'dunamai,' which means 'I am able.' The reader will therefore appreciate why the Oxford English Dictionary defines the word 'dynamic' as 'constantly changing' or 'in motion.'

### THE SCIENCE

Aerodynamics is a branch of gas dynamics, which itself is a branch of fluid dynamics. In physics, a fluid is defined as any gas, liquid or plasma that cannot sustain a shearing force when at rest, and which undergoes a continuous change in shape when subjected to such a stress. For the purposes of this book, we are only concerned about aerodynamics as it applies to the passage of the X-BOW through the Earth's atmosphere; the KTM X-BOW is not amphibious, and we therefore do not have to concern ourselves with its motion through liquid; it is also a terrestrial vehicle, confined to Earth, so we do not have to concern ourselves with its passage through the carbon dioxide and methane-rich atmosphere of Mars (although on the actual day of this paragraph being written – December 23, 2018 – space scientists using the European-Russian spacecraft ExoMars Trace Gas Orbitor have just reported that they have been unable to detect any Martian atmospheric methane – a huge departure from the long-standing belief that Mars has a methane-rich atmosphere) or the hydrogen-dense atmosphere of Saturn. We need only study how the KTM X-BOW moves through the Earth's atmosphere: the 78 per cent nitrogen, 21 per cent oxygen, 0.9 per cent argon, and 0.1 per cent trace gases mixture.

Aerodynamics studies the properties of moving air and the physics of how this moving air interacts with a solid object. The fundamental forces here include weight, lift, thrust and drag: weight is a product of gravity acting upon the mass of an object; lift is the force that moves an object upwards; thrust is the force that moves an object forwards; drag is the resistance force that opposes an object's forward motion.

## THE SCIENTISTS

The study of aerodynamics has been underpinned by pioneering science done by some of the greatest physicists the world has ever known. Five of them are particularly important here:

Sir Isaac Newton
1642-1726

Sir Isaac Newton (1642-1726), a fellow Cantabrigian – albeit the Lucasian Professor of Mathematics at Trinity rather than a lowly undergraduate at Pembroke – was the first person to postulate the theory of air resistance, otherwise known as drag: a fundamental cornerstone of aerodynamics. He laid out this idea in his book *Philosophiae Naturalis Principia Mathematica*, which was published in 1687. The contents of this book established some of the most fundamental laws of physics governing the universe, including the Laws of Motion and Newton's Law of Universal Gravitation.

Newton was an interesting person; born premature on Christmas day, his early academic achievements were partly motivated in response to schoolyard bullying. There was some nepotism involved in his admission to Trinity as a subsizar (thought-provokingly, 80 per cent of sizars who entered Cambridge in the seventeenth century took their degree, while only 30 per cent of gentlemen did), in that his uncle, who had also studied there, recommended him. As a Fellow at Trinity, Newton was required to take Holy Orders, but he refused to do so, and King Charles II gave him a special exemption from this ordination, on the excuse that Newton needed every available moment to study the Natural Sciences. Less commonly known is that approximately 10 per cent of all Newton's writings pertain to alchemy, some of which would have been considered heretical by the Church. Newton, arguably, was one of the greatest scientists of all time, and Albert Einstein hung a portrait of Newton on his study wall. Newton's Laws of Motion and Universal Gravitation and his ideas on air resistance are fundamental to the study of aerodynamics and its real world application in car design.

Daniel Bernoulli
1700-1782

Daniel Bernoulli's work is integral to understanding aerodynamic lift. Bernoulli (1700-1782) was born in Holland into an acclaimed family of mathematicians. He first studied mathematics, and then medicine in Venice, before settling down in Switzerland. In 1738 he published Hydrodynamica, a study of how fluids behave in motion, which asserted that as a fluid moves faster, it produces less pressure. Known today as Bernoulli's Principle, it describes the relationship between pressure, density and flow velocity, and explains how lift is generated on an aircraft's wings, why petrol flows through a carburettor, and what causes the canvas soft top of a Lamborghini Murcielago Roadster to lift upwards away from the cockpit as the car's speed increases. Lift is undesirable in a KTM X-BOW, as it lowers the maximum possible cornering speed.

Sir George Cayley
1773-1857

Sir George Cayley (1773-1857) is considered by many to be the father of aviation. He identified the four vector forces of flight – weight, lift, drag and thrust – and worked on measuring drag on objects at different speeds and at different angles of attack, and on the science and aerodynamics of cambered wings. His work, fundamental to aircraft design, is directly applicable to racing car design and the X-BOW.

Lord Rayleigh
1842-1919

Lord Rayleigh (1842-1919) was another important contributor to the field of aerodynamics, developing drag theory and contributing extensively to fluid dynamics, and in particular formulating the circulation theory of aerodynamic lift. Born John William Strutt, he, like Isaac Newton, had a distinguished academic career at Trinity, Cambridge, where he was Cavendish Professor of Physics, and

Opposite page and left: Extensive aerodynamic wind tunnel testing was undertaken by Dallara during the X-BOW's research and development phases. KTM points out: "The monocoque is essential to high torsional stiffness and the remarkable power to weight ratio. This is why the main chassis was built as a double wall monolithic structure made of carbon fibre-reinforced-plastic. In order to fulfil legal requirements for the vehicle and exploit optimum potential, dynamic and static loading conditions were simulated and compared to realistic conditions."

later Chancellor of the University. He received the 1904 Nobel Prize for Physics for his "investigations of the densities of important gases, and for his discovery of argon." The science underpinning the KTM X-BOW's contradictory requirements of low drag and high downforce are partly Rayleigh's work.

Henri Coandă
1886-1972

**Henri Coandă** (1886-1972) was a Romanian aerodynamicist, who some people say preceded both Dr Hans Von Ohain and Sir Frank Whittle in building the first jet-powered aircraft. He apparently crashed this plane in 1910, and, unable to get further funding, nothing further became of his jet plane. He did, however, make a very important contribution to the field of aerodynamics when he described the Coandă Effect. The Coandă Effect describes the tendency of a fluid stream, when in contact with a curved surface, to follow the curvature of that surface rather than continue in a straight line; it also explains how the curvature and profile of an aircraft wing produces lift. The Coandă Effect also underlies the technology behind the Dyson Airwrap Hair Curling Styler, the Dyson Bladeless Fan, various experimental flying saucers, echocardiogram discrepancies that cardiologists use to diagnose heart disease and how the front splitter of the KTM X-BOW generates downforce.

## THE GOVERNING LAWS

Of the four fundamental forces of flight (lift, thrust, drag and weight) two – lift and drag – are aerodynamic forces: forces that owe their existence to airflow over a solid body. Studying the movement of air around a solid structure (often referred to as a flow field) allows the forces and the moments acting upon that object to be calculated.

Four important Laws of Physics are especially relevant to the aerodynamics of cars: the Law of Conservation of Mass, which states that mass is neither created or destroyed; the Law of Conservation of Momentum (a derivation of Newton's second Law of Motion), which states that momentum within a flow can only be changed by work performed on that system by external forces; the Law of Conservation of Energy, which states that energy can neither be created nor destroyed within a flow; and Bernoulli's Principle, which states that pressure decreases when flow speed increases.

With particular regard to automotive aerodynamics, both external and internal aerodynamics are important. External Aerodynamics studies the airflow around solid objects of various shapes, for example over and around the wheelarches and the rear wing of the KTM X-BOW. Internal Aerodynamics studies airflow through passages in solid objects, for example through the numerous vents and ducts found on the front and the sides of the X-BOW.

Flow speed is another important classification criteria in aerodynamics. Flow issues are classified as subsonic if the flow problem happens below the speed of sound, transonic if the flow speed is just below or just above the speed of sound, supersonic when the flow speed is consistently above the speed of sound, and hypersonic when the flow speed is about five or more times greater than the speed of sound.

Fluid Viscosity and Fluid Compressibility are the final two variables that we need to mention in this extremely brief discourse on automobile aerodynamics. If the influence of the viscosity of the fluid within a given flow system is very small, then it can be considered as negligible and completely discounted, and such flow systems are called inviscid flows. Flows where the viscosity of the fluid is too large to be neglected are called viscous systems, and in these cases the viscosity of the fluid (in the case of the KTM X-BOW, this is air) needs to be taken into account when calculating the aerodynamic profile around that particular part of the car.

Incompressible Aerodynamics takes place in a flow system in which the density of the fluid is constant in both space and time. This is generally the case when fluid flow speeds are at or below 0.3 Mach (0.3 times the speed of sound). Compressible Aerodynamics takes place if and when the density of the fluid changes during the course of a flow system. At speeds above 0.3 Mach, there is generally a 5 per cent or more change in fluid density, and so compressible aerodynamic considerations come into play at and above this flow speed threshold.

## REAL WORLD APPLICATION OF AERODYNAMICS

Race car aerodynamicists have two major objectives: to reduce drag, which is a product of air resistance, and thereby increase top speed; and to increase downforce, which will further push the tyres onto the tarmac, and thereby increase cornering speed. Current (2018) Formula 1 cars are capable of generating 3.5G of lateral cornering force largely due to aerodynamic downforce.

The principles underlying aerodynamics have been employed by man for thousands of years, for example in sail boats and in windmills, and aerodynamics has also been recognised as an important consideration since the dawn of the motorcar. The cigar-shaped Cooper racing cars of the 1950s, and the wedge-shaped Lamborghini Countach of the 1970s and '80s (which, incidentally, despite its spectacular angular profile, has an awful drag coefficient, even without its large rear wing and wide Pirelli P7 tyres) were respectful nods to the importance of aerodynamics.

Aerodynamics became a serious consideration in the late 1960s, when Formula 1 teams started to test and deploy racing cars with rear wings. These aerofoils are, in effect, reverse aircraft wings, and create negative lift or downforce. The problem with wings or aerofoils is that they substantially increase drag, which in turn decreases performance.

Lotus, under the tutelage of Colin Chapman and Peter Wright, introduced ground effect technology to the Formula 1 world. The beauty of ground effect technology is that downforce is achieved with minimal additional drag. In the late 1970s Lotus designed the entire underside of their Type 78 race car to act like a giant reverse wing that would accelerate the air passing underneath the car, and so create a partial vacuum there. The higher air pressure present on the top surface of the car would then force the car downwards onto the road. The tyres would then be better able to bite into the tarmac, thereby enabling higher cornering forces to be achieved.

Brabham, under the guidance of Gordon Murray, took this idea to its logical extremity by using a fan to extract air from a sealed area underneath the car to create a partial vacuum, and therefore an area of enormous downforce. This Brabham BT46(B) fan car was only entered for one race – the 1978 Swedish Grand Prix, driven by Niki Lauda – which it won.

Today, the front and rear wings of a 2018 Formula 1 car together account for about 60 per cent of the total downforce generated, with the flat underbody floor responsible for the majority of the remaining 40 per cent.

Every surface, duct and vent of a racing car has to be designed with aerodynamics as the primary consideration. The design not only needs to reduce drag, and increase downforce evenly over the entire length and width of the car, but also needs to manage and optimise the airflow at the boundary layers, where the airflow over the body separates at the end of the car. This airstream separation causes turbulence, which in turn creates drag, which then slows down the car. All this is further complicated by the need for the car's aerodynamics to direct a good quantity of air to the radiators to cool the engine. The KTM X-BOW needs generous servings of ambient temperature air to keep its turbocharged Audi engine cool, and so needs large, exposed dual radiators on either side of the car. This critical requirement had a major impact on the design and the final appearance of the X-BOW.

Road car aerodynamics has assumed growing importance in recent years. Traditionally, road car aerodynamics was aimed at maximising performance figures, and top speed in particular. Today, aerodynamics is seen as a key way of reducing fuel consumption and emissions, which is so important in our current, environmentally conscious world. While population restriction is the only true way of controlling the ticking time bomb that is climate change, few, if any, world leaders dare to talk about this indisputable fact, as it goes directly against millenia-old religious and monarchial doctrines; both of which demand a large, constantly renewed, preferably ignorant, and therefore compliant, population base.

## AERODYNAMIC PARTS OF THE KTM X-BOW

Both aerodynamic drag and aerodynamic downforce increase with velocity, and the X-BOW uses various aerodynamic addenda to decrease the former and increase the latter.

## THE FRONT SPLITTER

The X-BOW's front splitter is the flat extension jutting forwards from the very bottom of the front bodywork-air dam. This splitter generates downforce by creating an air pressure differential between the upper and lower surfaces of the car when the car is in motion. As per the Bernoulli Principle and the Coandă Effect, faster-moving air exerts lower pressure than slower moving air, and the fluid stream in contact with the curved surfaces of the X-BOW will tend to follow these curvatures. To get maximum downforce one therefore needs slow-moving high-pressure air acting on the top of the car, and fast-moving low-pressure air underneath the car. A properly designed front splitter should be just one part of a greater ground effects system – which might include a flat underfloor, a rear diffuser or a rear wing – to ensure that there is an even distribution of downforce throughout the entire length and width of the car. When a car is travelling at speed, a wall of air pressure builds up immediately in front of the car. The front splitter acts as a wedge and forces the majority of this oncoming

high-pressure air to go over the top of the vehicle, only allowing a small amount to pass underneath the vehicle. This pressure differential creates downforce. Additionally, when the front splitter redirects this relatively small quantity of air underneath the car, it accelerates this underbody airflow, and so creates a high-speed low-pressure area underneath the car, further increasing downforce. The height of the splitter above ground level is critical to its effectiveness. The lower the splitter is to the ground, the greater the downforce it will generate; this is true right up to a critical point after which the splitter is so close to the ground that insufficient air is able to pass below. At this point, the air speed underneath the car will suddenly decrease, which will cause an increase in undercar pressure and drag, neither of which is desirable. Aerodynamics is a complex science as well as a dark art, and deviation from the KTM factory geometry settings is only for the brave.

## THE FRONT AIR DAM

The front air dam is the lower part of the front face of the vehicle, and is the first part of the car that encounters the oncoming airstream. It therefore has a great influence on the car's overall aerodynamics. With most ordinary cars, the front air dam is formed by the front bumper and grill, but in the case of the X-BOW it is formed by the front of the crashbox, the front body panels and additional front spoiler extensions. The front air dam is carefully designed to direct the airstream to maximise aero efficiency by reducing drag and increasing downforce; to ensure that adequate cool air reaches the side-mounted radiators and the engine intake snorkel; and to minimise in-cockpit turbulence. The air dam and the front splitter work together to control the degree of understeer and the car's front end turn in response. The design of the front air dam also determines how the airstream interacts with the undertray, the rear wing, and the rear diffuser, which again illustrates the joint up nature of car aerodynamics.

## THE VORTEX GENERATORS

Later X-BOW's could be specified with an optional splitter that features a middle plate carrying what looks like a row of six shark's teeth. This option changes the already threatening frontal appearance of the X-BOW to one of malign aggression. But these six shark teeth have more than simple cosmetic value. They are vortex generators. Vortex generators are aerodynamic devices found in civilian and military planes to counter shock-stall problems at transonic speeds; in large passenger planes like the Airbus A320 to reduce noise pollution; and on wind turbine blades to improve efficiency. In the KTM X-BOW the vortex generators are used to delay, limit and control what is known as airflow separation.

As an airstream meets the surface of a car, the atom of air nearest to the car surface, can, for purposes of physics, be thought of as effectively attached to that surface point, and thus be thought of as stationary. This effect decreases the further one gets from this stationary point: the flow velocity of the airstream progressively increases the further away the airstream gets from this static surface point, finally reaching what is known as the freestream point, where there is unimpeded flow of the fluid. The boundary layer refers to the layer of fluid in the immediate vicinity of a bounding surface, and its importance lies in the fact that the viscosity of

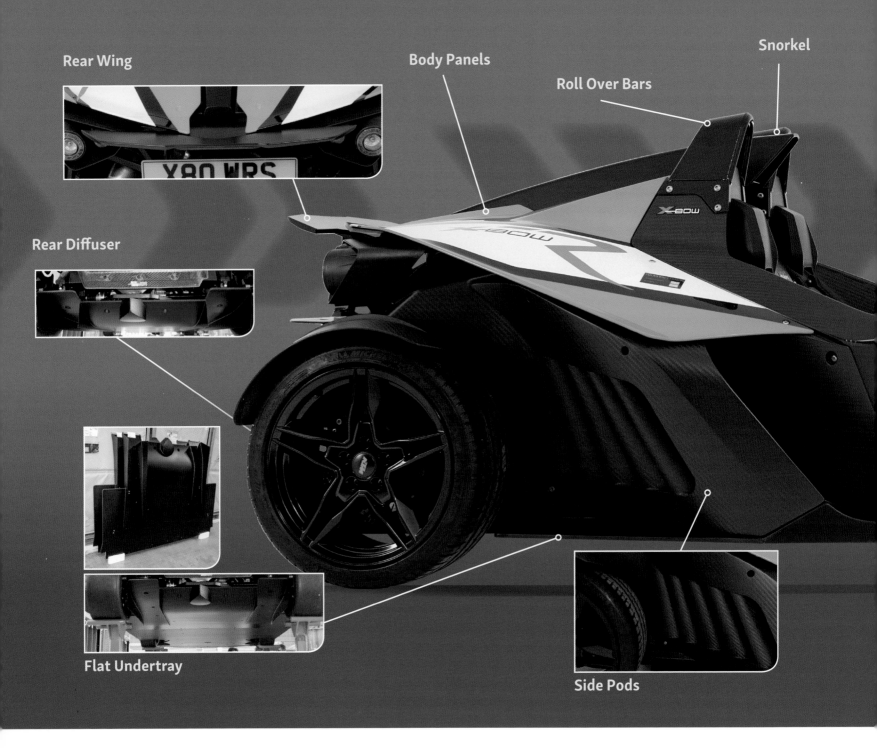

**Rear Wing**

Y80 WRS

**Rear Diffuser**

**Flat Undertray**

**Body Panels**

**Roll Over Bars**

**Snorkel**

**Side Pods**

the airstream can become significant here, which can have a deleterious effect on the car's aerodynamics.

Ideally, the airstream moving over the KTM X-BOW should have a high flow efficiency, gliding across the car as quickly as possible with minimum friction, and following the surface curvatures of the X-BOW as closely as possible, in what is known as 'attached flow.' However, at some point the X-BOW's bodywork must end, and at this point the clean, efficient airstream reaches a 'separation point,' where the airflow can no longer

follow the curvature of the car, but must instead suddenly diffuse out into free airspace. At the separation point undesirable turbulent air and uncontrolled aerodynamic forces come into being. Reaching a separation point is inevitable, because a KTM X-BOW, like every other vehicle, has a finite length, width and height, so the best that can be hoped for is that the airstream boundary layer is controlled and altered to get attached flow for as long as possible, and to engineer the separation point so that it has the least disruptive effect.

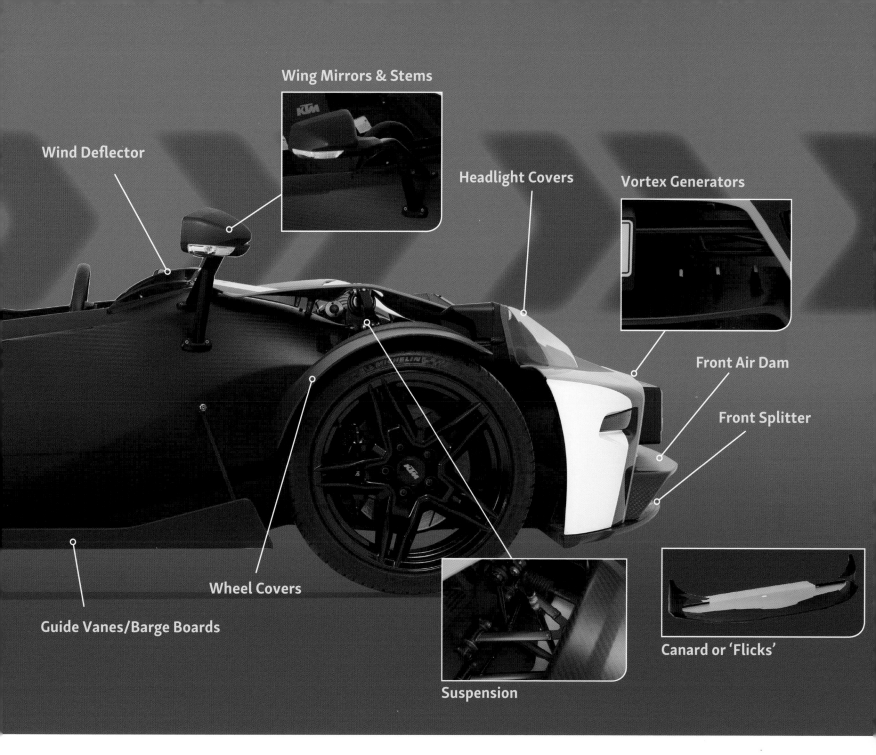

**Wing Mirrors & Stems**

**Wind Deflector**

**Headlight Covers**

**Vortex Generators**

**Front Air Dam**

**Front Splitter**

**Wheel Covers**

**Guide Vanes/Barge Boards**

**Canard or 'Flicks'**

**Suspension**

Vortex generators disturb the airflow stream that they encounter, and produce a swirl of high-energy air. This chaotic high-energy airflow mixes with, and integrates into, the boundary layer, and thereby increases the boundary layer's energy. High-energy boundary layer air is better able to follow the contours of the X-BOW's bodywork, and so allows attached flow to take place for longer, which translates into enhanced aerodynamic efficiency.

Vortex generators work best in very high airflow conditions: that is, at high speed. They also work best when they are very sharp-edged as they are then able to produce the greatest turbulence to the oncoming airstream. Vortex generators in aircraft and Formula 1 cars have very sharp profiles, but in the X-BOW they have been rounded and smoothed-off in the name of road-safety, which makes them less effective.

FLAT UNDERTRAY

The X-BOW has a full-length flat undertray, which is also known as a flat underfloor or a flat underbody. Without an undertray the lower parts of the X-BOW's engine and gearbox, exhaust system, suspension and other ancillaries would be hanging down into the airstream, which would disrupt the airflow and increase drag. A flat undertray shields the airstream from all this unevenness, and so improves the car's aerodynamics. It has been estimated that in the average modern road car, up to one third of all drag originates from disrupted underside airflow. Just to add a bit of complexity to this chapter, in cars with highly optimised flat undertrays, a very low front splitter can actually increase drag. If the undertray is very smooth, and the splitter directs a very large proportion of the oncoming airstream over the less smooth top surface of the car, then a greater proportion of the airflow will be disrupted, hence inducing more drag. It is interesting to note that the front splitter on the flat-undertrayed KTM X-BOW is actually quite high above the tarmac. The undertray extends laterally past the monocoque, and this is deliberate and serves two functions. Firstly, it serves as a mounting platform that allows the driver and passenger to more easily climb into the cockpit; the maximum permitted load here is 100kg. Secondly, by extending the flat undertray beyond the width of the monocoque, the designers have significantly increased the area over which the high-velocity, low-pressure air travelling under the car can act. This markedly increases the maximum potential downforce that the X-BOW can generate. This very visible part of the undertray also adds to the drama and aggression that is the X-BOW.

## THE BARGE BOARDS AND GUIDE VANES

The X-BOW has a rudimentary barge board in the form of the undertray extending past the monocoque, and at the leading edge of this there is a triangular vertical extension that acts as a guide vane. When the oncoming airstream collides with the front of the car, the front splitter, the air dam, the tyres, and the front suspension components all disrupt the airflow and generate turbulent air. The barge boards and the guide vanes collect and channel this air so that it regains a smooth and laminar flow, and then redirects this now-controlled air stream to the more rearward aerodynamic devices, like the rear wing and the rear diffuser.

## WHEEL COVERS

The smooth wheel covers of the X-BOW have an intricately shaped top surface to control and deflect the airflow in the optimal manner. A 2004 research paper by Volvo analysing the drag of an unnamed prototype Volvo road car, found that 13.1 per cent of the total drag was due to the front wheel and tyre package, and 7.1 per cent was due to the rear wheel and tyre package. The wheel covers enable the oncoming airstream to encounter a smooth surface, rather than the uneven, grooved surface of a tyre (and its attendant turbulent air when rotating at high speed).

## THE WIND DEFLECTOR

One of the most intriguing features of the X-BOW, which caught my attention when I first saw one in the flesh at the 2008 Birmingham NEC Autosport Show, is its wind deflector. While the part of the wind deflector that projects into the airstream is only 70mm in height, the whole deflector measures 110cm in width and 27cm in height.

It features numerous complex curves, which would have been very expensive and very difficult to manufacture in glass, particularly for series production. The wind deflector is made from injection-moulded Makrolon AG2677 by Plastic Design GmbH of Bad Salzuflen, in Germany, with extensive input from Bayer MaterialScience AG. The translucent grey deflector is 40 per cent lighter by virtue of being made in Makrolon polycarbonate rather than glass. Additionally, Makrolon has greater impact stability in case of an accident, and is more stable over a wider range of temperatures, which is important when dealing with a part featuring complex three-dimensional geometry. Even the anchoring of the wind deflector to the monocoque was challenging, as carbon fibre and Makrolon have different coefficients of thermal expansion, and the wind deflector has to remain firmly in position over the entire lifetime of the vehicle, despite being assaulted by vibration and wind forces when driving. Very unusually, the part of the wind deflector projecting into the airstream curves forwards and then downwards. To a layman, this would appear to be aerodynamically inefficient, as it would cause a lot of wind turbulence and drag, and my first thoughts were that it was designed in this manner to increase front axle downforce. I was surprised when the people I spoke to at KTM and KISKA rejected this idea, and I am still unsure as to why the deflector has the unusual shape that it has. The top edge of the deflector is rounded for safety reasons. The wind deflector reduces in-cockpit turbulence and also controls and directs the oncoming airstream over the rear body panels and the rear wing, as well as into the snorkel intake. The optional racing windshield is made of carbon fibre, and has a much simpler profile with a gently rising slope. It is said to be more aerodynamic, and to decrease in-cockpit turbulence. Airstream-induced head buffeting is one of the few problems with driving the X-BOW at speed, and sadly, most people that I have spoken to say that the racing screen does little to resolve this issue.

## THE SUSPENSION

The front suspension components in particular are very exposed to the airstream. The wishbones and suspension links have aerofoil-shaped profiles to maintain laminar flow and to delay flow separation, thereby reducing drag. Some parts of the pushrod suspension and both front shock absorbers are very visible, and though they contribute to the beauty of the X-BOW, are, therefore, in the direct line of fire of the airstream. Aesthetics over function carries an aerodynamic penalty.

## THE HEADLIGHT COVERS

Expensive optional headlight covers are available for the X-BOW. KTM call them racing headlight covers and they fit precisely over the existing headlights and are held in place by four small screws. They have a three-dimensional contour with a conical front end to progressively and efficiently deflect the airstream.

## THE WING MIRRORS AND STEMS

The wing mirrors and stems are also a source of turbulence and drag, but are essential for road use homologation. The stems are aerodynamically shaped with flattened profiles, as are the mirror covers. Interestingly, and as an illustration of just how exposed wing mirrors in general are to the airstream, the wing mirrors on the original Series 1 Mazda MX5 prototypes caused so much airstream disruption and secondary in-cockpit turbulence that they had to be redesigned and repositioned to improve their aerodynamics. On the KTM X-BOW, the wing mirrors project far outwards, and so have a very significant affect on the airflow to the radiators, the rear body panels, and the rear wing.

## THE ROLL-OVER BARS

The roll-over bars are safety-critical items in an exposed road-racer. They are positioned high up in the airstream and inevitably induce significant drag. This drag is minimised by the bars having a rounded front-facing profile.

## THE SNORKEL

The air intake snorkel rises high between the seated driver and passenger and projects directly into the oncoming airstream. It provides copious amounts of air for the turbocharged Audi TFSI engine, so much in fact that it need not be as high as it is in the earlier models. The later models have a much lower air intake. The snorkel, for me, is a key design feature of the X-BOW, but it is also a huge source of turbulence and drag in this road-racer. A prominent member of staff at the Graz factory described the aerodynamics of the original snorkel using a word of four letters synonymous with human discharge.

## THE FOUR BODY PANELS

All four body panels, which were originally made in glass-reinforced plastic with the option of carbon fibre, and latterly are made exclusively in carbon fibre, have aerodynamic profiles to maximise downforce and minimise drag.

## THE SIDE PODS

The side pods on either side of the X-BOW each house dual radiators, and as a deformable structure, also help protect the driver and the passenger in the event of a collision. The side pods and the radiators in the X-BOW are (due to necessity) large, and are also highly exposed to the oncoming airstream. They therefore generate significant drag. This penalty has been minimised by designing the side pods to be as smooth-walled, low, and narrow as possible, while still being able to accomplish the necessary cooling.

## CANARDS OR FLICKS

KTM can provide optional canards which they call 'flicks.' Canards are small winglets attached to the front air dam to increase downforce. Canards also create vortices, and these spiralling jets of low pressure air can be redirected to reduce drag. Canards only generate modest amounts of downforce, but are useful in optimising front to rear aerodynamic balance.

## THE REAR WING

The base X-BOW comes with a small rear wing, but there are a variety of rear wings that the factory and the aftermarket will supply on demand. A rear wing is a device that intentionally creates downforce.

In the X-BOW, the rear wing therefore has a reverse wing profile. This profile means that the top surface of the wing offers greater resistance to the airflow while allowing relatively free passage to the air passing underneath the wing: this, in turn, causes a high pressure to exist on the top surface of the wing and a relatively low pressure to exist underneath the wing. This causes a net downward force on the rear wing. Sadly, every rear wing induces some degree of drag. For a wing of given dimensions, the amount of downforce generated and the amount of drag induced is largely determined by angle of attack of the rear wing.

## THE REAR DIFFUSER

The KTM X-BOW has an aggressive looking rear diffuser carrying four vane dividers. The key role of a rear diffuser is to accelerate the flow of air underneath a car, creating an area of even lower pressure there, and thus increasing downforce. The rear diffuser acts as an expansion chamber to control the air as it exits from underneath the car, and it also works to reintegrate this low pressure, high velocity air into the ambient high pressure, low velocity atmosphere. The rear diffuser increases in volume along its length, and works according to the Venturi Effect. The diffuser progressively decreases the velocity of the air underneath the car, from the inlet of the diffuser to the outlet of the diffuser. Another way of thinking about a rear diffuser is to look at it as a wing: as air travelling underneath the car reaches the diffuser, the diffuser progressively curves upwards, creating more physical space for the same amount of air, and so creating a relative vacuum. This relative vacuum then pulls more low pressure air through the underneath of the car, thereby further increasing the car's downforce. Downforce is greatest at the entrance of the diffuser, and the air progressively increases in pressure as it passes through, before finally reaching ambient atmospheric pressure.

The four vane dividers control the airstreams and only allow the air to move in a linear fashion, thereby limiting turbulence and so increasing aerodynamic downforce and optimising aerodynamic efficiency.

Aerodynamic addenda all work together as one integrated package, and it is hard to believe that the average aftermarket tuner would have the ability, or the facilities, to improve upon the work done by the legendary Dallara Research and Development Centre. An owner would be well advised to stick with the optional aerodynamic packages offered by KTM, and to stick with the suspension geometry settings recommended by the factory.

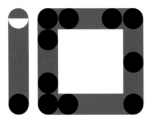

All the X-BOWs share essentially the same chassis architecture, the same basic drive-train, and the same suspension, electronics and safety underpinnings. Each of the models is different, as they are adapted to best serve their specific roles: for example, the Street variant is cheaper and more comfort orientated, while the RR and GT4 variants are adapted to chase the fastest lap times in a more dangerous environment, and so are more powerful and carry additional safety modifications.

However, the commonality between the various models greatly outweighs their dissimilarities, and because of this we can describe the technical details of the X-BOW within this one chapter, before describing how each variant is different in a later chapter.

Stefan Pierer's and KTM's determination that the X-BOW should be a cutting-edge 21st-century car can be seen in its many technological innovations. To hone the X-BOW further towards perfection, KTM put its prototypes and test mules through over 1,000,000km of testing, of which 100,000km were on the racetrack.

OVERVIEW OF THE X-BOW'S BODY PARTS

MONOCOQUE

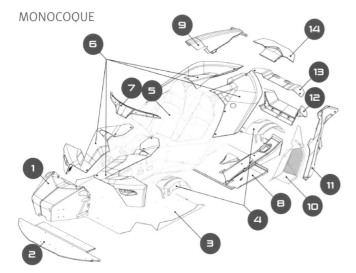

Body parts are as numbered above.
1: Crashbox
2: Front Splitter
3: Main Underfloor
4: Front/rear fender
5: Monocoque
6: Hoods
7: Wind deflector
8: Rear diffuser
9: Airbox
10: Radiator duct
11: Sidepod
12: Muffler cover
13: Rear intermediate fin
14: Rear spoiler

The 81kg wholly carbon fibre monocoque is made of four layers of carbon fibre ply and epoxy resin, and has a torsional rigidity of 35,000Nm per degree. It is in two parts, with the horizontal joint running the whole length of the tub. The upper and lower halves are joined together with high-strength epoxy resin glue. The monocoque arrives at the Graz factory pre-drilled.

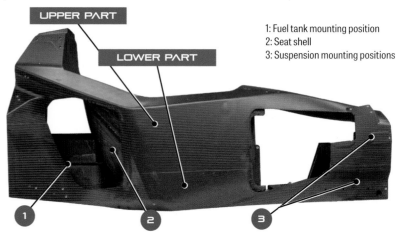

1: Fuel tank mounting position
2: Seat shell
3: Suspension mounting positions

| | | CFK |
|---|---|---|
| Upper part | | 1. Carbon lay |
| | | 2. Carbon lay |
| | | 3. Carbon lay |
| | | 4. Carbon lay |
| Bottom part | | 1 Carbon lay |
| | | 2. Carbon lay |
| | | 3. Carbon lay |
| | | 4. Carbon lay |
| Weight | | 81kg |

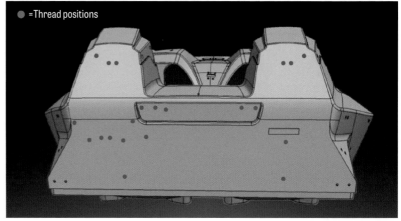

● =Thread positions

Wethje and Carbo Tech also pre-place aluminium threaded inserts so that various safety, suspension and other components can be bolted directly onto the monocoque. The all-important rear aluminium subframe is also bolted to the carbon tub in this way.

Aluminium inserts shown in place within the threaded inserts. Accurate positioning is key and the process for plotting these is extremely precise.
Below: Threaded inserts M5, M6 and M8 with cutaway diagram.

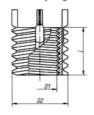

If an X-BOW suffers damage to the carbon fibre monocoque that cannot be repaired by the KTM service partner, a dedicated carbon fibre repair specialist is available in each country. In severe cases, the chassis makers (Wethje/Carbo Tech) will operate a 'Flying Doctor' service of specialist technicians.

## CRASHBOX

The crashbox is a safety-critical part of the X-BOW and has two functions. Its primary purpose is to deform and break up in a defined manner during a crash, thereby absorbing energy, as well as deflecting energy transmission away from the driver and passenger in the cockpit. Its secondary function is to reduce any energy that does get transmitted to the monocoque, so that the more expensive monocoque is either not damaged at all, or at least can be repaired.

The energy absorption and dissipation performance of the X-BOW's crashbox has been tested in numerous high-speed simulated crashes, and this crucial component meets FIA crash standards.

The 10.5kg crashbox is made of a carbon fibre sandwich with a 25mm aluminium honeycomb in the middle. In the event of a crash that involves any part of the crashbox, KTM stipulate that the whole crashbox must be replaced, and that no repairs or modifications should be performed on it.

The crashbox is mounted onto the monocoque with four bolts. It is designed to be easily and quickly removable for service and repair work to the battery and movable pedal box, both of which lie immediately behind the crashbox.

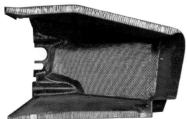

| | CFK |
|---|---|
| Outside | Carbon lay |
| Middle part | 25mm aluminium honeycomb |
| Inside | Carbon lay |
| Weight | 10.5kg |

## FRONT SPLITTER

The front splitter is mounted to the underside of the crashbox. It comes as standard in fibreglass-reinforced plastic, weighing 9.9kg, or can be ordered as an optional extra in carbon fibre with a 2kg weight-saving. It carries an aluminium element for additional strength, and is foam-filled to bulk out the structure.

Laminate construction

| | GFK version | CFK version |
|---|---|---|
| Main component | 1 Glass lay<br>2 Glass lay<br>3 Glass lay foam-filled<br>4 Glass lay<br>5 Glass lay | 1 Carbon lay<br>2 Basalt lay foam-filled<br>3 Carbon lay<br>4 Basalt lay |
| Ground component | 1. Glass lay<br>2 Glass lay | 1 Carbon lay<br>2 Carbon lay |
| Weight | 9.9kg | 7.9kg |

Frontsplitter construction

1: Aluminium reinforcing element 2: Main component 3: Foam-filled reinforcing element
4: Ground component

THE MAIN UNDERFLOOR

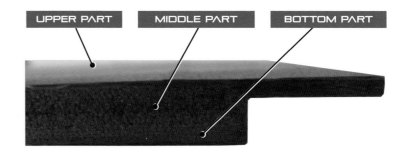

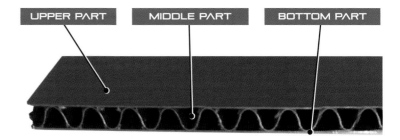

The two types of main underfloor shown as sections. They are constructed differently, with substantial weight differences. Top: GFK version, Bottom: CFK version.

The main underfloor was designed to be completely flat, and is an essential aerodynamic component of the X-BOW. It is a primary contributor to the enormous downforce that the X-BOW is able to generate. As mentioned in the previous chapter, the main underfloor extends laterally past the borders of the monocoque, to the space between the front wheels and the radiators. By doing this, KTM and Dallara have achieved two things: the extended underfloor serves as a mounting platform to aid the driver and passenger getting in and out of the car, and the extension increases the downforce generated by the underfloor, as the negative pressure created by the Bernoulli effect is in direct proportion to the total underfloor area.

The main underfloor is bolted to the underside of the carbon fibre monocoque, and is available in two versions. The standard version is made of black painted aluminium and weighs 17kg, while the carbon fibre version has a foam centre and weighs 10.30kg.

|  | Aluminium version | Aluminium version |
|---|---|---|
| Upper part | 0.5mm aluminium plate | Carbon lay |
| Middle part | 9mm aluminium plate | Foam-filled |
| Bottom part | 0.5mm aluminium plate | Carbon lay |
| Weight | 17kg | 10.3kg |

## THE REAR DIFFUSER

The rear diffuser is mounted to the rear of the rear frame with bolts, and can be easily and quickly removed for repair or maintenance work without disassembling the main underfloor. This is particularly useful for racing, in case of an accident on circuit that involves the back of the car. The rear diffuser is available in an aluminium version weighing 16.25kg, or a carbon fibre version with a foam-filled centre weighing 11.40kg.

## THE REAR FRAME

The aluminium rear frame is one of the major components of the X-BOW, and carries the engine, the torque arm and the rear suspension. It is mounted to the back of the monocoque with eight nuts and bolts on each side. In addition to this, there are three struts that also connect the top of the rear frame to the top of the monocoque. The X-BOW's transversely-installed Audi engine is carried on the rear frame by engine mounts, and the engine is further connected to the bottom of the rear frame by a torque arm.

The rear frame, shown in position on the monocoque.

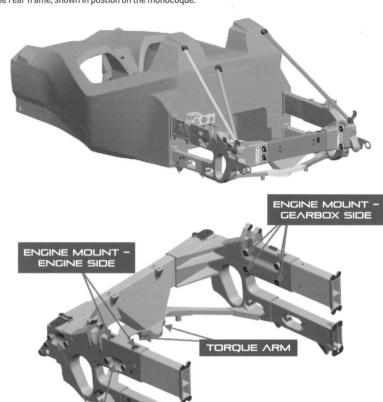

ENGINE MOUNT – GEARBOX SIDE

ENGINE MOUNT – ENGINE SIDE

TORQUE ARM

SUSPENSION

The rear frame is a safety-critical component, and was designed to meet FIA crash demands. It is made by welding together twenty-one different profiles and castings, with additional reinforcing strips mounted at high stress points. The construction of the rear frame requires complex machining and assembly, as tight tolerances are demanded for the alignment of the rear suspension pick-up points and for the positioning of the engine.

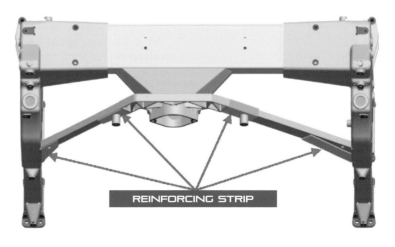

REINFORCING STRIP

Stassin and KISKA's masterpieces of minimalist body design were conceived with aerodynamics in mind, and to maximise where possible, the view of some of the internal components. The style is almost architectural in its approach, lending itself to an array of configurations; hence the GT4, and the Street versions of the car – whatever will they think of next?

## THE FLOATING BODY PANELS

The floating body panels were designed by Sebastien Stassin, Gerald Kiska and their team at Anif, just outside Salzburg. The only firm guideline from KTM to the designers at KISKA was that the X-BOW should look like "a true KTM, 'Ready To Race' product." KISKA applied deliberate minimalism to the whole of the X-BOW's design, just as you would find in a competition-orientated motorcycle. KISKA further emphasised the car's motorcycle roots by designing its few body panels so that they appear to float in free air, which gives the impression of lightness and transparency. These floating body panels also expose the car's mechanical components, and this gives the X-BOW a truly distinctive and radical appearance – a mix of visual brutality and advanced technology that ensures it has an almost unnerving and deeply striking presence.

While the floating panels have been designed taking into account their aerodynamic profiles, they have no direct mechanical function.

Initially, they were made of glass-fibre-reinforced plastic as standard, with carbon fibre panels available as an expensive optional extra. However, KTM found that the logistics involved in procuring and storing two different types of body panels were not economical, and now all these floating panels are made solely in carbon fibre form.

## THE FRONT SUSPENSION

The X-BOW has a classic, yet advanced, chassis set-up, which is directly descended from the highest echelons of motorsport technology. This allows the car to have a low centre of gravity and a well-adjusted weight balance, which are both prerequisites for excellent driving dynamics.

Specifically, the front suspension of the X-BOW features aerodynamically profiled double triangular wishbones, which are directly bolted to the carbon fibre monocoque, and which act on the spring-damper units through a pushrod system. Pushrod type suspensions are rare in road cars, and this system is derived from the world of formula racing. The springs and dampers are made by WP Suspension GmbH, a highly respected suspension specialist based in Mattighofen, Austria. WP has a stellar motorsport record, with bikes featuring its suspension components winning in numerous disparate categories – WP boasts over 300 motorcycle World Cup titles.

The front suspension of the X-BOW can be easily adjusted for height, camber and castor.

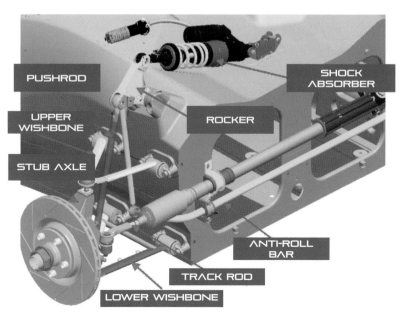

## THE FRONT AXLE ANTI-ROLL BAR

The front axle anti-roll bar acts on the pushrod suspension system through coupling rods. The standard front anti-roll bar is fixed, but a three-stage adjustable anti-roll bar can be specifies as an optional extra.

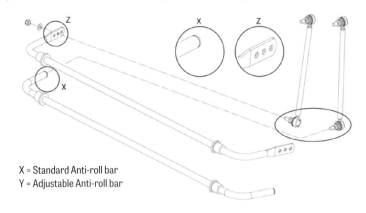

X = Standard Anti-roll bar
Y = Adjustable Anti-roll bar

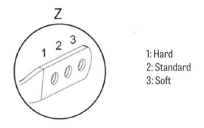

1: Hard
2: Standard
3: Soft

## CRASH-OPTIMISED WISHBONES

The front upper wishbones have been designed to minimise the accident loads that are transmitted to the expensive carbon fibre monocoque. These two wishbones have been mounted to the monocoque in an offset fashion. In the event of an accident this design allows the upper wishbone to deform relatively easily and quickly, so lessening the forces transmitted to the monocoque, and thereby minimising damage to the tub.

All the other six wishbones are mounted centrally, to retain the suspension-chassis rigidity that is important for the car's handling and roadholding.

## THE REAR SUSPENSION

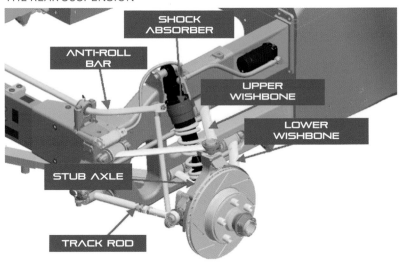

The rear suspension also features aerodynamically optimised double triangular wishbones. At the rear, these are connected to the aluminium rear frame in association with WP-derived spring-damper units. The rear suspension geometry can be adjusted for height and camber.

## THE REAR AXLE ANTI-ROLL BAR

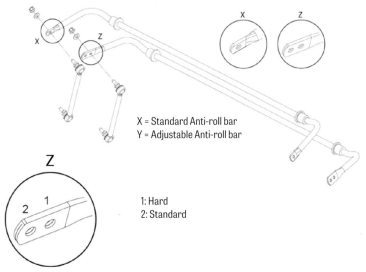

X = Standard Anti-roll bar
Y = Adjustable Anti-roll bar

1: Hard
2: Standard

The rear anti-roll bar is connected to the rear axle through coupling rods. The standard front anti-roll bar is fixed, but a two-stage adjustable anti-roll bar can be specified as an optional extra.

## SPRINGS AND DAMPERS

WP Suspension GmbH specially designed and developed four different spring and damper combinations for the X-BOW.

A car's safety, roadholding, handling, performance and ride comfort are all dependent on a well-functioning chassis, which in turn is dependent on a well-tuned suspension system. The X-BOW's suspension has a co-axial spring and damper system. The spring absorbs the wheel's movement as the car follows the undulations of the road, while the dampers control the spring movement. The stroke of the spring-damper combination in the X-BOW has been tuned as follows to get a safe, balanced and comfortable car:

– the first 25 per cent of the stroke mainly takes care of comfort
– the middle 50 per cent of the stroke takes care of balance
– the last 25 per cent of the stroke ensures safety

Ride comfort is determined by the amount of vehicle movement transmitted to the driver and passenger. Vehicle balance is determined by the weight distribution between the front and rear wheels. A car is primarily balanced on its springs. For safety, all the tyres should always be in contact with the underlying road surface, which in turn requires a small amount of suspension travel to always be held in reserve. If all the suspension travel is used up (which happens when the suspension 'bottoms-out'), grip, and hence safety, are severely compromised.

The springs have four functions:

– to support the car's weight at standstill, and when it is in motion
– to absorb the wheel's movements
– to prevent the damper being fully compressed
– to return the car to its 'neutral' position after a compression

The spring combinations available for the X-BOW have been developed to meet these four objectives by having different spring rates and spring preloads, so that any given car can be tailored either for the road or for individual race tracks.

### TYPE 1

Setting:

- Spring preload adjustment

|  | Front Axle | Rear Axle |
|---|---|---|
| Spring Rate | 16 N/mm | 80 N/mm |

### TYPE 3

Setting:

- Hydraulic Spring preload adjustment
- Rebound
- Compression High-speed
- Compression Low-speed

|  | Front Axle | Rear Axle |
|---|---|---|
| Spring Rate | 16 N/mm | 80 N/mm |

### TYPE 2

Setting:

- Spring preload adjustment
- Rebound
- Compression High-speed
- Compression Low-speed

|  | Front Axle | Rear Axle |
|---|---|---|
| Spring Rate | 16 N/mm | 80 N/mm |

### TYPE 4

Setting:

- Spring preload adjustment
- Rebound
- Compression High-speed
- Compression Low-speed

|  | Front Axle | Rear Axle |
|---|---|---|
| Spring Rate | 70 N/mm | 120 N/mm |

The spring rate is the force (N) needed to compress the spring by a specific amount (mm), and is measured in N/mm.

The spring preload is the amount (mm) the spring is compressed (which in the X-BOW's case can be done through the preload adjuster or by turning the adjusting ring).

The spring rate is a fixed value that remains constant, while the spring preload can be altered to set the desired drive height. The spring preload also alters the X-BOW's suspension sag. Each vehicle needs to have a predetermined amount of suspension sag to allow a wheel to move down as it passes over a hole in the road. Without any sag, a wheel would only be able to move upwards, which would compromise safety and comfort. By fine tuning the car's spring preload, the vehicle's drive height, and steering and suspension geometries – including sag – can all be optimised.

The dampers have two functions: control of wheel movement and control of spring movement.

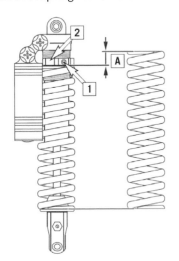

A wheel can move in two different directions (up or down), and ideally, each of these two movements requires a different damping rate. When a wheel moves up, the damper is compressed against the spring, and the damping that controls this movement is called compression damping. When a wheel moves down, the damper extends (this extension is forced by the spring), and the damping that controls this movement is called rebound damping.

The KTM X-BOW can be specified by its owner to have dampers with adjustable compression and rebound damping. The front and rear dampers in the X-BOW can be individually tuned for rebound damping, and both high-speed and low-speed compression damping. An owner can also specify springs with a preload adjuster.

The KTM X-BOW's WP dampers are filled with highly compressed nitrogen gas. The spring preload is adjusted by removing the

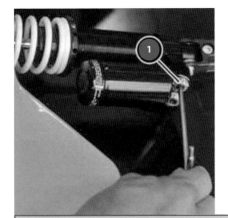

| Compression damping, front axle, low speed | |
|---|---|
| Standard | 16 clicks |
| Sport | 11 clicks |

damper and adjusting the spring length before reinstalling the damper.

The low-speed compression damping of the front suspension is set by turning the top adjusting screw clockwise with a hexagonal screwdriver until the last noticeable click, and then back anti-clockwise to the desired setting. Turning the screw clockwise increases the suspension damping, which makes the chassis harder, and vice-versa.

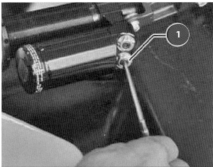

The high-speed compression damping of the front suspension is set by turning the bottom adjusting screw clockwise with a hexagonal screwdriver until the last noticeable click, and then back anti-clockwise to the desired setting. As above, turning the screw clockwise increases the suspension damping.

| Compression damping, front axle, high speed | |
|---|---|
| Standard | 9 clicks |
| Sport | 10 clicks |

The rebound damping of the front suspension is set by turning the screw at the other end of the co-axial assembly (where it is directly

connected to the pushrod system) clockwise with a hexagonal screwdriver until the last noticeable click, and then back anti-clockwise to the desired setting. Again, turning the screw clockwise increases the suspension damping.

| Rebound damping, front axle | |
|---|---|
| Standard | 5 clicks |
| Sport | 5 clicks |

Altering the low-speed compression damping of the rear suspension requires removal of the engine cover. Then, the bottom adjusting screw is turned clockwise with a hexagonal screwdriver until the last noticeable

click, after which it is turned back anti-clockwise to the desired setting. Turning the screw clockwise increases the suspension damping.

Altering the high-speed compression damping of the rear suspension also requires removal of the engine cover. Then the

| Compression damping, rear axle, high speed | |
|---|---|
| Standard | 5 clicks |
| Sport | 5 clicks |

top adjusting screw is turned clockwise until the last click, after which it is turned back to the desired setting, and turning the screw clockwise increases the suspension damping. The rebound damping of the rear suspension is altered in the same way as the front.

| Compression damping, rear axle, high speed | |
|---|---|
| Standard | 5 clicks |
| Sport | 5 clicks |

| Rebound damping, rear axle, high speed | |
|---|---|
| Standard | 15 clicks |
| Sport | 12 clicks |

## SUSPENSION VALUES AND TOLERANCES
Setting value and tolerances

| Suspension alignment KTM X-BOW | | | | Rear | | | |
|---|---|---|---|---|---|---|---|
| Front | | | | Chassis clearance: 110mm | | | |
| Chassis clearance: 100mm | | | | | | Optimum | Tolerance |
| | | Optimum | Tolerance | Camber | Left | -1°12' | 0°20' |
| Camber | Left | -1°30' | 0°10' | Camber | Right | -1°12' | 0°20' |
| Camber | Right | -1°30' | 0°20' | Camber | Left to right | | 0°10' |
| Camber | Left to right | | 0°10' | Collective track | | 0°17' | 0°12' |
| Castor | Left | 5°45' | 0°30' | Drive axle angle | | | 0°10' |
| Castor | Right | 5°45' | 0°30' | | | | |
| Castor | Left to right | | 0°45' | | | | |
| Collective track | | 0°00' | 0°12' | | | | |
| Steering axis inclination | Left | 12°30' | 0°30' | | | | |
| | Right | 12°30' | 0°30' | | | | |
| | Left to right | | 0°45' | | | | |

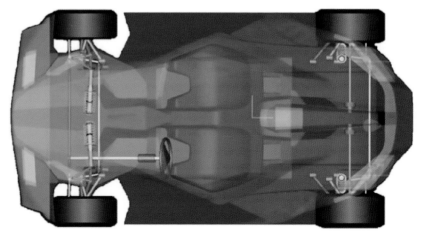

One of the notable aspects of the KTM X-BOW is its classic double wishbone set up, which allows for easy and fast fine-tuning of its suspension geometry.

CHASSIS CLEARANCE REAR 110MM

CHASSIS CLEARANCE FRONT 100MM

## GROUND CLEARANCE FRONT AND REAR

The ground clearance is set using the spring preload adjuster or by turning the adjusting ring. The clearance is measured by using reference points at the very front and rear of the underfloor.

## TRACK AND CAMBER ADJUSTMENT OF THE FRONT AXLE

The front axle track is adjusted by twisting the spur at the end of the front trackrod. The front axle camber is adjusted using shims under the mounting points of the wishbones. Each shim is 1mm in thickness.

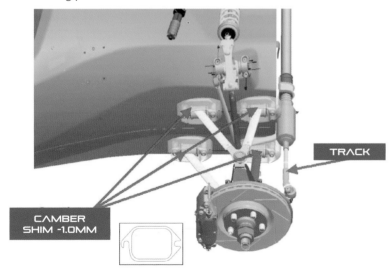

TRACK

CAMBER
SHIM -1.0MM

## TRACK AND CAMBER ADJUSTMENT OF THE REAR AXLE

The rear axle track is adjusted by twisting the spur at the end of the rear trackrod. The rear axle camber is also adjusted using shims under the

mounting points of the wishbones, but the shims available for the rear axle comes in thicknesses of 0.3mm, 0.5mm and 1mm.

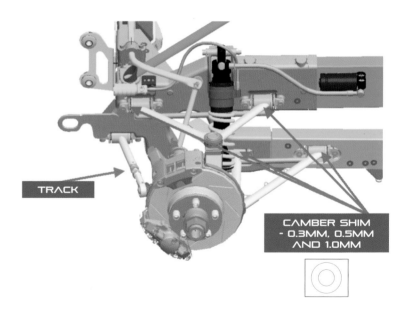

TRACK

CAMBER SHIM
- 0.3MM, 0.5MM
AND 1.0MM

## THE FRONT BRAKE SYSTEM

The brakes on the front axle are made by Brembo, and feature a four-piston fixed calliper system. The 305mm diameter front brake disc is both slotted and ventilated.

## THE REAR BRAKE SYSTEM

The brakes on the rear axle are also made by Brembo, and feature a two-piston fixed calliper system. The 262mm diameter rear brake disc is both slotted and ventilated.

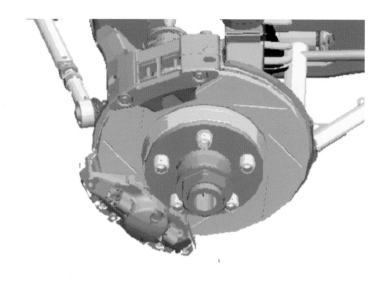

The X-BOW's front and rear Brembo brakes feature four-piston calipers, giving plenty of stopping power when needed (see photograph on pages 54-55).

The parking brake is also mounted on the rear, and has a mechanical calliper with a self-adjusting mechanism.

## WHEELS AND TYRES
### Rims

| | 5-hole connection | Central connection |
|---|---|---|
| Front | 7.5Jx17 H2 ET25 | 7.5Jx17 H2 ET32 |
| Rear | 9.5Jx18 H2 ET42.65 | 9.5Jx18 H2 ET42.65 |

### Tyres

| | Front | Rear |
|---|---|---|
| Continental Sport Contact 2 | 205/40ZR 17 max 500kg | 235/40ZR18 95 Y |
| Michelin Pilot Exalto PE2 | 205/40ZR 17 84 W | – |
| Michelin Pilot Sport PS2 | – | 235/40ZR18 91 Y |
| Toyo Proxes 888 GG | 205/40ZR 17 84 W | 235/40ZR18 91 Y |
| Michelin Pilot Sport Cup* | 205/50ZR 17 89 Y | 235/40ZR18 91 Y |
| *Not homologated for street use, only homologated for motorsport use. | | |

### Tyre pressures

| | Cold condition | Warm condition |
|---|---|---|
| Front | 1.7 bar | 1.95 bar |
| Rear | 1.5 bar | 1.85 bar |

## BRAKE PADS
With warm brakes and tyres, and standard KTM road brake pads, the KTM X-BOW can be brought from 100km/h to a standstill in only 32.8m. Optional racing brake pads, can better this. The racing pads have a significantly higher proportion of metal, which causes a high-pitched brake squeal when the pads and discs are not yet up to temperature.

## THE ADJUSTABLE PEDAL-BOX
A mechanically movable pedal box with a range of 280mm (210mm in right-hand drive form) allows the driver to customise the driving position.

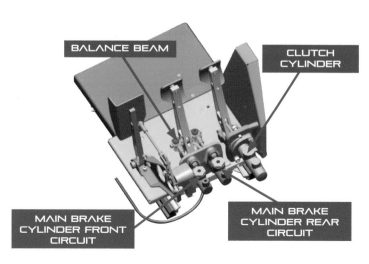

The foot brake system has two main brake cylinders: one for the front circuit and one for the rear circuit. Both master cylinders are connected to the pedal via a balance beam. A cockpit-mounted dial that alters the front to rear brake balance is available as an option. The brake master cylinder and the clutch cylinder have flexible hoses.

## THE STEERING SYSTEM

The KTM X-BOW has unassisted steering through a rack and pinion system with a ratio of 11.05:1. The steering column is unusual for this class of car, in that it's adjustable for both reach and rake. It has a 34mm range of height adjustability, and a 69mm range in length adjustability.

The steering wheel comes fixed as standard, but an optional removable steering wheel can be specified. The removable steering wheel system is of a quick-release type, and it works by releasing or re-engaging a collar on the steering column. The steering wheel boss holds ten buttons, which control the turn indicators, the horn, the lighting system, and the multi-function instrument display.

In the case of the fixed steering wheel, these buttons are connected to electrical wires and a winding spring, which leave through the centre of the steering column.

In the case of the removable steering wheel, KTM were concerned that these wire and spring connections would, in time, through the repeated removal and refitting of the steering wheel, get damaged. KTM therefore elected to design and fit a novel system through which the steering wheel buttons would link up with the rest of the car's systems through an infra red connection. There is an electronic module at the steering wheel end, and another at the steering column end, to modulate these infrared signals.

Both the steering wheel and the steering column incorporate deformable elements within them, so as to protect the driver in the event of an accident.

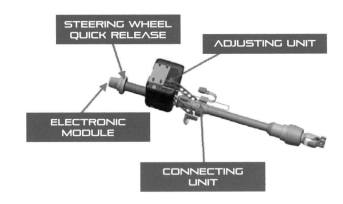

## SEATBELTS

The X-BOW is equipped with H-style four-point driver and passenger seatbelts, made by Schroth. A six-point belt system is available as an option. These belts feature an 'anti-submarining' system, which significantly reduces the risk of the car's occupants sliding under the seatbelt. In the event of a frontal collision, the inboard shoulder belt is designed to extend more, which in turn allows the inboard shoulder to move further and absorbs some of the energy. This reduces the amount of forward energy that is transmitted to the pelvis and so reduces injury.

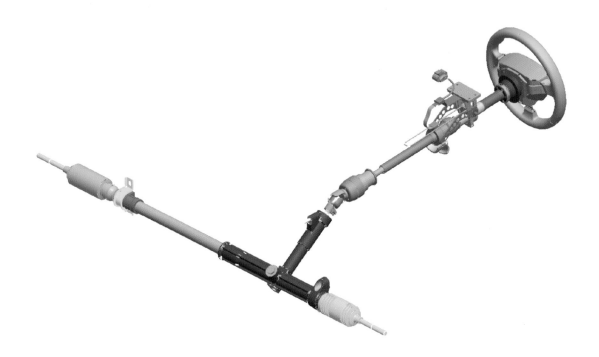

X-BOW complete steering column assembly, showing the connecting and adjusting units (see detailed illustration above) and the rack and pinion connection.

Harness-style four-point seatbelts come as standard on the X-BOW, more than enough to keep the occupants safe in the event of a collision; although a racing harness with six-point fixtures is also available if further restraint and reassurance is required.

**E**very KTM X-BOW produced to date has been powered by an Audi TFSI engine.

The X-BOW's engine is a 1984cc, four-cylinder, 16-valve, long stroke, Audi turbocharged engine featuring TFSI technology. The engine boasts a unique exhaust turbocharger and intercooler system, with fine-tuned engine mapping to minimise turbo lag and to sharpen throttle response. This engine is made up of an aluminium cylinder head carrying special mounts for high pressure direct injectors, and an iron block. It weighs 171.5kg, and features conventional wet-sump lubrication with a dedicated oil cooler. In its most basic form, it produces a peak power of 237bhp (177kW) at 5500rpm, and a peak torque of 310Nm across a wide rev range (2000-5500rpm). TFSI engine technology, variable valve timing and two counter-rotating balancer shafts allow for high power and torque outputs, and excellent driveability and response, from a compact, low capacity engine, all while achieving exceptional fuel and emissions figures: an official EC combined fuel consumption of 7.2 litres/100km, with emissions of 171g of $CO_2$ per kilometre.

Audi was not the only engine supplier that KTM considered for the X-BOW. Stefan Pierer was very clear that the X-BOW should be a premium product in every conceivable way, and that only the very best specialist partners would have the privilege of having an input in KTM's first four-wheeled product. A car's engine is one of its key components, and it either gives credibility and desirability in the eyes of potential owners, enthusiasts and the motoring press, or it does the reverse.

KTM never considered a motorcycle engine for the X-BOW. Although there were off the shelf KTM motorcycle engines that could have been suitably modified, a motorcycle engine was deemed as being just plain wrong for the premium super sports car that KTM wanted to build. Mercedes and BMW engines were briefly considered and rejected. Mercedes as a company did not want to get involved in the KTM X-BOW project, and BMW did not produce an engine that would fit the dimensions specified for the optimum X-BOW chassis. The engine powering the X-BOW had to be compact, lightweight, powerful and compliant with current and anticipated emissions legislation worldwide. The power plant also had to be tuneable, so that greater power outputs could be extracted from it as the product range expanded.

Audi had been closely involved with KTM as an actual corporate partner in the very early stages of the X-BOW's conception. When Audi decided that the X-BOW was too radical for its corporate image, and that the X-BOW exposed the company too much in terms of corporate liability, they did not abandon the project completely. It was Audi that suggested that Dallara had the research facilities, the development capabilities, the expert aerodynamic and carbon fibre specialists, and the necessary wind tunnel to engineer the X-BOW concept into life. It was Audi that was originally going to market and service the X-BOW in the many markets worldwide where Audi had a presence. Audi also had the capability to supply KTM with a complete drive-train for the X-BOW, rather than just an engine, and also had the capability to supply the complex and expensive-to-develop electronic ancillaries that the X-BOW would need. Audi was therefore a natural choice as an engine supplier for the X-BOW project, but it was only after careful deliberation that the two-litre, four-cylinder TFSI engine from Ingolstadt was decided upon. The 'T' in TFSI stands for 'Turbo,' and the 'FSI' stands for 'Fuel Stratified direct fuel Injection.'

Audi reinvented its image in the 1980s by dominating the World Rally Championship with the legendary all-wheel drive turbocharged Audi Quattro, which was tarmac and dirt-road capable. In the early 2000s Audi dominated the prestigious Le Mans 24-Hour race with cars powered by TFSI engine technology.

A Le Mans Audi R8 won this demanding race (possibly the most celebrated event on the motorsport calendar other than the Monaco F1 Grand Prix) every year between 2000 and 2005, except for 2003, when a Bentley Speed 8 won. All these Audi R8s were powered by 3.6-litre V8 engines using FSI technology, and produced 610hp (455kW) in 2000, 2001 and 2002, 550hp (410kW) for 2003 and 2004, and finally just 520hp (388kW) for 2005.

So the engine that KTM chose for its X-BOW featured technology of the highest pedigree, tested in full sight of the public over a continuous 24-hour race distance, on one of the world's most demanding circuits. All this was a marketing god-send for KTM and the X-BOW.

| Technical Data | |
| --- | --- |
| Engine code | BWA |
| Type | 4-cylinder in-line engine |
| Displacement [mm³] | 1984 |
| Bore [mm] | 82.5 |
| Stroke [mm] | 92.8 |
| Compression ratio | 10.5:1 |
| Maximum output | 177kW at 5500rpm |
| Maximum torque | 310Nm at 2000-5500 |
| Engine management | Bosch Motronic MED 9.1 |
| Variable camshaft settings | 42° Crank angle |
| Exhaust gas recirculation | Inside exhaust gas recirculation |
| Fuel quality | Superplus unleaded ROZ 98 |
| Exhaust gas treatment | 3-way catalytic converter |
| Exhaust emission standard | EU4 |

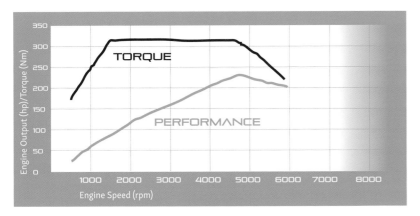

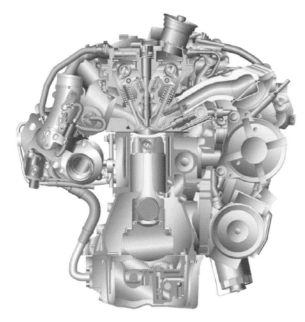

compression ratios cause premature spontaneous ignition of the fuel-air mixture at given hot spots within the combustion chamber. When this happens, some of the fuel-air mixture burns in an uncontrolled manner ahead of the flame front, producing high frequency pressure waves which cause the engine to vibrate and make a knocking sound. Knocking causes sparkplug point overheating, as well as damage to the combustion chamber surfaces, which in turn leads to reduced power and torque output, increased emissions, premature wear of the engine's internal components and excessive fuel consumption.

What lies beneath? Just under 240bhp, and maximum torque of 310Nm, that's what. An impressive equation, when added to the rest of an X-BOW.

Top: The graph shows the impressive torque and engine output of the Audi TFSI engine, whilst below, some of the detail of the engine block is shown; the valve positions and injector position can clearly be seen. A compact and efficient design, perfect for adoption by KTM for the X-BOW.

## FUEL STRATIFIED DIRECT INJECTION

Fuel Stratified direct Injection (FSI) is a novel engine technology, in which highly pressurised fuel from a common rail is injected directly into the engine's combustion chambers, rather than the traditional manner in which fuel is injected into the intake manifold.

Audi, in 2004, became the world's first manufacturer to combine forced induction by way of a turbocharger with FSI. Turbocharging and direct injection are complementary engine technologies that work together to increase engine efficiency and output, while simultaneously reducing the undesirable engine phenomenon known as 'knocking.'

Ideally, in a properly functioning engine, a flame front progresses smoothly from the point of ignition within the combustion chamber to encompass the whole of that chamber. Knocking happens when high

Knocking is more likely to occur in a turbocharged engine than in a normally-aspirated engine, simply because turbocharging produces higher compression ratios within the combustion chamber. Fuel Stratified Injection technology counters this tendency of knocking because the directly injected fuel swirls intensely around the combustion chamber, so cooling the chamber walls. The lower temperature makes premature spontaneous ignition of the fuel (and therefore knocking) less likely.

The Audi TFSI engine employs a fuel/air mixture in a stoichiometric ratio of 1kg of fuel to 14.7kg (which approximates to 12,400 litres) of air. By combining FSI with turbocharging, Audi is able to manufacture engines running high compression ratios without knocking. These engines exhibit high quality combustion characteristics, which means that they are thermodynamically very efficient and able to produce a lot of power and torque while being very fuel efficient and compact.

The KTM X-BOW's transversely mounted turbocharged Audi engine has a capacity of 1984cc, and the direct fuel-injection takes place at a pressure between 30 and 110bar. Its maximum power output of 237bhp (240hp/177kW) is produced at 5500rpm, with a maximum torque of 310Nm produced between 2000 and 5500rpm. All this is achieved with a fuel consumption averaging 7.2 litres per 100km, and $CO_2$ emissions of 171g/km – quite remarkable for a two-seater street legal race car that is able to accelerate from standstill to 100km/h in just 3.9 seconds.

## ENGINE BLOCK AND CYLINDER HEAD & PISTONS

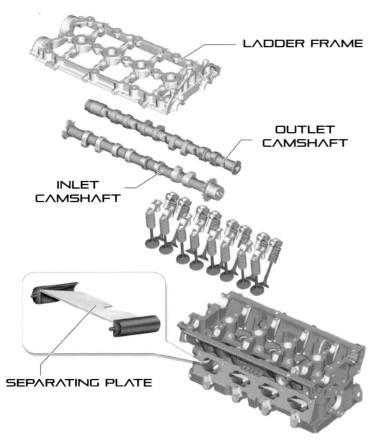

LADDER FRAME

OUTLET CAMSHAFT

INLET CAMSHAFT

SEPARATING PLATE

The X-BOW's engine block is made of cast iron, while its cylinder head is made of aluminium. It features four valves per cylinder technology, and the valves are operated by two overhead camshafts mounted on bearings in a ladder frame to ensure torsional stiffness. The outlet camshaft is driven by a toothed belt, while the inlet camshaft is driven by the outlet

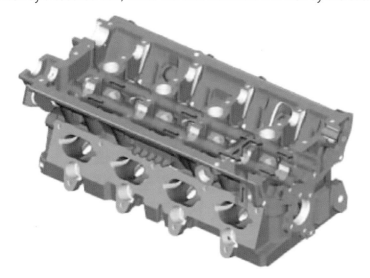

camshaft via a simplex chain. The mounts for the high pressure injectors are integrated into the cylinder head, with the actual injectors projecting directly into the combustion chamber. The exhaust valves are sodium-filled, and the inlet and exhaust valve seats are armoured.

The pistons are made of lightweight aluminium alloy to reduce oscillating mass, and the piston crown is specifically designed to achieve optimum fuel-air turbulence within the combustion chamber.

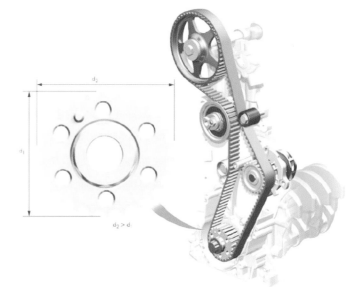

$d_2$

$d_1$

$d_2 > d_1$

## VARIABLE VALVE TIMING

The Audi TFSI engine in the X-BOW features variable valve timing that is controlled by an electronic control unit (ECU). This ECU receives information

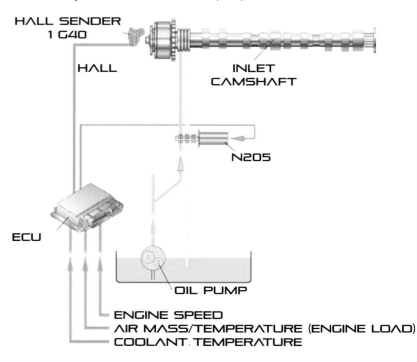

HALL SENDER 1 G40

HALL

INLET CAMSHAFT

N205

ECU

OIL PUMP

ENGINE SPEED
AIR MASS/TEMPERATURE (ENGINE LOAD)
COOLANT TEMPERATURE

about the engine speed, the engine load, the ambient temperature and the positions of the crankshaft and the camshafts. The ECU then adjusts the camshafts' position through N205 solenoid valves, which by opening and closing control the flow of pressurised engine oil through fluted variators. These fluted variators turn and so adjust the camshafts' positions.

## BALANCE SHAFTS

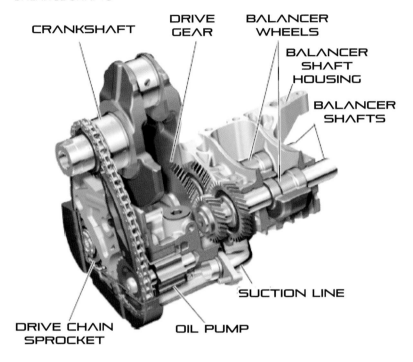

CRANKSHAFT
DRIVE GEAR
BALANCER WHEELS
BALANCER SHAFT HOUSING
BALANCER SHAFTS
SUCTION LINE
DRIVE CHAIN SPROCKET
OIL PUMP

Large capacity four-cylinder in-line engines, like that found in the X-BOW, are inherently unbalanced due to their design asymmetry. Such engines exhibit an intrinsic second order vibration (vibrating at twice the engine speed), which cannot be eliminated even with meticulous assembly and careful blueprinting of the engine's internal components. This vibration pattern is generated because the movement of the connecting rods is not symmetrical throughout the crankshaft rotation. When the ascending and the descending pistons are not always exactly opposed, a net vertical inertial force develops twice during each crankshaft revolution. In 1904, Frederick W Lanchester invented the balance shaft: an eccentric weighted shaft that offsets these unbalanced and undesirable vibrations. In essence Lanchester's idea was that two balance shafts rotating in opposite directions at twice the engine speed would cancel the inherent second order vibrations. The advantages in engine smoothness and balance conferred by these balance shafts is tempered by the extra cost, complexity and frictional losses that they bring with them. In the latter half of the 20th century, Mitsubishi and Saab both developed Lanchester's design to further refine and engineer out these second order vibrations. The X-BOW's engine features two balance shafts, which are driven by a chain from the crankshaft. This chain also drives the oil pump.

## THE TURBOCHARGER/EXHAUST MANIFOLD MODULE

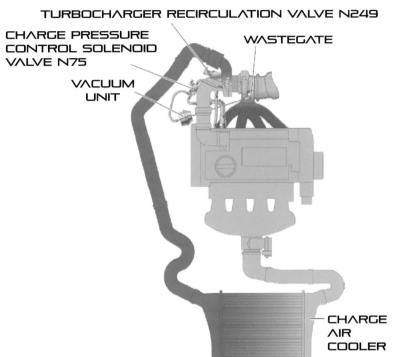

TURBOCHARGER RECIRCULATION VALVE N249
CHARGE PRESSURE CONTROL SOLENOID VALVE N75
WASTEGATE
VACUUM UNIT
CHARGE AIR COOLER

The water cooled turbocharger in the X-BOW runs to a maximum boost pressure of 1.07bar. The boost pressure is regulated by a wastegate that is controlled by a N75 boost pressure control solenoid valve. Adjacent to the N75 valve, and also mounted on the turbocharger, is an N249 valve that controls the turbocharger air recirculation. The turbocharger is attached to the cylinder head by five bolts. The exhaust manifold is specifically designed to be fluted, and also to take the engine's firing order into account. The resultant flute channels confine the exhaust gas pressure within their individual cylinder ports, ensuring that the exhaust gases have a smooth, consistent and equal flow over the turbocharger turbine blades.

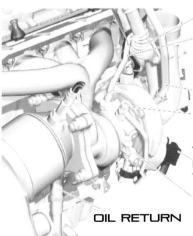

CRANKCASE BREATHER CONNECTION
COOLANT FLOW TO RADIATOR AND FROM AUXILIARY WATER PUMP
ACTIVE CHARCOAL FILTER CONNECTION
PRESSURISED OIL SUPPLY
TURBOCHARGER RECIRCULATION VALVE N249
COOLANT SUPPLY TO ENGINE BLOCK
OIL RETURN

This allows the turbine blades to maintain their speed for longer once the driver lifts off the accelerator, and the turbocharger's response time is thus minimised when the accelerator is next pressed down.

The Audi TFSI's turbocharger system has its own cooling circuit. To prevent oil deposits from burning onto the turbine shaft, an auxiliary water pump runs-on for up to 15 minutes after the engine has been switched off.

The auxiliary pump draws coolant from the cool side of the radiator and sends it to the turbocharger cooling circuit, which is incorporated into the engine block's cooling system. Having absorbed heat energy from the red-hot turbocharger system, this now-hot coolant is sent directly back to the radiator, so as to get rid of as much heat as possible, as quickly as possible. (See illustration below)

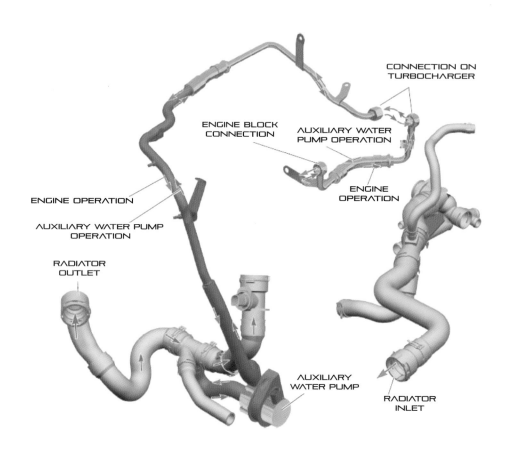

The KTM X-BOW turbocharger cooling system.

## FUEL SUPPLY

All the KTM X-BOW road-homologated models have 40-litre fuel tanks (the GT4 has a 70-litre tank). Located within the fuel tank are the electric fuel pump and the fuel level sensor. The power supply and the electronics for both these, as well as the fuel filters, are mounted on the top of the fuel tank.

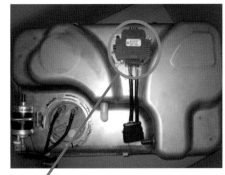

The fuel supply system consists of a low and a high pressure section. In the low pressure circuit, the fuel is conveyed at anywhere between 0.5 to 5.0bar depending on the engine load, from the fuel tank via the fuel

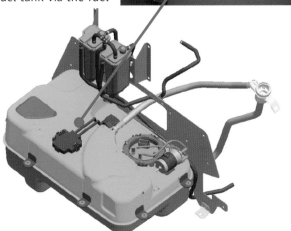

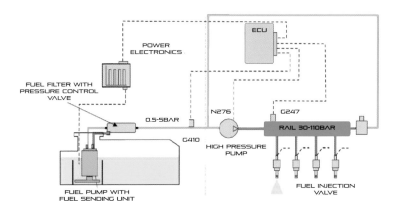

filter to the high pressure fuel pump (HPFP). The engine ECU activates and controls this fuel pump.

In the high pressure circuit, a single-plunger type high-pressure fuel pump generates the extreme pressure required in the fuel rail for the FSI system to function. The high pressure fuel pump works by a four-lobe cam follower riding on a camshaft lobe via a linearly driven plunger, and pressurises the fuel to a pressure of between 30 and 110bar.

The fuel rail is designed to distribute a defined fuel pressure to the high-pressure fuel injectors. The four high-pressure injectors act as the interface between the fuel rail and the combustion chamber. They meter out the fuel, and also create a specific fuel/air mixture within the combustion chamber. The pressure within the rail (30-110 bar) is higher than the pressure within the combustion chamber, and when the engine ECU generates the necessary voltage of 50V-90V to actuate the solenoid within the injector, the injector nozzle opens and high-pressure stratified fuel is injected directly into the chamber.

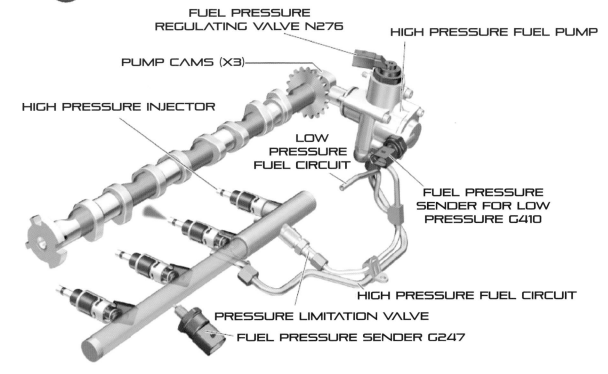

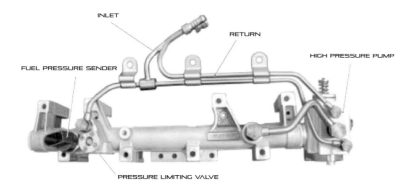

INLET
RETURN
HIGH PRESSURE PUMP
FUEL PRESSURE SENDER
PRESSURE LIMITING VALVE

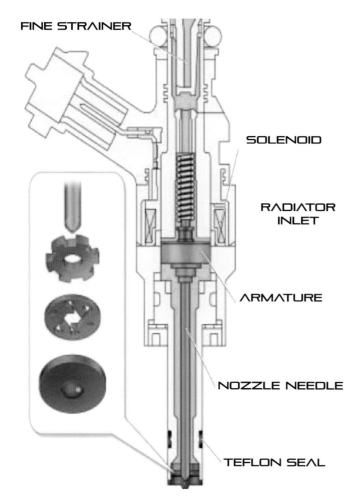

FINE STRAINER
SOLENOID
RADIATOR INLET
ARMATURE
NOZZLE NEEDLE
TEFLON SEAL

The turbocharger cooling circuit begins working at a lower temperature (about 40°C), while the engine cooling circuit begins working to maintain an engine coolant temperature of about 98°C.

Depending on the coolant temperature, the engine ECU activates the radiator fans through a power control unit.

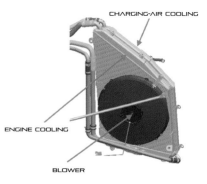

CHARGING-AIR COOLING
ENGINE COOLING
BLOWER

There is one power control unit for the right radiator fan, and another for the left.

◄ Power Control Unit, left side.

Power Control Unit, right side. ►

Engine coolant cycle

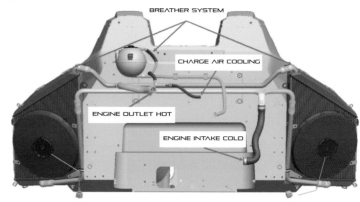

BREATHER SYSTEM
CHARGE AIR COOLING
ENGINE OUTLET HOT
ENGINE INTAKE COLD

Air charging coolant cycle

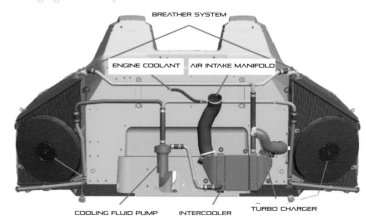

BREATHER SYSTEM
ENGINE COOLANT
AIR INTAKE MANIFOLD
COOLING FLUID PUMP
INTERCOOLER
TURBO CHARGER

## COOLING CIRCUIT

There are two sets of dual radiators, one on each side of the KTM X-BOW. The front radiator is responsible for the turbocharger cooling circuit, and the back radiator is responsible for the engine cooling circuit. The two radiators on any given side are connected in a parallel circulation, so each radiator takes on 50 per cent of the cooling function on that given side.

## EXHAUST SYSTEM

The KTM X-BOW's exhaust system features a three-way primary catalytic converter with upstream and downstream probes to monitor its functioning.

The back box has a control valve within it, which alters the exhaust sound to get the sportiest and loudest exhaust note possible within legal limits.

This control valve diverts the exhaust gases through either a 'long' or a 'short' exhaust tract. It is the engine ECU that determines, based on vehicle speed and engine load, whether the control valve is activated.

When the control valve is activated the exhaust gases are routed through the 'long' exhaust tract, first going through the resonance chamber, then through the muffler, before exiting through the tailpipes.

When the control valve is not activated, the exhaust gases are routed through the 'short' exhaust tract, only going through the muffler before exiting trough the tailpipes.

The 'long' tract therefore involves the exhaust gases taking a more circuitous route through the resonance chamber, and unsurprisingly the resulting exhaust sound is more restrained. The 'short' exhaust gases circuit results in a louder and more sporty exhaust sound.

Two-way muffller

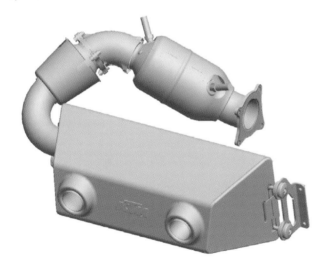

Rear view with exhaust valve actuation

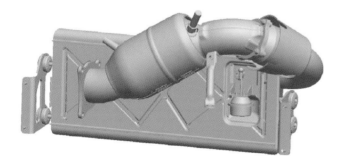

Exhaust position

Short exhaust tract

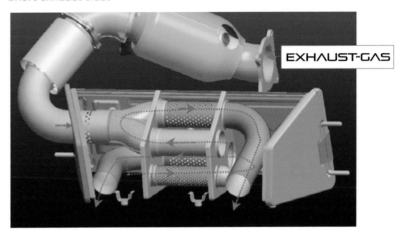

## THE GEARBOX
### Ratios and layouts

|  | Ratio | Overall ratio |
|---|---|---|
| 1st gear/drive pinion set I | 47:14 = 3.357 | 13.240 |
| 2nd gear/drive pinion set I | 48:23 = 2.087 | 8.231 |
| 3rd gear/drive pinion set I | 47:32 = 1.469 | 5.794 |
| 4th gear/drive pinion set I | 45.41 = 1.098 | 4.330 |
| 5th gear/drive pinion set II | 41:37 = 1.108 | 3.420 |
| 6th gear/drive pinion set II | 38:41 = 0.927 | 2.681 |
| Reverse gear/drive pinion set II | 34:23x14:14 = 3.990 | 12.317 |
| Ratio, drive pinion set I | 71:18 = 3.944 |  |
| Ratio, drive pinion set II | 71:23 = 3.067 |  |
| Mode | Sport |  |

The KTM X-BOW uses an Audi 02Q transversely-mounted gearbox with six forward gears and one reverse gear. It weighs 48.5kg and is rated to cope with a maximum input torque of 350Nm.

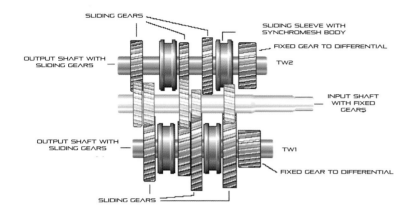

SLIDING GEARS

SLIDING SLEEVE WITH
SYNCHROMESH BODY

FIXED GEAR TO DIFFERENTIAL

OUTPUT SHAFT WITH
SLIDING GEARS

TW2

INPUT SHAFT
WITH FIXED
GEARS

OUTPUT SHAFT WITH
SLIDING GEARS

TW1

FIXED GEAR TO DIFFERENTIAL

SLIDING GEARS

a single output shaft. The various gears are mounted on the output shaft, and the more gears there are, the longer the output shaft has to be, and the longer the gearbox itself will be.

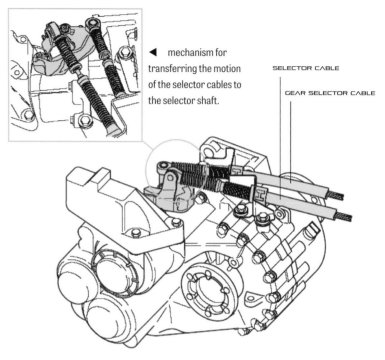

◄ mechanism for transferring the motion of the selector cables to the selector shaft.

SELECTOR CABLE

GEAR SELECTOR CABLE

KTM was keen that the X-BOW's gearbox should be compact, so that the whole drive-train package could be placed as centrally and as low as possible within the chassis, to optimise vehicle dynamics. This was a major reason why the Audi 02Q gearbox, a so-called 'short gearbox,' was chosen.

In a conventional gearbox, the input shaft transfers the driving force to

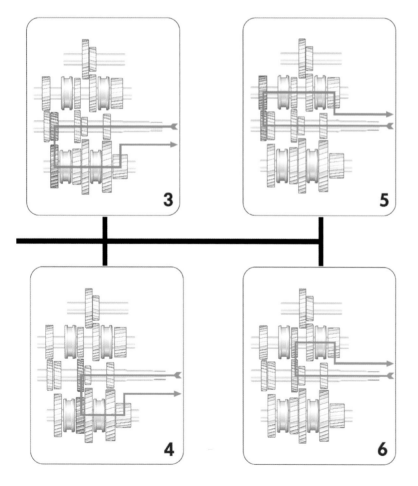

The Audi 02Q gearbox has the gears mounted on two different output shafts, which means that the output shafts can be shorter, which in turn means the gearbox can be shorter and more compact.

The gears are mounted on the output shafts as follows: output shaft one carries forward gears one to four; and output shaft two carries forward gears five and six, and the one reverse gear.

The X-BOW has a cable-operated gearshift mechanism. Movements of the gearlever in the cockpit are translated to movements of the selector shaft in the 02Q gearbox by two adjustable selector cables.

## THE LIMITED-SLIP DIFFERENTIAL

Early KTM X-BOWs could be specified with an 02Q Drexler mechanical limited-slip differential as an optional extra. This limited-slip differential is both torque and speed sensitive, works even if a driven wheel has no road contact, and has a very soft and quick response.

**Technical Data**

| Pull in (ramps angles) | Pull in % (locking values) | Coasting in (ramps angles) | Coasting in % (locking values) | Preload |
|---|---|---|---|---|
| 80° | 8% | 80° | 78% | 50Nm |
| Laminated disc pack 2+2 | | | | |

## THE BATTERY

The KTM X-BOW can be specified with either a 12V dry cell battery or a 12V lead acid battery with leakage protection. The battery is mounted on the monocoque floor, in front of the passenger footrest. KTM recommend that any operations on the battery or its connections should only be done from the front of the car. This means that the crashbox needs to be dismounted for battery replacement or repairs to the battery connections, which is both time-consuming and labour intensive.

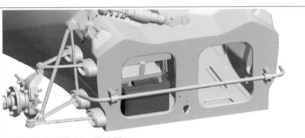

### TECHNICAL DATA

| | |
|---|---|
| Lead acid battery | 12V / 69 AH 520 A EN |
| Dry cell battery | 12V / 34 AH / 450 A SAE |

## THE E-BOX

KTM call the box containing the fuses and relays the 'E-Box.' This white humidity-protected rectangular box is mounted on the left side of the car, on the rear subframe. Within the E-Box is a circuit board, which is connected to the car's wiring harness.

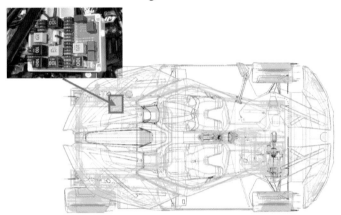

## Overview fuses

| | | | | | |
|---|---|---|---|---|---|
| F1 | 10A | Air-flow meter | F17 | 25A | Body control unit and hazard lights switch |
| F2 | 15A | Water pump | F18 | 40A | Heater unit |
| F3 | 15A | Tank control unit, relays EKP | F19 | 5A | Fan control unit left and right |
| F4 | 15A | Immobiliser system, multi-fuction steering wheel, combi-instrument, engine control device | F20 | 25A | Singular ignition coil |
| F5 | 10A | Diagnostic and vehicle control unit | F21 | 10A | Terminal 87 – Main relay |
| F6 | 25A | Horn | F22 | 10A | Terminal 87 – Fuel pump relay |
| F7 | 25A | Headlamp right | F23 | 10A | High pressure control valve |
| F8 | 15A | Headlamp left | F24 | 25A | Engine control unit |
| F9 | 25A | Heating ventilator | F25 | 10A | Exhaust control cap |
| F10 | 25A | Electric socket 12V | F26 | 10A | Lambda probe (LSU) |
| F11 | 5A | Relay multi-function steering wheel, combi-instrument | F27 | 10A | Lambda probe (LSF) |
| F12 | 10A | Tank control unit | F28 | 10A | Relay water pump turbocharger |
| F13 | 10A | Diagnosis | F29 | 10A | Radiator fan |
| F14 | 5A | Coupler point pedal box-brake, clutch | | | |
| F15 | 25A | Terminal 75 – Relay immobiliser system | | | |
| F16 | 5A | Main relay – Engine control unit | | | |

## Overview relays

| Position | Name | Information |
|---|---|---|
| K1 | RE1 Starter relay 1 | |
| K2 | RE1 Starter relay 2 | |
| K3 | RE3 EKP-Relay | Fuel pump relay |
| K4 | RE4 Terminal 75 Relay | |
| K5 | RE5 Terminal 15 Relay | |
| K6 | RE6 Main relay | Engine control unit |
| K7 | RE7 water piump relay | Turbocharger cooling pump |
| K8 | RE8 MFL realy | Multi-function steering wheel |
| K9 | Z_RT additional relay mounting | Horn |
| K10 | Z_RT additional relay mounting | Headlamp right |
| K11 | Z_RT additional relay mounting | Headlamp left |
| K12 | Z_RT additional relay mounting | Heater unit |

## THE ELECTRONIC CONTROL UNITS

The KTM X-BOW has three major electronic control units: the engine ECU, the body control ECU (FSG), and the immobiliser control ECU (FBS).

The engine ECU is also located on the left rear side of the car. It receives information from multiple engine and mechanical sensors. It then sends out instructions to control and optimise the performance of the engine depending on the data received from the engine sensors, as well as the data received about the vehicle's real time dynamics. The engine ECU is in direct communication with the immobiliser control unit, and also checks the status of the brake, the clutch and the starter systems. There is continuous two-way data transfer between the engine ECU and the body control ECU.

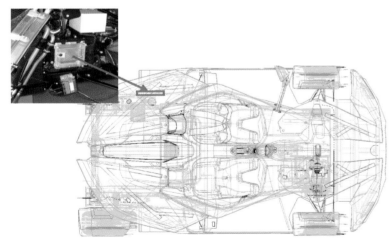

The body control unit (FSG) and the immobiliser control unit (FBS) are both located just to the right of the centre line at the front of the car.

The body control unit (FSG) is the master control unit that oversees, amongst other things, the following functions: gateway CAN data bus system; exterior lights; signal and warning codes; fuel tank level calculation; outside temperature measurement; heater control unit; vehicle speed data; vehicle mileage data; oil pressure and engine speed codes; heater unit control; and communications between the multi-function steering wheel, the instrument cluster and the rest of the car (through an infrared transmitter and receiver system).

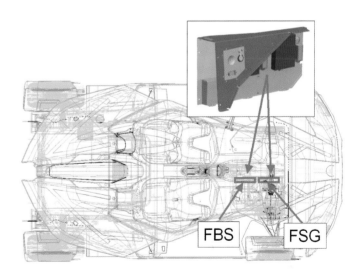

The immobiliser control unit (FBS) controls an anti-theft system that is made up of a Keyless-Go system (adapted from the Audi A8; see below), and an electronic gearshift locking system. This immobiliser control unit receives transponder signals from the chip embedded within the X-BOW's car key, and also communicates with the engine ECU. When the correct transponder signal from the key is received, and when the driver performs the correct sequence of actions necessary to start the car, the immobiliser

## Assembly mounting positions

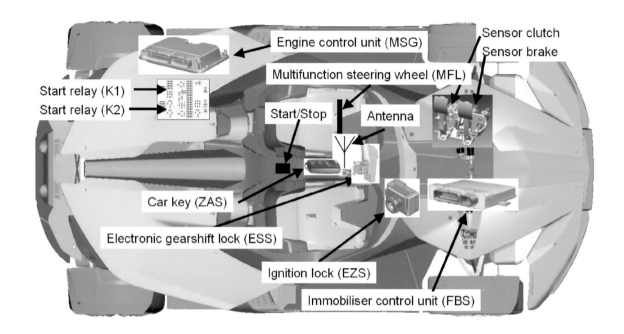

Engine control unit (MSG)

Sensor clutch
Sensor brake

Multifunction steering wheel (MFL)

Start relay (K1)
Start relay (K2)

Start/Stop

Antenna

Car key (ZAS)

Electronic gearshift lock (ESS)

Ignition lock (EZS)

Immobiliser control unit (FBS)

## Overview data communication

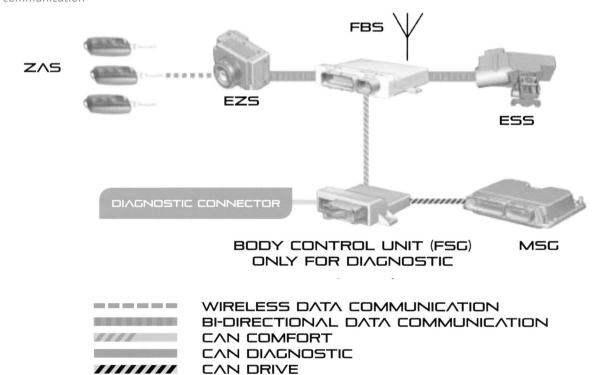

ZAS

FBS

EZS

ESS

DIAGNOSTIC CONNECTOR

BODY CONTROL UNIT (FSG)
ONLY FOR DIAGNOSTIC

MSG

WIRELESS DATA COMMUNICATION
BI-DIRECTIONAL DATA COMMUNICATION
CAN COMFORT
CAN DIAGNOSTIC
CAN DRIVE

control unit deactivates the electronic gearshift lock, and also allows the engine ECU to fire up the engine.

### THE CAR KEY

Although the X-BOW comes with what looks like a conventional car key, it in fact utilises a Keyless-Go system adapted from Audi's flagship A8. To start the car, KTM recommend that the key fob is inserted into the pocket located on the central console, after which the driver has to perform a complex sequence of actions involving the brake and clutch pedals, the steering wheel controls (twice!), and the starter button on the central console. When all the required signals are received, and all the correct actions are performed, the engine ECU and the immobiliser control unit allow the car be started and moved.

In an emergency, when the Keyless-Go system fails, there is an ignition barrel in the passenger compartment, where a conventional key can be inserted into a barrel lock to start up the car. This requires much dexterity and suppleness of body, as the driver has to lean across the cockpit and reach low down into the passenger footwell to insert and turn the key, while simultaneously pressing down on both the clutch and brake pedals! It is simply impossible to do all this once the driver has done up the four-point seatbelt.

### THE CAN BUS SYSTEM

The KTM X-BOW uses a standardised data bus arrangement, with four different CAN bus systems feeding into the body control unit (FSG), which then acts as the master unit that controls the car's electronics and mechanics:

#### CAN engine

The CAN bus engine system is responsible for the communications between the engine ECU and the body control unit, and has an average transfer rate of about 500kB.

#### CAN diagnostic

The CAN bus diagnostic system allows a two-way transfer of data between the diagnostic port and the body control unit, with an average transfer rate of 500kB.

#### CAN private

The CAN bus private system is responsible for communications between the multi-function steering wheel, the cockpit dash display and the body control unit. Again, it has an average transfer rate of about 500kB.

#### CAN comfort

The CAN bus comfort system allows for data transfer between the immobiliser system and the body control unit, with an average transfer rate of 100kB.

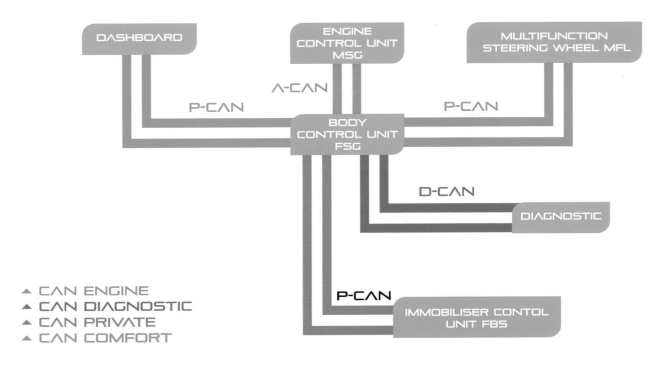

MODEL VARIANTS

## PROTOTYPES

Three prototype KTM X-BOW cars were built, all three by Dallara Engineering at its Research and Development Centre factory in Varano de' Melegari outside Parma in Italy.

These were the only X-BOWs ever built by Dallara. Every other X-BOW, including the first 100 production units which were called the 'Dallara Edition,' were built at the dedicated KTM X-BOW factory in Graz, Austria.

One of these prototypes is now the centrepiece in the foyer of the KISKA headquarters in Anif, just outside Salzburg. Sebastien Stassin, KISKA's chief designer, was kind enough to show the author around this car in detail during a visit to KISKA in August 2018. The KISKA prototype has been significantly modified since it was first built, as it was used as a test mule for testing various development ideas. Although the KISKA car has

'Dallara' and '100' stickers on it, it is in fact one of the three prototype cars built in Varano.

Sebastien was at pains to point out that the prototype cars all had a one-piece carbon monocoque made by Dallara, unlike the production cars which have two-piece monocoques (a top half and a bottom half that are later bonded together) made either by Wethje or CarboTech. Other notable differences on the KISKA car compared to the production cars are the shallow, clear, non-curled wind-deflector; the wing mirrors; the snorkel; the rear wing; and, notably, the suspension measurement devices (so that the suspension geometry could be adjusted and optimised during testing).

Reiter Engineering, which is based in Kirchanschöring, north of Salzburg, which was instrumental in developing the X-BOW racing programme, also has one of the prototypes.

The KTM X-BOW factory in Graz also holds one of the three prototypes, and again, this car has been significantly modified since it left Dallara. The wind deflector, wing mirrors, cabin architecture, pedal box arrangement, snorkel, and dash display are all very different to their counterparts found in the production cars.

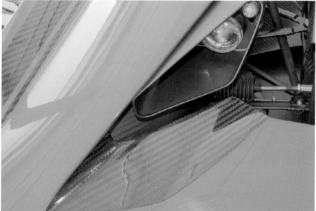

Sebastien Stassin giving a tour of the prototype Dallara X-BOW in the foyer of KISKA's HQ at Anif.
Detailing on the first 100 (Dallara) cars differ from the KTM production version, but there's no mistaking that this is the one and only X-BOW.

## CRASH-TESTED MONOCOQUE

Taking pride of place, and mounted high up on a pillar between the warehousing area and the pre-production assembly area in the Graz factory, is the KTM X-BOW monocoque that underwent crash testing. Crash testing was initially carried out by Dallara Engineering. Later crash tests were carried out to FIA Article 258a standards. The X-BOW's carbon fibre monocoque passed these tests with relatively little damage to the tub, and no intrusion into the passenger compartment. The carbon monocoque is one of the X-BOW's unique selling points, and the crash tests justified the additional cost of using this expensive and labour intensive material.

The Crash-tested monocoque is testament to the strength behind the core of the X-BOW.

## THE DALLARA EDITION KTM X-BOW

The first 100 production X-BOWs were called the 'Dallara Edition' in honour of, and to acknowledge that, Giampaolo Dallara and his team in Varano de' Melegari had succeeded in the difficult task of bringing an unusual concept car to production reality.

The Dallara Edition cars made their debut at the Geneva Motor Show in March 2008.

This limited edition was packed as standard with desirable options: a removable steering wheel, carbon fibre mud guards, quick release and locking devices for the wheels, adjustable suspension, a mechanical limited-slip differential, unique 'Dallara' and '100' body decals, and a metal plaque in the cockpit with the car's serial number.

All 100 Dallara Edition X-BOWs were pre-sold before the car made its Geneva Show debut.

## THE KTM X-BOW GT4

Motorsport is the blood that runs in KTM's veins. KTM has earned its 'Ready To Race' motto the hard way, and numerous World Championship trophies stand testament to this.

It therefore comes as no surprise to learn that KTM, right from the concept stage, planned for the X-BOW to participate – and to dominate – on the race track. The KTM X-BOW GT4 was the racing variant with which KTM would seek racing dominance. Dallara was heavily involved in designing and developing the GT4. This car was first tested in February 2008, and went through the compulsory FIA crash test in March. It passed the Article 258a safety test on its first attempt, thus achieving the same safety credentials as dedicated open-wheel FIA-certified race cars and American Le Mans Series race cars.

In April 2008, the GT4 competed in its first race: the legendary Tourist Trophy at Silverstone. The KTM X-BOW GT4 won the Super Sport category of this race, and was also in the top five overall – and on its very first race outing, too. As all this had happened before the first road car left the production line, KTM could justly claim that the X-BOW was born on the racetrack. Lessons learnt on the track were quickly translated into modifications for the road cars – competition does indeed better the breed.

The X-BOW GT4 cost €82,900 (before national taxes and import duties in 2009), but came with significant safety modifications as standard. As well as the carbon monocoque, and steel roll-over bars, the flanks of the car were protected against penetration by sharp objects with extra layers of Kevlar and Zylon fibres. Zylon, a liquid-crystalline polyoxazole, has a tensile strength 1.6 times that of Kevlar, and a Young's modulus of 270GPa, which means that it is very stiff. Zylon, which was invented in the 1980s, was used for the tether along which the Martian Lander carrying the Martian Rover descended onto the surface of the Red Planet. Zylon tethers are also used in Formula 1, to secure the wheel to the chassis, to prevent a wheel being ejected into a crowd of spectators in that case of an accident. Special side-impact drop links behind the front wheels came as standard in the GT4; these prevent the wheels of other vehicles becoming entangled with those of the GT4.

The GT4 has a 70-litre safety fuel tank – with openings on both sides of the car for rapid refuelling – a racing exhaust system, special aerodynamic bumpers and headlight covers, a racing suspension set-up with adjustable pushrods and shock absorbers, and a limited-slip differential. Other standard features include a dry battery, a removable steering wheel, an ignition master switch, a fire extinguisher system, steel towing eyes front and rear, and a racing head guard. In the GT4, the body panels, the mud guards, the front splitter, the rear diffuser, the rear bumper and the racing underbody are all made of carbon fibre. An air-jack system is also available as a factory-fitted option for fast and simple lifting of the vehicle during pit stops.

## THE KTM X-BOW CLUBSPORT

The Clubsport model was designed for those owners who wanted to use their X-BOW regularly on the race circuit. Stefan Pierer – a keen motorcyclist – and KTM wanted the X-BOW to be a car that fitted with the company motto of 'Ready To Race.' Thus the Clubsport variant was a natural product for KTM to design and manufacture. This model boasted the same carbon monocoque and the same 2.0-litre 240hp Audi TFSI engine found in the other variants.

Priced at €59,980 (before national taxes and import duties in 2009), the X-BOW Clubsport offered its owners additional safety features: the roll-over bars were made from steel, the front roll-over protection structure was further strengthened, and side 'protection drops' were added immediately behind the front wheels to prevent the wheels of other vehicles becoming entangled with the Clubsport's own. This track-orientated model also had as standard a six-point safety harness, an emergency stop switch, racing head supports, a handheld fire extinguisher and a dry battery. The Clubsport's chassis employed adjustable shock absorbers with modifiable compression and rebound damping, adjustable pushrods, preload adjusters, and adjustable front and rear anti-roll bars, so that ambitious amateurs and semi-professional racers could fine-tune the cars to their own driving style, as well as to any given race circuit. In the Clubsport, the flat racing underbody and the rear diffuser were made of aluminium composite, the front splitter was made of carbon fibre, and a mechanical limited-slip differential was fitted as standard.

## THE KTM X-BOW SUPERLIGHT

Stefan Pierer's vision for the KTM X-BOW was a re-interpretation of a super sports car designed for the 21st century: "We took Colin Chapman's idea of a spartan, lightweight sports car reduced to the bare essentials, and transferred it into the new millennium – with as many technological innovations as possible."

Colin Chapman was not only a true engineering genius, but was a marketing one too – it was Chapman who introduced big money sponsorship into Formula 1 motorsport. He designed and engineered the cigar-shaped Lotus 25, which was the world's first stressed monocoque racing car. Then he took advantage of the car's shape and painted the cars to resemble cigar tubes – pure marketing brilliance at a time when cigarettes, cigars and smoking were the norm in high society.

The two quotes that Chapman are best known for are: "Simplify, then add lightness," and: "Adding power makes you faster on the straights. Subtracting weight makes you faster everywhere."

Weight reduces performance, and detracts from driving pleasure by reducing the immediacy of a vehicle's response to the driver's input.

The X-BOW was conceived to be a lightweight car, and this goal was achieved, without sacrificing safety, through the extensive use of carbon fibre. The Superlight model took this weight-saving idea to the next level. Here – in addition to the carbon monocoque – the smooth racing underbody, front splitter, rear diffuser, major body panels and mud guards were all also made of carbon fibre. Lightweight alloy wheels with a single central wheel nut also reduced unsprung mass.

At €79,980 (before national taxes and import duties in 2009), the Superlight was substantially more expensive than the Street and Clubsport models, but carbon fibre is an expensive material. The Superlight partially makes up for this by having an even more spectacular appearance than normal: its black body panels of visible carbon fibre give it a unique, menacing, technoid presence.

While it still features the standard 240hp 2.0-litre Audi TFSI engine, the Superlight gets a removable steering wheel, a limited-slip differential, and shock absorbers adjustable for compression and rebound as standard.

## THE KTM X-BOW ROC

Here, 'ROC' stands for 'Race of Champions.' The Race of Champions was first run in 1988, having been organised by Michèle Mouton, the French female rally driver who was runner-up in the 1982 World Rally Championship administered by the FIA.

The ROC is an annual event in which the world's best rally and racing drivers compete against each other in identical cars. The 2008 ROC took place on December 13-14 at London's Wembley Stadium, with racing legends like Michael Schumacher, Jenson Button, Sebastian Vettel and David Coulthard taking part. The chariot of choice for this race was the KTM X-BOW. David Coulthard said on seeing the X-BOW: "This is really an ingenious car concept. I think it looks absolutely stunning – I can't wait to get behind the wheel." Michèle Mouton said: "The X-BOW generates an incredible furore with its spectacular design alone," while Sebastien Vettel said: "Driving the KTM X-BOW is incredible fun." Sebastien Loeb, a Frenchman who was a gymnast before becoming the most successful driver in World Rally Championship history (he has won the World Championship a record nine times in a row), was finally crowned the 2008 'Champion of Champions.'

The KTM X-BOW received numerous plaudits for its design and its performance during the 2008 ROC, and, in recognition of this, KTM decided to produce a special limited series of cars called the X-BOW ROC. Just 30 units were produced, featuring all-carbon body panels, specially painted lightweight alloy wheels with a single central wheel nut, a specially tuned sports exhaust, and exclusive paintwork in a ROC design with associated decals. The same 240hp Audi TFSI engine remained. The flat underbody, front splitter, rear diffuser, and mud guards were all made of carbon fibre, and the ROC had a removable steering wheel, a limited-slip differential and a fully adjustable performance suspension as standard. The 2009 price for this exclusive, limited edition car was €69,980 (before national taxes and import duties), which included a Schuberth helmet and an indoor car cover.

## THE KTM X-BOW STREET

The 2009 KTM X-BOW product line-up had as its base model the X-BOW Street. The Street was designed as the cheapest and most road-biased variant, but it still featured a full carbon monocoque, the same Audi 2.0-litre TFSI with 240hp, and the basic aerodynamic addenda that is integral to an X-BOW. Thus the Street had a smooth racing underbody, and a front splitter, and a rear diffuser made of aluminium composite material. Factory-fitted optional extras for the Street included a removable steering wheel, a limited-slip differential, and street-homologated semi-slick tyres. The Street was designed to be the most cost-accessible entry point into the X-BOW range – at a base price of €49,980 (before national taxes and import duties) – without sacrificing the purist and unfiltered driving pleasure that an X-BOW brings with it: the immediacy of response and the exposure to the elements that comes from driving a very lightweight and open-cockpit car. KTM wanted to build a car that gave the feeling of riding a motorcycle, or driving a single-seater racing car, and with the Street they succeeded, and at a relatively affordable cost.

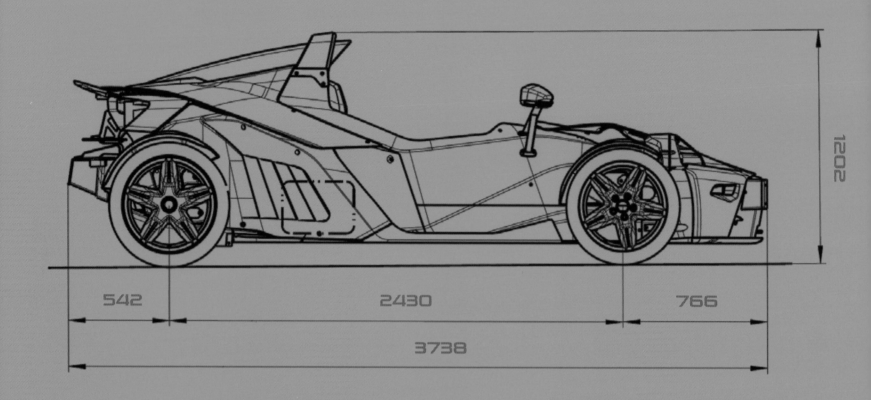

542     2430     766

3738

1202

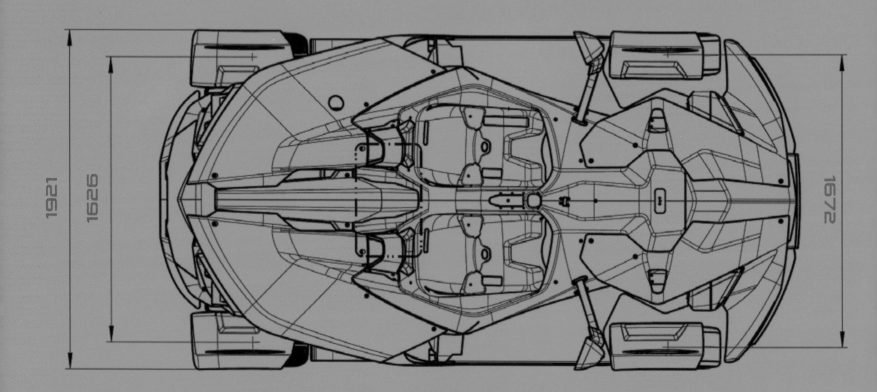

1921

1626

1672

The GT4 carries an inherent advantage as a race car, by virtue of its modular construction. In the event of an accident, as long as the monocoque is not damaged, and the mounting points are not deformed, damaged parts can be replaced in a matter of minutes, leaving the X-BOW 'Ready To Race' in record time. Not only does this increase the chances of race success, but it also reduces the cost of running. Another important factor in cost reduction is the use of the standard 240hp Audi TFSI engine in the GT4: it is a crate engine so is relatively affordable, and is reliable and fuel-efficient, while the TFSI engine technology has been proven with numerous overall wins in the 24-hour Le Mans race.

## THE KTM X-BOW R

In the summer of 2010, rumours started percolating that KTM were preparing to launch a new, more powerful and more refined X-BOW.

The X-BOW was the world's first production vehicle to boast a monocoque made entirely of composite carbon fibre, and additionally was relatively affordable for such a revolutionary product. It therefore deserved success in the marketplace. This it achieved with the first 100 Dallara Edition cars, all of which were pre-sold. But then the effects of the 2008 global financial crisis began to take hold. What had been planned as a production run of 1000 cars every 12 months dwindled down to single figure monthly sales. Series production had begun at the Graz factory in August 2008, but by November 2009 less than 500 X-BOWs had been built, of which over 80 were rumoured to have remained unsold. This sorry tale was re-emphasised by the X-BOW sales figures for the United Kingdom. The UK, with its strong track-day presence, had been identified by KTM as one of the X-BOW's biggest markets. But 18 months after launch, KTM had only sold 28 cars in the UK despite fairly aggressive marketing. This was partly due to loss of consumer confidence because of the recession, partly because of the sinking value of the Pound Sterling against the Euro, and partly because of the very high costs of desirable optional extras. What had been projected in April 2007 as a £37,000 base car had, by August 2008,

| X-BOW | Street | Clubsport | Superlight/ROC | GT4 |
|---|---|---|---|---|
| Bodystyle | Two-seater sports car | | | Single-seater race sports car |
| Chassis | Carbon-Monocoque | Racing Carbon-Monocoque | Carbon-Monocoque | Racing Carbon-Monocoque |
| Powertrain | Transverse mid-mounted engine and rear-wheel drive | | | |
| Engine | Make:<br>Type:<br>Capacity:<br>Bore and stroke:<br>Max power:<br>Max torque:<br>Valves:<br>Materials:<br>Emissions class: | | Audi TFSI<br>Turbo-charged, 4-cylinder petrol with direct fuel injection<br>1984cc / 2.0Litres<br>82.5 x 92.8mm<br>240ps (177kW) at 5500rpm<br>310Nm (229lb/ft) from 2000 to 5500rpm<br>16 (4 per cylinder)<br>Cast iron block, aluminium alloy cylinder head<br>Euro 4 compliant | |
| Transmission | Type:<br>Ratios:<br><br><br><br><br><br><br><br>Reverse: | | 6-speed manual<br>1st: 3.36:1<br>2nd: 2.09:1<br>3rd: 1.47:1<br>4th: 1.09:1<br>5th 1.11:1<br>6th: 0.91:1<br><br>3.9898:1 | |
| Limited-slip differential | | X | X | X |
| Suspension | Fully independent double triangle wishbones | | | |
| WP-spring elements | Fix | Adjustable with preload-adjuster | | Adjustable |
| Pushrod-layout | Front | Front adjustable | Front | Front adjustable |
| Anti-roll bar | Fix | Adjustable | Fix | Adjustable |
| Steering | System<br>Turning circle<br>Steering wheel | | | Rack and pinion (unassisted)<br>10.8 metres<br>290mm diameter |
| Brakes | System<br>Front<br><br>Rear<br><br>Parking brake | | | Hydraulic (unassisted)<br>Brembo 305mm ventilated discs with 4-piston fixed calipers<br>Brembo 262mm ventilated discs with 2-piston fixed calipers<br>Calipers on rear disc (not GT4) |
| Wheels and tyres | Front<br>Rear | | | 17x7.5in alloys with 205/40 tyres<br>18x7.5in alloys with 235/40 tyres |
| Dry weight | 790kg | 805kg | 785kg | 825kg |
| Front/rear % split | 37/63% [static]  35/65% [aerodynamic] | | | |

| X-BOW | Street | Clubsport | Superlight/ROC | GT4 |
|---|---|---|---|---|
| **Fuel tank capacities** | 40 litres [98 RON] unleaded petrol] | | | 70 litres [98 RON unleaded petrol] |
| **Performance** | 0-100km/h 3.90s<br>60-100 km/h 2.80s<br>80-120 km/h 2.97s | | | 0-100 km/h 3.90s<br>0-200 km/h 18.60s |
| **Lateral acceleration/ speed** | Series tyre 1.50g max<br>Semi-slicks 1.80g max | | | 2.00g max |
| **Vmax** | 220 km/h | | | 235 km/h |
| **Braking to standstill** | 100-0 km/h 32.9 metres [series tyre, warm brakes] | | | TBD |
| **Downforce** | At 100 km/h 48kg<br>At 200 km/h 193kg | | | |
| **Fuel consumption** | CO² mass emissions (urban conditions) 231g/km<br>(extra-urban conditions) 135g/km<br>(combined) 171g/km<br>Fuel consumption (urban conditions) 9.8L/100km<br>(extra-urban conditions) 5.7L/100km<br>(combined) 7.2L/100km<br>Range > 500km | | | Racing:<br>35L/100km<br>Range:<br>200km |
| **Emissions class** | Euro 4 | | | |
| **Warranty and servicing** | Legal warranty: two years<br>Service intervals: Every 12 months or 5000km | | | TBD |

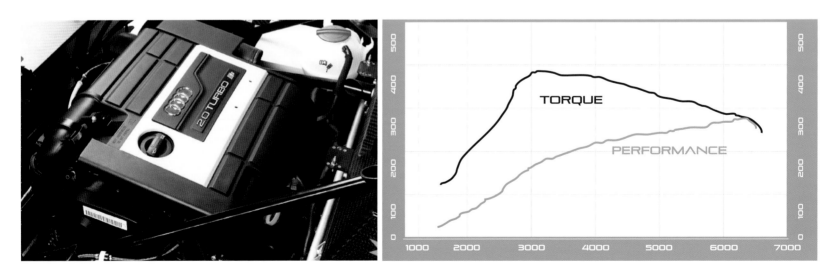

Audi's TFSI engine, the power plant for every X-BOW from the debut model to the GT4.
An obvious choice if the torque curve is anything to go by; a pretty perfect mix that lends itself so well to the life of a road-racer.

become a £50,000 base car, and by the middle of 2009 many motoring magazines were road-testing factory-supplied X-BOWs with price tags in excess of £80,000, once optional extras were accounted for.

In August 2009, KTM called a temporary halt to X-BOW production, with the stated intention of restarting in January 2010, but at a much reduced level. KTM's share price plummeted from a high of €59.50 in 2007 to €18 in late 2009, and KTM's autumn 2009 financial statement included this ominous line: "A sale of the entire Sports Car Division will also have to be considered."

Given this backdrop, it was both surprising and heartening to hear, in mid-2010, that KTM was continuing to fund research and development of the X-BOW. Owners, enthusiasts and the motoring press had long concluded that the X-BOW's Dallara-engineered chassis could easily cope with more power and torque. A more powerful, capable and refined X-BOW would be better able to justify its premium price against its cheaper rivals, and thereby retain, and hopefully increase, its market share.

In the summer of 2011, the new KTM X-BOW R made its debut. In keeping with its parent company's motto of 'Ready To Race,' the 'R' stood for 'Racing.' The R variant was the performance-orientated model, and was designed to liberate the latent potential of the X-BOW. This car was fully homologated for road use, and fully conformed to the requirements of the prevailing European Union Small Series Production Standards.

The modifications and the developments seen with the R were extensive, and included changes to the engine, the chassis attachments and the suspension.

The X-BOW R used the Audi CDL engine, which was a derivation of the engines from the Audi S3 and the Audi TTS. While still carrying a capacity of 1984cc and TFSI technology, it now boasted a larger Garrett T4 turbocharger,

reprogrammed Bosch engine management, and an uprated fuel-injection system with new fuel injectors. The blow off valve was now positioned in front of the throttle body to get the turbocharger to spool up more quickly when the throttle pedal was depressed. With this new modified engine the R variant's headline figures were now boosted to 296bhp (300hp) at 5500rpm and 295lb/ft (400Nm) of torque at 3300rpm. With this almost 25 per cent increase in power and torque output over the base car, KTM claimed that the 0-60mph dash now took 3.6 seconds rather than 3.8 seconds, and the top speed increased from 137mph to 144mph.

The power and torque produced by the X-BOW's engine has to be absorbed by the engine mounting points on the aluminium rear subframe. To cope with the extra power and torque in the R variant, KTM fitted modified and strengthened engine mounts to this model.

The torque support arm, which had previously been attached to the rear subframe, was now attached directly to the carbon fibre monocoque in the R variant. This alteration allows the engine's torque and power to be transferred to the chassis more quickly and with less vibration, so allowing the R to accelerate out of corners faster and with more refinement.

The repositioning of the torque support arm also allowed the engine in the R variant to be sited 19mm lower in the chassis bay. This had the direct effect of lowering the overall centre of gravity of the car by 15mm – something that greatly enhances the car's stability, agility and roadholding.

Stiffer springs and uprated shock absorbers (adjustable for compression and rebound) are standard on the R. Fibet bushings with Teflon shims are used on all the wishbones to reduce axial deflection, which optimises the suspension and steering responses. A Drexler limited-slip differential, and a unique tri-colour (orange, white and black) body panel design with red, italic 'R' decals, come as standard with the X-BOW R.

The R from 2011 looks every bit the road-racer, and with its larger T4 turbocharger, improved engine management systems and fuel injectors, manages 0-60mph in just 3.6s, stepping on the toes of far more expensive rivals from the likes of Porsche, Lamborghini, Ferrari and Lotus to name but a few. The X-BOW had arrived.

The 2011 price for the KTM X-BOW R (before national taxes and import duties) was €64,900. The motoring press was unanimous that the R variant was substantially better than the base car, and that its higher price was totally justified.

With the launch of the KTM X-BOW GT, the R variant underwent a facelift. The headlight surrounds and the front body panels were redesigned to improve the car's aerodynamics, and to give it a sleeker, more modern look. Ditto the rear body panels, which gained shark-gill-like ventilation slits. New bilateral air intakes were developed in the space immediately below the roll-over bars. The trademark snorkel, very sadly in my opinion, was deleted in the name of reducing drag.

## THE KTM X-BOW GT

The base KTM X-BOW looks like almost nothing else on the road. Only a Lamborghini Countach could compete with it in terms of dropping jaws. Its startling, predatory, technoid appearance is partly because it does not have a windscreen. Its transparent, double-curved, injection-moulded Makrolon AG2677 wind deflector is only 70mm high. This makes it look like a Formula 1 car when viewed from the outside, and makes the driver feel like a Formula 1 World Championship contender when seated in the fixed, hip-hugging Recaro seats.

The lack of a windscreen comes at a price, however. Although European Union rules do not force an X-BOW driver or passenger to wear a crash helmet, real-world driving experience dictates that it would be a folly not to wear a crash helmet. Rain drops at 30mph are an exquisite torture without a helmet, and tiny stones flicked up by the car in front can hurt and scar, and most definitely detract from the pleasure of driving. Most importantly, a penetrating eye injury is a very real possibility, and I can assure you, after over 30 years as an eye surgeon, that putting a broken eye together again can make reassembling Humpty-Dumpty look very easy in comparison.

Wearing a crash helmet is therefore essentially mandatory in the X-BOW, but this puts off many potential owners, and so limits the X-BOW's share of the super sports car market. Furthermore, the various X-BOWs that were available in the first four years of production were all hardcore cars that required an unusual degree of dedication from their owners. At the X-BOW's price-point, a significant proportion of potential owners would be 'senior,' and less amenable to a lack of creature comforts than they would have been a decade or two previously. An added bonus would be to capture those in this niche market who also wanted to use their road-racers for touring – better weather protection and better luggage carrying capacity would help here.

KTM recognised this, and introduced the X-BOW GT in 2013, specifically to capture this segment of the market – the target audience being customers who wanted a more user-friendly X-BOW that could be enjoyed without having the bother and discomfort of donning a crash helmet, and with both a roof and a boot.

The GT variant was based on the X-BOW R. The key feature that the KTM X-BOW GT brought over and above the base car was a windscreen and side windows-cum-doors.

KTM designed the GT's windscreen to envelop the driver and passenger in much the same manner that a helmet visor wraps around the wearer's

On top of the world: Chassis 0642. Sometimes parking spaces aren't easy to find ...

face. There were also many similarities in the curvature and shape of the GT's windscreen to that of the iconic Lancia Stratos.

The addition of a windscreen and the side windows/doors to the X-BOW was only possible by making fundamental changes to the X-BOW's carbon fibre chassis. This is the reason why the windscreen and doors of the GT cannot be retrofitted to existing X-BOWs.

KTM have done a very thorough job with the GT variant. The windscreen and the doors are high quality items made of laminated safety glass, and the fit and finish is exemplary. The frameless wraparound windscreen features integral heating elements for quick defrosting, and the GT has a single arm windscreen wiper with a windscreen washer spray system. The A pillars are narrow, and do not restrict vision even when cornering. The doors open and close with the aid of gas struts

The road-orientated GT is geared towards comfort (everything in life being relative), and it has a heater and air-conditioning. An optional removable roof, which KTM calls the X-TOP, can be used at speeds up to 80mph, and is small enough to be folded and stowed away in the cockpit when not in use. The cockpit is more plush than the base car, with detachable sun-visors and a more complete central console carrying the switches for the windscreen wiper, screenwash/wipe system, and windscreen heater, as well as the interior ventilation and heating system. Leather seats with contrast stitching are available as an optional extra. The GT's air-conditioning system is designed to reduce the in-cockpit temperature to about 15°C, even in the ambient temperatures of early afternoon in the Middle East and South-East Asia.

The GT loses the large central snorkel and has flatter revised rear body panels. This allows for a detachable, streamlined luggage pod, with a capacity of 50-litres, to be securely mounted on the rear deck.

The new rear body panels, which together form the engine cover of the GT, have shark-gill-like ventilation slits, and present a quite different rear appearance compared to the earlier, snorkel-carrying R version.

The front of the car has also been subtly altered with new narrower and more angular headlamps, new larger front wheel fairings, and new front body panels that slope more steeply to the front splitter. These changes give the GT a more muscular, yet more streamlined appearance.

It is no surprise to learn that all these body changes were done with keen attention to the car's aerodynamics, and the GT generates less drag and more downforce than the previous generation R model.

The GT retains the 1984cc Audi TFSI of the R model, but the engine ECU has been reprogrammed to favour driveability over maximum performance. The power output falls to 281bhp (300hp) at 6400rpm, but the maximum torque figure increases to 310lb/ft (420 Nm) at 3200rpm to improve dynamic flexibility.

New colours were made available for the GT variant. There is a choice of two standard colours (Electric Orange and Pure White), or five extra-cost options (Python Green, Fusion Orange, Original Blue, Combat Grey and Carbon Black).

The GT's base price, before options, in 2013 was €72,500.

### The KTM X-BOW RR

KTM look upon their X-BOW RR model as the ultimate weapon in the fight for hundredths of a second on the race track. The RR continues with the veteran Audi 1984cc TFSI engine and the same basic chassis architecture as every previous X-BOW, but is tuned uncompromisingly for victory on the circuit and is almost limitlessly customisable. This race-specific car is the perfect choice for KTM's own one-make race series (the KTM X-BOW Battle), but the RR has also proven itself in competition against long-established names like Ferrari, Lamborghini and Porsche.

As can be seen from the technical data sheet that KTM produced for the RR, the specialists from the X-BOW Motorsport Division will tailor each RR to the requirements of that customer. In particular, the engine power and torque outputs can be modified and tuned according to the customer's specification. While the rear tyre size remains unchanged compared to the R variant at 255/35/R18, the front tyre size increases to 215/45/R17. On semi-slick tyres the KTM X-BOW RR can generate in excess of 2.0G of lateral acceleration. This is a bespoke racing car at a relatively affordable price.

## THE CLOSED BODY KTM X-BOW GT4

An excellent book – titled *GT4 X-BOW: Designed to Race* and written by Alexandre Rossier – that focuses purely on the track-only closed body GT4 already exists. It is a book that I would recommend to readers seeking more information on the closed body race car.

This book, on the other hand, concentrates on the open-cockpit, road-legal KTM X-BOW variants, but the closed body GT4 is an integral part of the KTM X-BOW family, and to not discuss it would be a grave omission. This is especially true as the closed body GT4 plays such an important role in the X-BOW Battle race series, and therefore in the X-BOW series in particular, as well as in KTM in general. So here are the bare bones on this closed body variant. (Please refer to Rossier's book for more details.)

This vehicle was designed as a pure race car for the GT4 European series, and was the brain-child of Hans Reiter. Hans is the founder of Reiter Engineering, which is based in Kirchanschöring, Bavaria, Germany. It was

This GT4 shows the simplicity with which the canopy opens. Noteworthy is the extensive race roll cage, which is unique to the race-only GT4.

designed by KISKA in 2014, over a period of less than two months. The closed body car is heavily based on the open-cockpit X-BOW, and shares the same basic carbon fibre monocoque and crashbox.

This race-only vehicle has a 170mm longer wheelbase and a lower ride height than the road-capable X-BOW variants. Quick and easy access to key mechanical components that might need replacing during the heat of a race, and top-flight aerodynamics were the two key design ambitions. This car is even more sensational in appearance than the road-homologated models, as it features a spectacular single-piece canopy to allow driver access. This one-piece Makrolon canopy is front-hinged, and rises high towards the sky when open, allowing the driver relatively quick and easy entry into the cockpit. It also allows the pit crew ready access to tighten the driver's seatbelts.

In the autumn of 2014, the first rolling chassis was assembled at the Graz factory. A completely new suspension system and new uprights had to be designed and manufactured because of the changes to the car's wheelbase and ride height. This closed body GT4 racer retains the same 1984cc four-cylinder in-line Audi TFSI engine seen in the open-cockpit models. The power and torque of the engine, and therefore the acceleration and top speed of the car, can be specified by the customer. Equally, the aerodynamic addenda, and hence the aerodynamic downforce generated by the car, is to customer specification. It does, however, feature a semi-automatic, racing grade gearbox as standard. Also standard are built-in air-jacks, to ease and quicken wheel changes and any other necessary in-race mechanical repairs.

The closed body GT4 was initially called the X-BOW GTR, and teaser photos were released online in late 2014. The first prototype X-BOW GT4 was put together by Reiter Engineering in March 2015. The first shakedown test was carried out at the Adria race circuit on April 1, 2015. Over a two-day test session, more than 400 laps, and in excess of 1000km, were covered by the two test drivers: Tomas Enge and Naomi Schiff. On May 24, 2015, the GT4 won its class at its debut race at the Zandvoort race circuit. Thus far, there have been three evolutions of this GT4 variant, principally with alterations to the bodywork. The closed body GT4 racer is currently produced at both the Reiter Engineering facility in Kirchanschöring, and the KTM X-BOW factory in Graz.

This is a spectacular and successful racing car, and with its massive, almost unique, front-hinged, transparent canopy, it fully lives up to its nickname: 'The Batmobile.'

GT4 dressed to kill. Naomi Schiff prepares to unleash the beast and join the battle.

Each KTM X-BOW is in very many ways bespoke, in that they are made to the exact demands of their first owners. At present, the Graz factory will only start the build process of an X-BOW after receiving a full specification for that order, and only after a substantial accompanying deposit has been received.

To date, after over 10 years in series production, only about 1300 units of the KTM X-BOW have been produced; this is an exclusive, special, and expensive car, although a detailed examination of its basic specification, and a close comparison of its design features relative to that of its rivals, show the X-BOW to be good value for money.

One of the most special things that strike an owner when ordering and specifying a new X-BOW, is just how bespoke the ordering, manufacturing and delivery processes for the X-BOW are. KTM invites every potential owner to visit its Graz production facility, and will organise a personalised tour of the production line with a senior staff member. The extensive list of optional extras can be seen, discussed and decided upon at this stage. Every car is built with the greatest of care, by engineer-technicians with specific expertise in each given area. Each X-BOW is assembled by hand – a real rarity in today's automotive world. In fact, one of KTM's slogans for the X-BOW is, "Produced Perfectly By Hand." The new owner can pick up his X-BOW at its birthplace in Graz, Austria, or at one of the limited number of KTM dealerships worldwide, or even have the car delivered to their home or business address.

Every factory production X-BOW to date has had three features that are not alterable. These three things work together to define the X-BOW: the first is the carbon fibre monocoque, and the second is the 1984cc Audi TFSI engine. Thirdly, each of these cars comes with a set of basic aerodynamic addenda – the front spoiler, the side barge boards, the rear wing and the rear diffuser.

Within these set parameters, the X-BOW can be extensively customised. KTM is able to modify the following aspects of each car: the engine, the gearbox, the aerodynamic package, the suspension set-up, the ancillary mechanicals, the paint and decals, and the interior with comfort-orientated optional extras. KTM also offer a choice of models that are either track-biased or road-biased.

KTM has put together various mechanical, suspension and aerodynamic packages to help customers navigate through the extensive list of optional extras available, so that they end up with the most appropriate car for their individual needs. Again, the customer is not limited by these packages, but can choose à la carte, or can have the whole tasting menu if so desired!

### THE ENGINE

The R and GT variants use the same subtly modified Audi TFSI engine. The engine electronics are tuned differently for each model – the R's to produce more power for the track, and the GT's to produce more easily accessible torque for greater dynamic flexibility during road use. The race-orientated RR can be specified with an engine extensively modified by KTM's Motorsport Division to suit the owner's demands and desires; this is limited almost exclusively by the size of the owner's wallet.

### THE GEARBOX

The author was fortunate enough to see the very first X-BOW equipped with a dual-clutch automated gearbox during his visit to the Graz facility in the autumn of 2018. This is a very important development, particularly for the goldmine that is the Chinese market. Apparently, wealthy young Chinese have little experience with manual transmission cars, and offering an automatic brings in a whole new potential customer base.

The new dual-clutch automated gearbox makes it possible to change gears under full load within milliseconds. This six-speed gearbox uses GT3-inspired technology developed by Holinger Europe, and has been extensively tested on the race track. Shift paddles mounted on the X-BOW's removable steering wheel pneumatically operate the shift fork functions in as little as 90 milliseconds. A 'selected gear' indicator is integrated into the car's dashboard display in all cars equipped with this optional gearbox.

The standard six-speed manual Audi gearbox weighs 53kg, while this new automated gearbox is substantially lighter at just 35kg.

### THE AERODYNAMIC PARTS

KTM have continuously honed the X-BOW's aerodynamics, and have taken particular care to ensure that any new aerodynamic parts can be retro-fitted to already existing cars.

As a road-racer, on-track performance is a vital part of the X-BOW's identity. Together with lightweight construction and smooth power delivery, the contradictory demands of high downforce and low drag dictate how quickly the X-BOW will lap any given racing circuit.

The R variant can now be specified with aerodynamic parts that give it up to 400kg of downforce at 200km/h. This is double the downforce that the first, standard R car was capable of generating. This enormous downforce is largely responsible for the high lateral acceleration that the X-BOW can achieve. The RR variant can, for example, exceed 2.0G of lateral acceleration on road-legal semi-slick tyres.

As of 2018, KTM offer four optional aerodynamic packages for the X-BOW.

Aerodynamic Package 1 consists of an additional carbon fibre front

splitter sporting shark-tooth-like projections (vortex generators), and two carbon fibre air guide vanes, all of which are fitted to the crashbox. These parts increase front axle downforce and also enhance engine cooling by optimising airflow into the radiators.

Aerodynamic Package 2 consists of two carbon fibre front-hood spoilers,

each of which has two flicks or canards. These front spoilers and their integrated flics further increase front axle downforce, and KTM therefore recommend that Aerodynamic

Packages 2 and 3 should always be fitted together, so that any additional downforce is spread equally over the whole length of the car.

Aerodynamic Package 3 consists of an additional carbon fibre

rear spoiler that increases rear axle downforce. The angle of attack of this spoiler can be easily and quickly adjusted to generate any one of three levels of downforce.

Aerodynamic Package 4 features a front splitter extension and

two gurneys for the underfloor, all of which increases front axle downforce.

Further optional aerodynamic addenda include a racing airbox, which is flatter than the standard item and so generates less drag, aerodynamic racing headlight covers, a carbon fibre racing windshield, a flat, fully-carbon underbody with

NACA ducts for enhanced airflow through to the engine compartment, and a 1.8-metre-wide adjustable racing rear wing (bottom picture).

## THE SUSPENSION SET-UP

The standard X-BOW can be further customised by choosing either a Performance Suspension Package (stiffer springs and WP-made shock absorbers with adjustable compression and rebound damping), or a Racing Suspension Package (which features even stiffer springs and modified WP dual adjustable shock absorbers to further increase roll stiffness).

Other optional suspension components include: adjustable front and rear anti-roll bars; a progressive

linkage system to improve the responsiveness of the front axle; adjustable pushrods that lower the X-BOW's ride height and thereby its centre of gravity; and racing wishbones with polyurethane rather than rubber bushings, which lead to quicker and more precise steering responses and more accurate handling. Michelin PS3 Summer tyres, Michelin Pilot Sport 4 or Michelin Pilot Sport Cup 2 threaded tyres can be specified. Other options include Michelin Rain tyres, Toyo R888R semi-slick road-legal tyres, and track only Michelin Full Slick Battle tyres.

set or with a central locking nut; the Street Wheel Set, also made of aluminium, can also be had as a 5-bolt set or with a central locking nut; and finally, the X-BOW can be specified with BBS lightweight aluminium wheels, which are unique in that they have a coloured wheel rim ring – a choice of Fusion Orange, Metallic Silver, or a personalised colour are all available.

## THE ANCILLARY MECHANICALS

KTM offers an optional black chromed Sports Exhaust System, which delivers a louder and throatier exhaust note than the standard silver exhaust system. The Sports Exhaust System is also 5kg lighter than the standard.

Further customisation is possible by opting for the X-BOW Racing Exhaust. This system, which includes a 100-cell catalytic converter, is designed purely for motorsport and is FIA homologated. It is 12kg lighter than the standard exhaust system. The engine ECU has to be reprogrammed if a 100-cell catalytic converter is used.

A Quick Shifter (see right) for the six-speed manual gearbox is available as an option. A more elaborate Racing Shifter is also available, which allows for even shorter throw gearlever movements, and also delivers faster and more precise gear changes.

Additional engine and gearbox oil cooler systems can be specified by the customer. These are particularly useful in the hot and harsh environment of the race track. Racing ABS is now available for the X-BOW. An optional Racing Intercooler System has been developed by WP Performance Systems for the X-BOW, and this significantly reduces the temperature of the intake air, and so delivers a power boost of up to 7 per cent. An optional Racing Water Pump is available, which enhances engine

efficiency, especially at high ambient temperatures.

An optional Air-Jack System (above) is available for the X-BOW. This system uses compressed air, and is designed specifically for the race track. It allows the car to be raised quickly and safely, so that jobs like changing wheels or replacing shock absorbers can be done in the least possible time.

A variety of brake discs and brake pads are available for the X-BOW. The Large Rear Brake Disc Set uses 305mm x 22mm rear discs that enhance braking power. The Racing Brake Disc Set reduces unsprung

mass through its use of an aluminium mounting bell and the specially slotted steel brake discs optimise heat conduction loss, and thereby reduce braking distance. A choice of touring brake pads, racing brake pads or long-distance racing brake pads are available. These have respective coefficients of friction of 0.49, 0.55 and 0.62 respectively. The X-BOW can also be specified with an in-cockpit adjustable brake balance dial. This allows adjustment of the brake balance between the front and rear brake circuits, thus allowing the car's set-up to be optimised for any given racer's driving style or for any given race circuit.

Two performance packs are also available as options on the X-BOW. Performance Pack 1 was developed for the R variant, and allows the engine to be lowered by 19mm. It incorporates a torque stay that is attached directly between the engine block and the monocoque, and features modified suspension geometry. This pack comes as standard on all cars as of model year 2011. Performance Pack 2 consists of a modified carbon fibre air filter housing, and a new chrome-molybdenum steel tubular space frame. The former optimises intake airflow to the turbocharger and also generates a sportier intake sound, while the latter strengthens the rear subframe of the X-BOW, and significantly increases the torsional stiffness of the whole car.

## THE PAINT AND DECALS

KTM offers a bespoke paint service for the X-BOW. Just about any colour is possible for the body panels, and just about any pattern can be entertained. Style and cost are the two main limiting factors, but as

Left: this is a very well specced interior indeed; Suede Racing steering wheel, anodised handbrake and gearlever with leather cover, comfort seats finished in alcantara with contrasting KTM Orange stitching and multimedia system.

Above: Ready to race. A statement, not a question.
Left: Multimedia syatem by Parrot. Ready to relax? Vivaldi please ...

the latter is often not a restraining factor on the former, some truly ugly, albeit striking, cars are sometimes let out of the Graz factory gates. As Marilyn Monroe said: "Imperfection is beauty, madness is genius and it's better to be absolutely ridiculous than absolutely boring."

The X-BOW can also be further customised with optional stick-on decal sets pre-made by the factory. Bespoke sticker sets are also available – designed and manufactured to the owner's personal taste.

Paint Protection Film for the front body panels, the crashbox, and the underfloor between the rear wheels and the radiator fairings is also available.

### INTERIOR AND COMFORT-ORIENTATED OPTIONAL EXTRAS
Optional Comfort Seats are available for the X-BOW and are designed to be a visual delight, while simultaneously able to hold the occupant comfortably, safely and securely in place. These Comfort Seats are made from a weatherproof anti-slip material that is waterproof and dirt-proof. Fully customised seats with special stitching or made of special material or to a special design are available upon request.

A black aluminium anodised gearshift lever is an option, as is a gearlever boot that matches the colour and stitching of the Comfort Seats. Alternatively, the gearlever boot material and stitching can be completely customised to the owner's specification. A matching black aluminium anodised handbrake lever is also available.

The optional Racing Steering Wheel, with a thinly padded rim covered in high quality full grain leather and carrying an orange 12 o'clock marking, will find particular favour with track-day diehards.

It might seem incongruous, but the road-racer is now available with air-conditioning. All is not lost though, as this option is only available with the touring-focussed GT variant. KTM claim that its air-conditioning system is able to maintain an in-cockpit temperature of 15°C even in the most extreme summer heat. Individual vents are present on both the driver and passenger's sides, and the system is simply and easily operated through a switch on the central console.

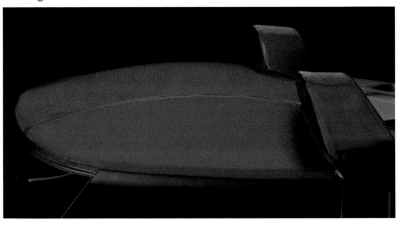

Surely, even more astounding is that the X-BOW can now be specified with the components and brackets to host a multimedia system! Using smartphone technology, 3G and 4G internet access, and a five-inch multi-touch screen, satellite navigation, music, and hands-free telephone conversations are now all available.

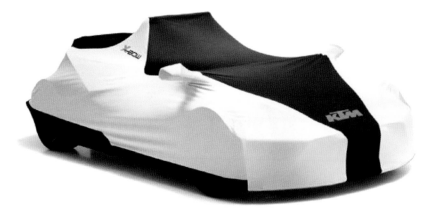

Bespoke hi-tech car covers are available for both indoor and outdoor use. KTM have thought everything through for enhancing your ownership experience, and your X-BOW.

Opposite page, left to right: Carbon fibre HANS-compatible racing headrest, FIA approved rain light, OMP plumbed-in fire extinguisher system, Arai racing helmet, Nomex racing suit, gloves and boots. Also shown is the Schuberth road helmet, which has a wider visor area for improved vision.

The GT variant also has a detachable soft top, which KTM calls the 'X-TOP.' KTM claim that the X-TOP is quick and easy to mount and demount. It is made of a water and dirt-repellent fabric and can be folded and stowed away in the passenger footwell when not in use.

The GT variant was also the first X-BOW to offer the genuinely useful option of having a demountable luggage carrying system. When accompanied by a passenger, in-cockpit storage space is very limited, which is a major problem when the X-BOW is used for long-distance,

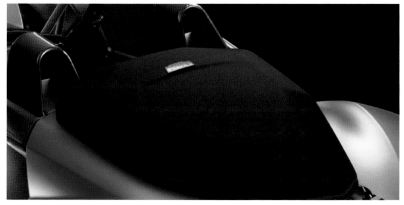

multi-day touring holidays. The GT's luggage storage system is a flexible fabric-like bag that sits atop the rear body panels. It has a luggage capacity of about 50-litres. This stowage system can now be fitted to any X-BOW variant, provided that the car in question is equipped with the low profile air box option. The old-style large snorkel and this luggage system are mutually incompatible.

KTM-logoed indoor and outdoor car covers are available. Just as the car itself can be clothed and protected, KTM also offers clothing and protection to the drivers and passengers of the X-BOW, by way of a three-layer Nomex racing suit, racing gloves, racing boots, and the choice of an X-BOW logoed road helmet made by Schuberth or a racing helmet made by Arai.

## SPECIALISED RACING OPTIONS

The X-BOW, true to its roots, can be specified with a variety of addenda that are particularly useful and desirable in a race setting.

An FIA-homologated six-point racing seatbelt is available, as is a racing headrest, to provide the driver with additional safety and stability by supporting his or her helmet. Both these options are fully compatible with a HANS system.

A handheld fire extinguisher mounted in the passenger footwell, or an OMP plumbed-in fire extinguisher system are available. The latter system is homologated to FIA standards, is electronically activated, and carries 4.25 litres of extinguisher material.

Racing rain lights, certified by the FIA and controlled through the steering-wheel-mounted foglight button, is another optional extra, as is an FIA-homologated battery cut-off switch. Front and rear steel racing tow hooks are stronger than the standard items, and are particularly important when an unfortunate X-BOW is being towed out of a gravel trap.

Racing roll-over bars made of steel, racing seat padding (which replaces the standard seat and allows the driver to sit lower within the car), and a carbon racing footwell cover (which seals the passenger footwell and optimises airflow around the cockpit), are all available to further customise this already bespoke road-racer.

KTM and Dallara are companies steeped in motorsport tradition: While KTM is 'Ready To Race', Giampaolo Dallara says, "our mission is to make race cars faster and safer." The X-BOW was conceived as a road-racer, so it is no surprise that KTM, pretty much immediately, organised a one-make race series just for the X-BOW: the X-BOW Battle.

The X-BOW Battle, which is commonly abbreviated to X-BB, is said to be Europe's largest and most successful one-make race series. It has been operational since 2008, and the author was fortunate enough to spend three exhilarating days watching the X-BB at the Panonnia-Ring in Hungary, between August 30 and September 1, 2018.

This was a great opportunity to meet fellow X-BOW owners who were merely spectators, X-BOW owners who were racing, drivers who had hired an X-BOW for the duration of the race meeting, and race team owners and members. Also present were almost all the staff from the X-BOW factory at Graz. KTM says that every one of its Graz staff has at least two roles, and this was clearly the case, with the factory workforce playing key roles in trackside marshalling, public relations and hospitality, preparing the race cars, pre and post-race scrutineering, repairing accident-damaged cars, refuelling, and generally keeping all the guests busy and happy.

This last point is very important. KTM, as is its tradition, is highly organised and meticulous in its preparation and execution. The X-BB is a beautifully professional event that is a joy to attend. But KTM wants the X-BB to be fun for its guests; it says, "Customer racing done differently." The X-BB is, by definition, a competitive event, but off-track, KTM tries to engender a kindred feeling and family atmosphere amongst the racers, the spectators and the Graz staff members. And it has been very successful in achieving this particular goal.

Keeping in mind that we were at a motor-racing circuit – with race cars moving in and out of the pits at speed, mechanics moving heavy equipment within confined spaces, and hot exhausts and fuel nearby – as long as we were being sensible, KTM pretty much allowed free access to every part of the pit garages and the pit lane throughout the three-day Panonnia-Ring event. This was fabulous for photography, and also for interviewing the drivers and the pit crew.

The X-BB was also an unexpected opportunity to see just how strong and well made the X-BOW is. For those of us who only use our X-BOWs on the road, and who feel no shame in keeping these road-racers polished and sparkling in heated garages, it was illuminating to see the X-BOWs shrugging off real physical abuse with ease. Hartwig Breitenbach, who is in charge of Customer Services at the Graz factory, and without whose extensive help (which was always served up in the most cheerful and generous manner) this book would not be in existence, is a very well-built gentleman, even by Austrian standards. And here he was in the Panonnia-Ring garages, both feet balanced on an X-BOW's front splitter, vigourously bouncing up and down, exposing the splitter to his full, not inconsiderable, weight. When I expressed surprise and concern at the delinquency being

An impressive line-up for the racing at the Pannonia-Ring in Hungary. Whether an owner, a hirer or a spectator, this is competitive , one-make racing for X-BOW enthusiasts Europe-wide.

# XBB
## X-BOW-BATTLE

Clockwise from top left: Naomi Schiff climbs into the cockpit of a beautifully turned out GT4, seemingly more than just ready to race.
Nose-to-tail, edge of seat racing is all part of the fun and participation.
Naomi checks lap times and telemetry , fuelled by pretzel sticks!

X-BB racers get almost as much support from KTM as an F1 team. The race series is extremely popular, well organised and heavily subsidised by KTM, providing everything a race team requires for a days safe and professional-style competition on the track. Nothing is left to chance.

inflicted upon the poor splitter, Hartwig's reply was pure KTM: "Better it fails here in the garage, than out there on the racetrack." Needless to say, the splitter survived both.

Both the closed cockpit KTM X-BOW GT4 racers and the open cockpit KTM X-BOW RR racers were present in abundance at the Panonnia-Ring event. The X-BB allows for a variety of on-track activities, including Free Driving, the Battle Sprint, the Battle Endurance, and the Rookies Challenge. The latter three are race activities, and the drivers need, as a minimum, a national or international D-class license. The races are time limited, with the Sprint, Endurance and Challenge being 25 minutes, 55 minutes and 25 minutes respectively.

The 2019 X-BB race calendar ran from March to September, and KTM organised events at Mugello in Italy, the Red Bull Ring in Austria, Brno in the Czech Republic, the Nürburgring in Germany, and the Hungaroring in Hungary.

The prices for taking part in these 2019 events ranged from €790 for a full day's free practice, to €9990 for full participation at all of the above events. These comparatively modest prices are only possible because the X-BB is heavily subsidised by KTM. Factory sources intimated that the cost of hiring the Red Bull Ring racetrack alone, for a three-day event, was about €120,000. On top of this, KTM also had to bear in mind staff and catering costs, as well as spare part support and transportation costs.

That said, the X-BB also serves an important function as a wonderful advertising platform for the X-BOW, for KTM Industries AG, and for Pierer Industrie AG.

Left, insets: The sights, sounds, smells and atmosphere of an X-BB are intoxicating, vibrant and exciting for all involved – if the X-BOW is the soul of each event, then at the heart of the matter there are people – and KTM, it would seem, recognise this.

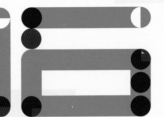

**F**ar too much of my misspent youth was spent fantasising over material from car magazines, and a good proportion of my pocket money was spent on the same. Three motoring publications have had, and continue to have, majority rights on both my time and my disposable income, namely *Autocar*, *Car*, and *EVO*. What their contributors have in common is the gift of analysing a motorcar, and then imparting the results to the reader in a most engaging way – and in doing so, they bring unseen cars to life in the reader's mind. Another thing that all three publications have in common is the generosity to allow this very enthusiastic amateur writer to use limited, selected excerpts. They have done this for the Murcielago book, and have pledged the same support for the Countach and Diablo books as well. I want to use these excerpts because their contributors capture the essence of the car and the driving experience better than anyone else. I want to thank Jim Holder and Olivia Pina of *Autocar*, Nick Trott, Stuart Gallagher and Jane Townsend-Emms of *EVO*, and Colin Overland of *Car* for their generosity in allowing me to use these selected excerpts.

*AUTOCAR, SEPTEMBER 11, 2008: Raining in the KTM X-BOW*
Dynamically, the KTM X-BOW has most things nailed. It rides, it steers, it grips and it handles. And it does them all with real ability. The X-BOW's biggest issue is wind buffeting. Up to 60mph or so it's fine, but above this your head can get bounced around by some pretty severe buffeting. It's a shame because in other respects, the KTM has got things absolutely spot on.

*AUTOCAR: KTM X-BOW Review*
And of course the KTM X-BOW is predictably fast, not to mention huge fun. It's also unexpectedly refined, with a supple ride, relatively muted exhausts and a body remarkably free of vibration. Draughts aside, in fact, the standard model almost seems tame. But build speed and confidence – not hard with a mid-engined chassis this friendly – and you realise that this is an utterly exhilarating weapon. Turn-in sharpens at speed, spearing the KTM through switchback twists that allow you to feel the car pivoting directly beneath your spine. You sense G-force too, of which it can pull as much as 1.5 on road tyres. The steering is quite heavy when loaded, slightly masking its fine sensitivity, and the servo-less, ABS-less brakes must be pressed hard, although the results are mighty effective if you can stay on the right side of locking a wheel. Oversteer moments are satisfyingly easy and unalarming to correct, making this a car that's easy to polish your skills with. But given its price, you've got to love the KTM X-BOW as a piece of engineering and product design as much as you've got to love the driving experience.

*AUTOCAR, MAY 18, 2011: KTM X-BOW R*
The headline news is a power upgrade to 295bhp. But there is more to it than that. The engine sits 19mm lower in the chassis, which brings a 15mm centre of gravity drop overall, and the donkey's now fixed rigidly to an aluminium rear subframe, rather than via flexible mounts. Springs are stiffer too, dampers are uprated, while to increase steering precision and reduce front-end stiction, the front wishbone washers are Teflon.

What's it like? Better. We've had a few issues with the X-BOW in the past, and these changes go quite a long way to curing many of them.

And to drive? The X-BOW R's now getting close to where it should be too. It's still a short, wide car so has lots of grip but less straight line stability than some cars. It's very agile, one thing that could get you into trouble: as the engine moved during cornering, particularly as you got back on the power, the weight shift could upset the cornering balance. And in a short, mid-engined car with what feels like some roll-steer and a limited-slip differential, that was never going to be a bundle of laughs. That's much less of an issue now. The changes to the front improve not just steering precision but also feedback, so it weights up nicely and passes on decent road feel through the rim. But the key is that the chassis is more progressive – you can more easily influence how both ends contribute to the grip levels. Give it a lift here, trail brake there, more throttle than might be sensible on the way out; you can do all these with the confidence that the chassis is working with you, rather than against you. The R is easily £8000 better.

*CAR MAGAZINE, JUNE 25, 2008: KTM X-BOW Review*
Are you sure that this is a car? It looks more like a detached cockpit from an F-117 Nighthawk. In the flesh it goes beyond that – almost defying description. The chassis appears to have been designed around a seated driver, which means that there's plenty of leg and elbow room. A perfect

driving position for just about anyone. How does it drive? The initial impressions are very good. The X-BOW's pedal action is slick and the steering nicely heavy – but the throttle response is vague and the gearlever throw is too long and imprecise. Above 30mph, the wind noise and buffeting makes the engine noise inaudible, and with such power available you rely heavily on the shift light to tell you when to change gear. Conversely, while the driver feels detached from the acceleration, the X-BOW decelerates with complete control, feedback and intimacy. The servo-less Brembos are superb, offering huge feel and massive retardation. Its not thrilling, tyre-curdling, eardrum-busting acceleration, just a confident, smooth and forceful increase in forward momentum. The handling is equally benign.

*CAR MAGAZINE, JULY 6, 2011: KTM X-BOW R Review*
The KTM X-BOW R, an even faster version of the sports car. So the KTM X-BOW R is quicker than most Ferraris? Yes. Prod the throttle and the R simply flies towards the horizon. There's so little weight on board – the skeletal X-BOW R weighs just 790kg dry – that it slingshots towards the horizon in short order. Turbo lag isn't an issue, although the most rabid acceleration doesn't arrive until nearer the 3000rpm torque peak. The basic 236bhp KTM X-BOW is no slouch, but to put the R's greater performance in perspective, it has a quarter more power. The gearlever is perfectly positioned for BTCC style knockshifts, keeping that Audi four-pot on the boil. Get in the groove, and the X-BOW R comes together beautifully. There's an extra urgency that makes the R noticeably faster than the regular X-BOW, and as a point-to-point device cross-country, few vehicles will touch it. Traction is excellent, and the R adds a limited slip diff to tame all that torque at the rear axle. The X-BOW R is a brilliant, idiosyncratic vehicle. The engineering is sublime, the carbon fibre tub a work of art. Clearly, it's a preposterously impractical car, and one only suited to the most committed of drivers, but we applaud its individuality. We loved it.

*CAR MAGAZINE, DECEMBER 10, 2014: KTM X-BOW GT Review*
How has the KTM X-BOW become an X-BOW GT? KTM hasn't just plonked a windscreen and doors on the X-BOW. There have been changes to the carbon fibre monocoque (which is why the windscreen and doors can't be retrofitted to an existing X-BOW) and the aerodynamics have been tweaked too, with KTM claiming there's now less drag and more downforce. KTM have also tweaked the electronics for better driveability. Do the windscreen and doors feel flimsy? Not a bit. The screen and door-window-things have the same level of fit and finish as the rest of the X-BOW: a quality feel that easily bests a Caterham, and would shame some manufacturers of "proper" cars too. The downside is that the windscreen's A pillars block your view of the exposed front wheels. As

for the roof, it's called the X-TOP, and all the tugging at straps, zips, rubber seals and tight leather that must be endured before your KTM is finally watertight will get even the most ardent bondage fetishist frothing through their gimp mask. There's no doubt the windscreen makes the X-BOW easier to live with, but I'm not sure it's the route KTM should have taken. The GT is £14,000 more than the standard R, so if you are going to spend £73,000 on a carbon fibre track-day toy you'll probably want it to be as extreme as possible. Yet the X-BOW, being turbocharged, and bigger and heavier than a Caterham, already couldn't match the visceral experience of the iconic Seven. And by fitting a windscreen and doors it's removed you still further from the puristic driving experience that these sorts of cars are supposed to deliver.

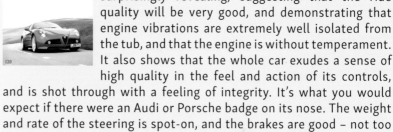

*EVO MAGAZINE, AUGUST 19, 2008: KTM X-BOW*
KTM has devised a short loop on the access roads around the back of the pits. It's not much, yet it's surprisingly revealing, suggesting that the ride quality will be very good, and demonstrating that engine vibrations are extremely well isolated from the tub, and that the engine is without temperament. It also shows that the whole car exudes a sense of high quality in the feel and action of its controls, and is shot through with a feeling of integrity. It's what you would expect if there were an Audi or Porsche badge on its nose. The weight and rate of the steering is spot-on, and the brakes are good – not too heavy with lots of feel and bite – and the clutch and throttle make a pleasingly consistent trio down in the footwell. In pure road-going spec it feels very poised and exploitable. What's most striking is that while most mid-engined lightweights have sensitive and often light steering, the front-end of the X-BOW seems planted, weighty and positive, even though at 37/63 front/rear, its weight distribution is little different. The X-BOW is remarkably friendly too. It's playfully oversteer-y in the slower corners, giving you the option of backing off and gathering up, or keeping it nailed and riding it out, and there seems to be a built-in calmness in most scenarios that gives you time to react. There is mid-engined attitude in there: steer sharply in a left-right flick and the pendulum effect can build momentum oversteer, but once you get to know the car, you can manage this so that you exit the sequence dealing with just as much attitude as you're happy with. The X-BOW remains a hugely attractive and desirable car, and I have an inkling it might just be brilliant on British B-roads.

*EVO MAGAZINE, APRIL 2010: X-BOW Clubsport to the Arctic Circle*
We're approaching the 800-square-mile Saltfjellet-Svartisen National Park. The KTM changes character. The track-orientated geometry encourages the car to sniff out cambers, but firm up your grip on the steering wheel and drive closer to the centre line, and you find it simply flows, turning-in with precision,

palming off mid-corner bumps and sucking in the horizon like a jet engine gobbles air. We find that selecting a higher gear and using the turbo's torque is the key to fast, smooth progress. It's a remarkably easy car to drive fast, with a neutral balance and zero understeer. In slower-speed corners, the KTM just grips and goes, but in the higher-speed corners – and there are many at the Arctic Circle Raceway – you invariably chicken out before the car runs out of grip. It simply monsters the high-speed bends; flick the wheel the tiniest amount and it turns, then zips through and joins the apexes like electricity through a circuit board. When the car finally starts to slide at high speeds – and I'm talking 120+mph – it does so consistently and from all four corners. For those who find sudden high-speed oversteer a trifle bothersome (like me), the KTM is that remarkably benign companion you've been looking for.

turns a gear higher than you otherwise might, but also because its a very feelsome, pointy and easy-to-place car. The brakes are also hugely impressive, so it feels cohesive. The springs and dampers are stiffer than before, which creates fast reactions to your inputs without losing the progressiveness of its slides. On the debit side, the six-speed manual gearbox remains numb and unfulfilling, and I'd prefer not to sit quite so upright. The pedals adjust rather than the seat, but I'm always too close to the seat with too much bend in my elbows. That aside, you'd have a lot of fun with one of these on a track day and it remains a unique and extraordinary object to ogle. KTM have made positive strides with the X-BOW R. It's a punchy machine that pummels the track into submission rather than dancing around the lap; you take it by the scruff of the neck rather than guide it round with your fingertips. If that's your thing, you'll get on well with the R.

*EVO MAGAZINE, JANUARY 2012: KTM X-BOW R*
*EVO Track Car of the Year 2011*
KTM even found funding to develop its first car, and the R is the result. It's got a load more grunt (almost 25 per cent more), and there has been a raft of revisions under its carbon skin too. The R is actually much faster than it feels, perhaps in part due to the torque of the motor allowing you to run through

*EVO MAGAZINE, APRIL 25, 2013: KTM X-BOW GT*
*Review*
The KTM X-BOW GT: a culmination of modifications and tweaks directed at making the four-wheeled KTM a more satisfying, rewarding and focused road car. This has been done through the provision of a frameless wraparound

The X-BOW is a regular jaw-dropper at shows throughout the world, attracting positive reviews wherever it shows up. This car, complete with imaginative 'CRO2BOW' number plate, showed up at a supercar show held at Wilton House in Wiltshire in 2010.
(Courtesy Ian Hunt)

windscreen (heated and equipped with a wash-wipe system), an optional removable soft top that stows in the cabin and can be used at speeds up to 80mph, and an optional streamlined luggage pod fixed to the engine cover. The GT gets a slightly retuned version of the X-BOW R's transversely mid-mounted Audi-sourced 2-litre turbocharged motor with 281bhp instead of 296, but a mildly pumped-up 310lb/ft of torque for better driveability. And the fact that you can now actually hear the engine's somewhat raucous full-throttle rage (admittedly hyped by a sports exhaust) is utterly transformative, immediately giving this X-BOW a sense of drama and character that

drivers of the screen-less versions are denied. Moreover, the lack of turbulence in the cabin verges on the miraculous. The styling has been tweaked too, with a new simplified engine cover, narrower headlight surrounds, and revised front bonnet panels, making the frontal aspect look even more amazingly low and aggressive than it was before. You can be sure that the X-BOW GT will collect more slack-jawed gazes than anything this side of a McLaren P1.

The KTM X-BOW, due to its wholly carbon fibre chassis and its top-flight aerodynamics, had, at its debut, no true contemporary rivals. It was track-day aristocracy, or for those of us who abhor every monarchial system and their attendant hangers-on, the X-BOW was the ultimate track-day car, based purely on merit. Dallara's genius in engineering, KISKA's talent in design, and KTM's vast resources, placed the X-BOW on a different, and higher, plane than any existing amateur race car in 2008.

There are, however, two cars that need immediate mention – one which inspired the X-BOW, and the other that evolved from it. The former is the iconic Lotus Seven, and the latter is the spectacular Dallara Stradale.

### LOTUS SEVEN

The Ford flathead engine with 49hp was the first engine to be used in the Seven, but later, Ford Kent/Crossflow engines produced up to 135bhp. One of the latest developments of the Seven, the Caterham 620, uses a two-litre supercharged Ford Duratec engine producing 310bhp at 7700rpm, for a power-to-weight ratio of 508bhp-per-tonne and a 0-60mph time of 2.79 seconds. The Seven and its derivatives have truly stood the test of time, and have spawned a whole host of imitators. The Seven was based on Chapman's other famous dictum, "Simplify, then add lightness," and this thinking was fundamental to the design philosophy underpinning the KTM X-BOW.

### DALLARA STRADALE

At the launch of the X-BOW, KTM's CEO, Stefan Pierer, said: "We took Colin Chapman's idea of a spartan, lightweight sports car reduced to the bare essentials and transferred it to the new millennium – with as many technological innovations as possible." The spartan sports car Pierer was referring to was the Lotus Seven. Lotus Engineering (later called Lotus Cars) produced the Lotus Seven between 1957 and 1972. Production of updated, ever more powerful and modern variants continues at the time of writing, under the aegis of Caterham Cars. Early Sevens only weighed about 500kg, and therefore had excellent low-speed acceleration despite their modest engines. As per Colin Chapman's dictum, "adding power makes you faster on the straights. Subtracting weight makes you faster everywhere," the Seven was renowned for its agility within its, admittedly limited, speed range.

The Seven had poor aerodynamics with the clamshell-style front wings causing drag and also generating lift at high speed.

The Dallara Stradale is the first road car built by the legendary Dallara motorsports company. Giampaolo Dallara cut his teeth as a young engineer at Ferrari, before moving on to become Lamborghini's first Technical Director. Dallara has enjoyed unparalleled success at the very highest echelons of motorsport, but it has always been his ambition to build a road car bearing his name. Speaking of the Dallara Stradale, Giampaolo has said: "I like to think that Colin Chapman, who I began to admire since the days of his Lotus Seven, would appreciate the essentiality and simplicity of this car." Dallara continues: "This project sums up everything we learned from racing and collaborations with our clients, and I am convinced that those who will use this car will be able to experience the pleasure of driving for the sake of driving."

In September 2018, the authors were fortunate enough to be given a detailed guided tour around the dedicated, stand-alone building in which the Dallara Stradale is built by a small, highly-select team of engineer-technicians. This is a truly special place, and it is the only small volume car production facility we have visited that betters the Graz X-BOW factory. This building is situated directly behind the actual house that Giampaolo Dallara was born in over 80 years ago. You enter this facility through a small door, which leads into an ante-room filled with finished cars awaiting delivery to their new owners. On the day we visited, there was a spectacular blue car waiting to go off to a very famous and successful French ex-Formula 1 driver of Italian origin.

Go through the next door, and you enter a small white-walled cavern, where expert mechanics murmur in hushed tones, and gently pad across the shop-floor in almost total silence. This is nothing like a factory floor, though: in cleanliness and organisation, this room looks more like a surgical operating theatre. Dallara Stradales, in various states of construction, rest on the factory floor, or are suspended in mid-air while the technicians work beneath them. It is a sight to behold, and an experience to savour.

Later that afternoon, we were taken out on a test drive into the hills and back roads surrounding Varano de' Melegari. The Dallara Stradale is a whole level better than our 2012 KTM X-BOW R. It pains to admit this, but it is quite simply true. The Stradale accelerates more aggressively, brakes more violently, and corners more fiercely; all the while being better damped and more composed than the X-BOW R, and while also ensconcing the driver and passenger in a more luxurious leather-covered cockpit.

The Stradale is pretty unique in that it can be easily and rapidly customised into any one of four interchangeable configurations, even after the car has been built. The base car is a Barchetta without doors or a windscreen, like a single-seater racing car. A windscreen can be added to make it into a Roadster. A T-frame can then be added to convert the Roadster into a Targa. Finally, two gull-wing doors can be added to convert the T-frame car into a Coupe – versatility indeed.

The interior of the Stradale is very, very similar to the KTM X-BOW, albeit exquisitely swatched in soft leather. The lessons Dallara learnt from the X-BOW are clearly evident in the interior architecture and ergonomics of the Stradale.

The mid-engined Stradale is powered by a transversely-mounted, modified, 2.3-litre Ford Ecoboost four-cylinder engine producing 395bhp. A six-speed Ford manual gearbox is standard, but a robotised gearbox with paddle actuation is available as an option.

With Dallara's established expertise, it is no surprise to learn that the Stradale is capable of enormous downforce. This car's dry weight is 855kg, and in its base configuration it can generate up to 400kg of downforce. A huge rear wing is available as an option, with which, when the rest of the car is set up in a maximum downforce configuration, the Stradale can generate up to 810kg of downforce.

The Stradale is a hugely impressive car, and one which is entirely worthy of the Dallara name. It shares many features with the KTM X-BOW, which is unsurprising as they share parentage. The Stradale is clearly the better road car on any objective assessment, but you could buy three KTM X-BOW Rs for the price of one fully-optioned Dallara Stradale.

## PROTOTYPE BROOKE 260 RR

I owned the prototype Brooke 260 RR for a decade, and only sold it to finance a 2005 Arancio Atlas Murcielago Roadster. This car set the context point from which one can really appreciate the design integrity and build quality of the KTM X-BOW. In truth, this was a car built by a couple of men in a shed, but it was a very pretty, and a very fast car. It could also go round corners well, which shows what two men in a shed can accomplish. Built in Honiton, a small town in Devon, the Brooke was powered by a mid-mounted, in-line, 260bhp, 200lb/ft Cosworth-fettled Ford Duratec engine. A right-hand gearlever controlled a five-speed Renault-sourced manual gearbox. While the interior and exterior finish on this prototype were superb, it only took a 300m drive in the KTM X-BOW R to recognise that Graz was producing a totally superior machine to what was being produced in Honiton. Component quality and expert development always shines through, and in this case the space-framed Brooke was put in the shadows when compared to the carbon fibre-tubbed X-BOW. The Brooke was a very honest and straightforward lightweight road-racer, and we thoroughly enjoyed our ten years with it. We once drove the 260 RR 650 miles in a day, from southern England, through the length of France, to the Spanish border; we did feel very sore and stiff the next day. This actual prototype 260 RR was tested by *Autocar* and found to do the 0-60mph sprint in 3.2 seconds and the 0-100mph sprint in 7.68 seconds. The claimed top speed was in excess of 155mph.

### THE MODERN CARBON-TUBBED LIGHTWEIGHTS
The KTM X-BOW was the first non-niche production car to feature a complete carbon fibre monocoque. Since then other road-racers with carbon tubs have been launched.

### BAC MONO

The Briggs Automotive company, based in Speke, Liverpool, England is unique in producing a road-legal single-seater. The lead author found the highly reclined seating position of the BAC MONO very intimidating. This and the huge price tag are the only cons to this car. It is exquisitely designed and put together, and a delight to behold. Originally powered by a Cosworth modified 2.3-litre Ford Duratec engine (very similar to that found in the Brooke 260 RR), the MONO has been powered by a 2.5-litre unit producing 305bhp since 2015. It has a pneumatically operated Hewland-sourced six-speed sequential gearbox. Rest to 60mph can take as little as 2.7 seconds, and a 170mph top speed is possible.

### CAPARO T1

The Caparo T1 is another road-legal racer with a kerb weight of 470kg, featuring a carbon fibre and aluminium honeycomb monocoque. Looking like a mutant Formula 1 car, the T1 is able to generate a maximum of 875kg of downforce at 150mph. It is powered by a 3496cc, all-aluminium, naturally aspirated, Menard V8 engine producing 575bhp at 10,500rpm and 310lb/ft at 9000rpm. Teamed up with a pneumatically operated 6-speed Hewland sequential gearbox, the T1 can go from 0-60mph in under 2.5 seconds, and in low-downforce configuration can reach 205mph.

### ZENOS

The Zenos road-racers have an extruded aluminium spine that is bonded to a carbon fibre composite tub. There are three model variants: the E10, the E10S, and the E10R. The E10R is the most powerful and fastest, and uses a 2.3-litre Ford EcoBoost engine producing 350bhp and 350lb/ft. Mated to a six-speed manual box, the R version does the 0-60mph run in 3.0 seconds, and the car can reach 155mph.

### ELEMENTAL RP1

The Elemental RP1 has a full carbon composite tub with steel sub-frames at either end. This British street-legal track car weighs 580kg and uses a two-litre Ford EcoBoost engine tuned for 320bhp, to accelerate the RP1 from rest to 60mph in 2.8 seconds. Elemental claim that the RP1 will generate 200kg of downforce at 100mph. With additional aerodynamic addenda, the RP1 can generate a maximum downforce of between 500kg and a phenomenal 1200kg.

### TRADITIONAL-CHASSIED LIGHTWEIGHTS

There are a large number of lightweight street-legal road-racers featuring non-carbon-tubbed chassis.

### LCC ROCKET

The legendary Light Car Company Rocket was designed by the equally legendary Gordon Murray, together with Chris Craft. Featuring tandem seating in a cigar-shaped body, similar to the Brooke 260 RR, but narrower, the Rocket weighed a miniscule 386kg and was powered by a 1000cc Yamaha engine producing either 143bhp or 165bhp. A total of 55 cars were produced between 1991 and 1998.

### RADICAL

Radical produce a variety of track-only and street-legal lightweight cars. Radical has the technical know-how to engineer its cars with advanced aerodynamics, which has translated into setting outright lap records at the Nürburgring Nordschleife for road-legal production cars.

### ARIEL ATOM

Scaffolding-tube-led technology, married to wonderful Honda VTEC engine technology. The scaffolding tubes make advanced aerodynamics difficult. The most attractive aspect of the Atom, for me, is the styling, which was developed by Nick Smart while he was a student at Coventry University.

Mazda MX-5

Toshihiko Hirai, the father of the iconic lightweight Series 1 Mazda MX-5, which made its debut in 1989, designed the car on the concept and principles of Jinba ittai – ''Unity of Horse and Rider.'' The MX-5 was a driver-focussed sportscar, but also aimed to be reliable, practical and affordable. An MX-5 with properly set up suspension geometry and premium tyres is a real joy to drive. This icon met all its design briefs, and now on its fourth iteration, it is the best selling two-seater convertible in history. The one millionth MX-5 was made on 22 April 2016, and production continues unabated.

LOTUS 340 R, EXIGE, 2-Eleven and 3-Eleven

Above: Lotus 3-Eleven. Below: Lotus Exige.

This chapter started with Stefan Pierer and Giampaolo Dallara expressing their respect for Colin Chapman and his Lotus Seven. It would therefore be fitting to close this chapter recognising that Lotus Cars is still a company led by research and development, and that its Engineering Division remains one of the most respected in the world.

The Lotus Elise of 1996 introduced revolutionary chassis technology to the world: extruded aluminium sections bonded with epoxy adhesive and rivets. This chassis technology is also used in the Lotus 340R, Exige, 2-Eleven and 3-Eleven. The Lotus 3-Eleven has been considered a world-class road-racer since it's inception in 2015, as the follow-up to the 2-Eleven – despite using this chassis technology, which is now almost a quarter of a century old.

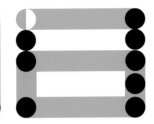

### MICHAEL WOELFLING

Michael Woelfling (pictured) is the very long-standing CEO of KTM Sportcar. He has nurtured the X-BOW almost from conception.

"When I started my journey at KTM, I couldn't even imagine where it would take me or where the project would go. We started with a different approach to that we ended up with, yes, but we succeeded and we achieved some amazing things. As one of Europe's last small-series manufacturers, we were able to sell more than 1200 vehicles all over the world over the past ten years. We conquered markets like China, the Middle East, and the United States. We created one of the biggest one-make racing series: the X-BOW BATTLE. And we developed an incredible, successful racing car for international racing series with the KTM X-BOW GT4. Moreover, we proved the amazing technical abilities and the incredible know-how of the KTM AG group by devising, implementing, developing, building and selling a street legal car, and by being the first Austrian company after 50 years to do so. We did this with a very small, but outstanding, team that was and will always be 'Ready To Race.' It makes me proud to be part of this team and that we've been able to write a small bit of automotive history with the KTM X-BOW. Now let's make sure to go on with the story!"

### MARK HOSKEN

Mark Hosken of Backdraft Motorsport is an acknowledged expert on aftermarket tuning and development the X-BOW. His company is based

in Milton Keynes, UK, and is actively involved in motorsport, as well as servicing, modifying, and upgrading supercars.

"Back in 2008 when the X-BOW was launched, we were busy tuning and upgrading the Mk5 Golf GTis, which shared the VW BWA 2-litre turbo engine. The X-BOW was a very well-engineered open top sports car, with great handling but very disappointing power-to-weight ratios. Especially when compared to its main rival at the time: the Ariel Atom. The BWA was the lowest power TFSI engine configuration. In order to be an authorised KTM dealer you were not allowed to mess with such things, so we stayed independent of KTM and set about tuning the X-BOW to be the car we believed it was supposed to be.

"We developed three stages of power upgrade: one, two and three. The first was a generic ECU map; the second was a map, downpipe and intake system; and the third was a full upgrade to the Audi S3 K04-64 configuration. Shortly after developing the stage three on the X-BOW, we realised a weakness in the charge cooler fitted as standard. We developed a new charge cooler that was not only stronger, but reduced the intake temperatures significantly.

"As a motorsport company, we didn't stop at engine upgrades: we developed suspension, braking and handling improvements to cater for the ever-increasing power boosts. In 2010 we developed our own 'Big Turbo' car, with full engine internals, huge turbo system, water methanol injection, suspension, braking and handling improvements. Based on a Clubsport model, the car is road legal and track focussed.

"Over the past ten years dealing with the X-BOW in fully tuned guise, we have been surprised at how robust the car is. The charge cooler we developed has been fitted to most X-BOWs in the world. The only other issue, which is a standard problem with the engine, is the wear that can occur on the camshaft-run, high-pressure fuel pump bucket. It needs regular monitoring and replacement. It is a low-cost component that will terrorise the top end of the engine if left unchecked. Regular cambelt changes are also recommended and unfortunately the engine needs to be lifted to do this job.

"I have very fond memories testing our own development car at amazing circuits like Spa Francorchamps, and UK circuits including Silverstone, Brands Hatch and Donington Park. Whilst most UK cars have been kissed by our upgrades, I have also travelled all over the world tuning X-BOWs – Dubai, Bulgaria, Spain, South Africa and the Dominican Republic, to name a few – meeting some fantastic enthusiast owners along the way and enjoying this fabulous motor car!"

### ERIC PARADIS

Eric Paradis is Vice President of Business Development at the Circuit of the Americas, and manages race track rentals for major car manufacturers, as well as Indycar and Formula One teams. He is a keen racer, and recently tested the 2012 F1 Renault car at Paul Ricard. This is what he says of the X-BOW:

"The KTM offers a visceral driving experience, but one that is as pure as they come. The KTM is fast, nimble and agile around corners. It is the best of both worlds: the conviviality of a GT, the speed and pleasure of driving an open-wheel race car. The design is unique and stands out, the noise is exciting, the driving position is perfect, and the feedback that the car provides to the driver is second to none. For any track enthusiast, it is the best bang for the buck!"

### GABOR HERGET

Gabor Herget is an Austrian racer who has tested in Formula 3000. Here are his thoughts on the four-wheeled KTM:

"The X-BOW is a perfect car for the race track. The stock setup also makes it drivable on a legal road. Even though its monocoque body makes it really safe, due to the lack of ABS and a traction control system, it's only good for driving in dry conditions on legal streets. On the race track, it's a superior car. The lightweight setup and turbo-powered engine make it a very fast racing machine. KTM chose an engine that is widely used in Audi S3 streetcars and brings down the cost of maintenance. It's not only a fast car but also cost efficient if you compare it to similar lightweight cars.

"If I compare it to Formula cars I've driven, I would say that the X-BOW is a little easier to start with and more fun to drive. It is also a mid-engined and well-balanced car. It's somewhere between a go-kart and a Formula car. It's also more cost-efficient and reliable than other lightweight cars due to its production-based parts"

### NAOMI SCHIFF

Naomi Schiff is a works racing driver for Reiter Engineering, and races the KTM X-BOW GT4. Of Belgian-Rwandan parentage and South African nationality, Naomi has raced in multiple categories throughout the world, and is particularly well placed to give an expert opinion on the X-BOW. Despite a punishing race schedule, she found the time – and the calm – to allow the authors a comprehensive interview amongst the frantic atmosphere of the pit garages at the Pannonia-Ring X-BOW Battle in September 2018. The following is an excerpt from that interview:

"I have been a racing driver for thirteen years, and feel very privileged to now have a contract with KTM and Reiter Engineering. The open-cockpit

X-BOW is great fun to drive on both the road and on the race circuit. It has an impressive power-to-weight ratio, as the Audi TFSI engine delivers the necessary power and torque for this lightweight, carbon fibre-chassised car. The open-cockpit X-BOW feels like a go-kart. It is very agile, but is also very manageable. Even on street tyres the open-cockpit car has good grip.

"The closed-cockpit GT4 is different in that it's heavier, has ABS, and has much more downforce. On slick tyres, the GT4 has incomparably more grip. The faster you go in the GT4, the greater the downforce generated, so paradoxically you have to drive faster to get around a tighter corner quickly. The closed-cockpit car is a much more physical car to drive, as it oversteers more, and you have to fight and manage the oversteer to get the best possible lap times."

### TOMAS KWOLEK

Tomas Kwolek is an amateur racer from the Czech Republic, who was interviewed at the same Hungarian race meeting:

"I like the open-cockpit car more as it has no driver aids, and it is therefore a straight fight between the car and driver. The GT4 is too heavy and has a paddle-shift gearbox, so the car is more detached from the driver. I get a better feeling from the open car: with the open car, it all depends on the driver."

### MADS SILJEHAUG

Mads Siljehaug was another works driver that we interviewed at the Pannonia-Ring in September 2018. Mads is a Norwegian racer who is contracted to Reiter Engineering, and in 2018 he raced a Gallardo in the Blancpain GT3 series and a KTM X-BOW GT4 in the GT4 European series. This is what Mads says of the X-BOW:

"The open-cockpit X-BOW comes with a really good base platform from which to start racing. To get the best out of it does not require the intensive set-up work that the closed version needs. The open car looks after its tyres much better, and is really quick as long as you do not exceed the tyre's capabilities. You have to manage the tyres carefully, especially the slick tyres, which have zero grip when they are cold. With the open car, even the slick tyres give you a lot of warning that they are reaching the limits of their adhesion, and the driver has plenty of time to react accordingly.

"The open car feels very much like a Formula car, but even so, it is less responsive than the GT4 car. At low speed, you have to work the steering wheel of the open car more. At high speed, you can feel that downforce is being generated, and the car actually feels more settled."

### MANFRED WOLF

Manfred Wolf is Head of Customer Racing and Public Relations at KTM Sportcar GmbH, and has been at the Graz facility from almost the very beginning. The authors were very fortunate to have this veteran X-BOW expert take us on a highly detailed, station-by-station tour of the X-BOW factory.

"When the KTM X-BOW was launched back in 2008, KTM CEO Stefan Pierer made a clear statement: creating the first KTM car, he was driven by the idea of making 'a 21st century version of Colin Chapman's revolutionary, spartan, lightweight sports car, reduced to the bare essentials with as many technological innovations as possible.' In the end, that's exactly what he and the whole KTM X-BOW team successfully achieved. With its unique carbon fibre monocoque, providing unmatched safety in the lightweight sports cars category, its unrivalled amount of downforce, and its uncompromised layout as a middle-engined, rear wheel driven, 800kg track weapon with European Small Series Homologation, KTM created a one-of-a-kind car that has been impressing petrolheads around the world ever since. Personally, besides being passionate for the KTM X-BOW for more than ten years on and off track, I especially and strongly believe in the future of our general concept. In times of tough discussions about fuel consumption, emissions and environmental safety, our lightweight technology is the one and only key to keeping the beloved sports car and super sports car market alive! So watch out, there will be more to come in the future."

ENRICO GIULIANI

Enrico Giuliani was the KTM X-BOW Program Manager at Dallara during the car's gestation, and was intimately involved with its development. He is an expert in vehicle dynamics and vehicle testing, and briefed the authors during their visit to the Dallara Research and Development Facility.

"X-BOW is, for me, first of all, the name of a beautiful journey.

"We had to put a 'technological skeleton' inside the creature that KTM and KISKA had dreamed up, which they had already given a new, innovative, disruptive and stylistic appearance. They knew what they'd like it to be and they asked Dallara for technical and technological help to turn it into a reality, without losing the character of their vision.

"The X-BOW was to be essential and light, a creature conceived for pure driving pleasure, able to deeply excite and redefine track-day cars with a sophisticated product. This was what had been asked of us, and we couldn't possibly say no – simply because it was what we had dreamed of doing for years.

"It had to have a monocoque and a carbon body, as well as sophisticated aerodynamics and suspensions in order to guarantee lateral accelerations never seen before in a road car.

"We left for a wonderful trip with the guys of KTM and KISKA, with a blank sheet of paper, and after ten months the first prototype was ready to start the set-up process. It was one of those very rare projects where the car is so deeply in the DNA of the team that has to engineer it, that you can only live it as a life experience, having fun along the way.

"We made choices that no one had ever made before, building a logical bridge between the world of motorcycles and the world of cars. When the technical choices you are called to make are so different from what exists around, you cannot be sure that the result lives up to expectations. But there is always a moment when you understand whether the direction taken is right or not. For the X-BOW, this moment was during the first test in Clermont Ferrand at the MICHELIN headquarters. We were there to conduct tire functionality tests; when the French engineers analysed the working conditions and performance of the tyres on the X-BOW, they were really impressed with how they – developed for high-performance road cars – had found a place on the X-BOW, supporting side accelerations never seen with tyres of that kind, and with any road tyre before then.

"In that precise moment, we understood that the technical direction taken for the KTM creature was correct, and we would have the chance to squeeze out the performance that the X-BOW has today.

"The carbon fibre, aerodynamics and suspension had become the technological skeleton of the KTM X-BOW, and its character was beginning to emerge.

"We created a car that you don't take out of the garage because you have somewhere to be; you take it out because you want to experience the pleasure of the journey."

CRAIG JOHNSON

Craig Johnson has been a car engineer-technician for 20 years, the last 12 of which have been exclusively with Audi. He holds the highest possible qualification within the Audi Technical-Service Department and is an Audi Master Technician. Craig has repeatedly won Audi competitions involving participants from 34 different countries, and has been rated as the best technician in Fault Diagnosis and Rectification world-wide. This is what he has to say about the X-BOW, having worked on Chassis 0642:

"Quite unexpectedly, I received a message from a bemused service advisor saying she had a chap on the phone with a KTM who wanted some advice. My curiosity about this unusual car was at least partly responsible for me calling him back. Path needed a spare key for his X-BOW, and his car also needed a full service, including a routine cambelt replacement. The key needed was from an Audi A8 (D3) model. The problems were immediately apparent: firstly, this type of key can only be ordered to chassis number from Audi, and secondly, these keys need special coding. This is done online though a system called FAZIT, which is a centrally held database of immobiliser and security information in Germany. I was perfectly happy with the servicing aspect of the drive-train, as this is exactly what I was trained to do, but as a precaution I made various online enquiries about the X-BOW, and also spoke to the local KTM franchise agent. I emailed with my findings to Path, together with the contact details of the franchised agent, and expected to never hear from him again.

"Much to my surprise, Path rang me back. He had been in contact with

the KTM factory who had told him that they could supply a replacement key already coded to the immobiliser of his car. He then asked that I personally carry out the full service and the cambelt change on his beloved X-BOW. He was very specific that he wanted only me, and no other technician, to work on the car: a highly unusual request, but then a highly unusual car and a highly unusual owner.

"For the majority of my career I have worked on Audis, specialising in the R8 and Audi Sport models. My passion for cars, and the friendships I have made through my more routine work, has also allowed me to work on various Lamborghini models, in particular the Huracan, Gallardo and the Aventador, all of which carry a large amount of Audi DNA. This gave me the confidence to work on the X-BOW – another car with Audi genes. I just had to work out exactly how I would lift the car and support the engine without damaging the very expensive carbon fibre, having heard horror stories from the franchised agent.

"Before committing myself to undertaking this task, I wanted to see the car first hand, and talk over what was needed and what technical information Path had on the car. This was also a great opportunity to see the other cars in his collection.

I was soon satisfied with the extensive and comprehensive technical information that Path had collected, and having examined the car carefully, I was happy that I could gain access to all the parts safely and without too much fuss.

"The engine was very familiar to me. The CDL type engine is used in the Audi S3 and TTS models, and was the latest incarnation of the belt driven 2.0 TFSI engine, which Audi had been using since around 2004.

"A date was set, and I eagerly waited for the car arrive. I envisaged that the job would take me around 8-10 hours to complete, and I wanted to make sure that we had the car in for at least two days, to allow for any unforeseen technical issues or parts issues.

"A KTM X-BOW is a very rare sight anywhere, let alone at an Audi dealership, albeit a major Audi dealership. The car created quite a stir with staff and customers on its arrival, and after a brief handover I finally had the keys to Path's beloved X-BOW. I was aware that Path spent a lot of

time at the dealership that day, watching my every movement from the large, glass-fronted customer viewing bay. Again, a bit unusual.

"My first task was to remove the full underbody tray. The car could be safely jacked at three specific points where it would not cause damage. The rear needed to be lifted first to increase the ground clearance and to slide the tray out. I did this by raising the car on a four-post lift and then reversing onto strategically placed wedges. The bolts were removed, and, with the help from two other technicians, the undertray was slid out very carefully. I was very surprised at the weight of it, but recognised that a car like this could spend some time in the gravel traps of race circuits due to over confident owners, so this piece had a dual role: establishing the aerodynamics of the X-BOW, as well as protecting the under body parts from costly damage.

"At this point, I drained the engine oil and replaced the oil filter. I then carried out a full underbody inspection. The car was in amazing condition and had obviously never seen a gravel trap, or, in fact, any race circuit in its 1000-mile life. The drained oil was still golden and the filter looked almost new. The sump plug and oil filter were replaced at this point. I lowered the car and removed both the rear upper body panels and the striking air intake snorkel. My first observation of the snorkel was that its main function appeared to be funnelling air down to the gearbox casing via a very large-diameter S-shaped Samco silicone hose. It looked like the snorkel's primary function was not to feed cold air to the turbocharged engine, which was a bit of a surprise.

"Having fitted protective covers to the rear fenders and radiators to stop any potential damage from dropped tools or bolts, I looked into the now exposed engine bay, and was greeted by a very familiar sight. The Audi rings on the engine cover were still in place. KTM obviously had no intention of hiding the X-BOW's power source – I later found out that KTM were actually very proud of this Audi connection. This engine cover is not just for show, and houses the air filter unit and mass airflow sensor. This type of airbox/cover is secured to the top of the engine by plastic 'mushroom mounts,' which locate into rubber grommets in the cover. Due to the heat that these grommets are exposed to within the engine bay, the rubber goes hard and the grommets can be notoriously difficult to remove. This X-BOW had covered such a short mileage, but the cover obviously hadn't been disturbed in the car's six-year life-span, so I wasn't surprised when one of the mushrooms was beheaded on removal. A replacement was easily sourced on a next-day order (funnily enough these are replaced fairly frequently, even on more normal Audi cars).

"I then split the airbox by removing the screws holding it in situ, and replaced the air filter.

"With the airbox removed, I now had adequate access to safely remove the four ignition coils, and could also easily access the spark plugs. These were removed and checked for condition: they looked fine. I then carried out a bore check with a video endoscope. These engines, even after very high mileages, are very strong and do not present issues, other than a thirst for oil. The bores were as new and showed no marking at all. I fitted the new spark plugs, refitted the four ignition coils and filled the car with 4.6 litres of engine oil.

"The next, and most complex, part of the job was the cambelt replacement.

I transferred the car to one of our scissor-action lifts, which, again, allowed me to raise the car via the wheels, and without needing to use the jacking points. This made it easy to raise the car a few inches off the ground and support the engine via the aluminium sump and gearbox using soft rubber pads. This is common practice for supporting the engine on Audi A3s and Audi TTs, and allows maximum access to the top of the engine.

"With the engine supported, I removed the auxiliary belt and tensioner, and could then get to work removing the engine mounts, which in turn would allow the cambelt covers to be removed.

"There was slightly less space between the engine and chassis than what I was used to, but with some jiggling the engine mount was soon out, allowing me to remove the upper plastic cover.

"Once again, I was presented with a familiar sight. The timing marks of the engine are very clear, with the camshaft pulley having a notch that aligns with the matching mark on the belt rear cover marked by OT and an arrow. The crankshaft timing mark is a notch on the outer auxiliary drive pulley which aligns with a mark on the lower outer cover. There are no special locking pins associated with a belt change on this type of engine. It is common practice, once the crankshaft is timed, to make a small reference paint mark in the crankshaft sprocket to the block. I replaced the timing belt and all associated rollers, as well as all the fitting nuts and bolts as required. I carried out an inspection of the water pump for leaks and smoothness, and, unsurprisingly, this was also as new (a common practice is to replace the water pump at the same time as the cambelt but this would really only be applicable on cars that had covered in excess of 50,000 miles).

"I confirmed all the marks were still correctly lined up, and then tightened the spring tensioner to the predetermined point. This is done quickly and easily by rotating an Allen key anti-clockwise in the tensioner against the spring while aligning a tooth with a slot. I rotated the engine four revolutions and confirmed that everything was spot on. This is the most critical part of the whole operation, as an incorrectly timed engine will, at best, not run correctly, which will bring on the engine warning light, and at worst will cause the pistons to impact with the valve gear, causing catastrophic (sometimes terminal) damage to the engine.

"I reassembled the timing covers and aligned the engine mounts, then inspected the auxiliary drivebelt for signs of perishing. Rubber has a habit of degrading if it isn't flexed or moved for long periods of time. The condition of the belt was testament to the car being run just enough to keep this degradation at bay, so the original belt was refitted and tensioned.

"The jacking up of the car was something I was apprehensive about. KTM are very specific about the three areas that the car can be supported on. I lifted the front of the car using the centre point under the towing eye. This allowed me to inspect the front wheel bearings/brake assemblies and suspension components. I removed the front wheels and checked the condition of the Brembo brake assemblies, which were all in great condition, displaying no real signs of wear. At this point I bled the fluid from the front callipers. A small amount of corrosion was cleaned from between the steel hub face and the alloy wheel.

"The only degradation I could see on the car was some cracking to the steering rack trackrod ends. I suspect this is due to the car being driven so little in its life. I didn't consider the cracking excessive, or needing immediate attention, so I will reinspect this carefully when the car is brought in for its service next year.

"I raised the rear axle using two trolley jacks on the specific tow eye points at the rear. I was very careful to ensure that the car was unladen, and that it was lifted perfectly square, and only just enough to remove the rear wheels. The brakes, again, were in great condition and just needed a quick clean before all was refitted and torqued up.

"I also changed the clutch's hydraulic fluid, checked the gearbox oil level and cleaned the steering wheel infra-red connection plate. The handbrake system was also tested, but no further adjustment was needed. I finished up by checking the coolant level and strength, which was very interesting as the car runs two radiators on each side. Additionally, the X-BOW has a water-cooled charge-air cooling system, which replaces the air-to-air intercooler system found in most Audi/VW cars. This is obviously down to the fact that the car is protected from the airflow by the cockpit rather than out in front.

"I was amazed by the quality of the car: the carbon fibre around the fuel tank was simply beautiful. All the pipework and wiring was tidy and up to the usual Audi quality that I see day in, day out. I was expecting to see something a little more 'kit car,' but I was very impressed with what I saw: mainstream premium quality.

"Once the car was all reassembled, it was time for the final road test; I was really looking forward to this bit. I'm used to being looked at in Audi R8s and the odd Lamborghini and Ferrari that I have had the privilege to drive, but the KTM was something else. I guess anything four-wheeled that you have to don a crash helmet to drive is going to turn heads. The car was obviously very well developed: the suspension, albeit hard, was supple, and soaked up the smaller pot holes with ease. The go-kart-like, quick steering rack and the tiny diameter steering wheel really made the whole experience very memorable. The X-BOW appears to have noticeably less turbo lag than the mainstream Audi models, which is not surprising considering that the X-BOW weighs less than half what an S3 weighs. The 2.0 TFSI engine has always been known for its very broad torque curve, but the X-BOW really shows what this engine can do. Another thing I was very surprised by was the feeling at speed. I've driven cars that feel like they are doing 100mph at 50mph, but the X-BOW was quite the opposite, feeling very comfortable at a 60mph cruise. One of the things I did like was seeing the front suspension in action on the road, the horizontally mounted coilover units compressing and extending constantly to smooth out the ride.

"I gave the car the once over after the road test, and checked the oil, coolant and brake fluid levels, and then reset the service indicator by pressing a sequence of buttons on the very basic instrument pod assembly. A quick check of the fault memory showed a sporadic issue with the Lambda probe, which monitors exhaust oxygen content after the catalyst. This fault code was cleared. Two months later, the same fault code returned. The failed Lambda probe was replaced, and this fixed the fault permanently.

"The KTM X-BOW: what a beautifully designed and built car, and what a joy to work on!"

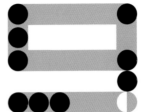

The KTM X-BOW has the power to induce automotive lust. It seduces with its dramatic and brutal beauty, tantalises through the sophistication of its carbon fibre monocoque, mesmerises with the potential of its advanced aerodynamics, dazzles because of its motorsport parentage, charms through its muscular build quality, enchants by virtue of its rarity, and quite simply bewitches the weak and the susceptible. It is temptation.

It bears repeating this again here, purely to try and explain my total captivation with the X-BOW, first upon reading its technical specification in 2007, and then upon seeing it in the flesh for the very first time in 2008.

The X-BOW enticed me, like only the Lamborghini Countach had before. There are so many parallels, links and associations between the two. However, there are also stark dissimilarities. The Countach has no motorsport heritage, while KTM and Dallara sweat racing through every pore. The Countach was always a coupé, while the X-BOW was launched as an extreme barchetta. The Countach driver sits in a cockpit swatched in the finest soft Italian leather, while the X-BOW driver is deprived even of a windscreen. The Countach launched a revolutionary drive-train with its massive-capacity, normally-aspirated, classic 60-degree V12 engine orientated south-north relative to its gearbox, while the X-BOW makes do with a much more prosaic, albeit mid-engined, drive-train layout, and features a lightly modified, off-the-Audi-shelf, small-capacity turbocharged four-cylinder engine.

Equally, there are close similarities and associations, most importantly in relation to the key people involved with each project.

Giampaolo Dallara, so critical in the gestation and delivery of the X-BOW, was Lamborghini's first Engineering and Technical Director at the tender age of 26. Although Dallara had left Lamborghini by the time the Countach was launched, his engineering ethos permeated through the company and into the Countach, not least by virtue of him training Paolo Stanzani, who later fathered the radical Countach.

Loris Bicocchi is the second person who needs to be introduced at this stage. In the same way that Paolo Stanzani was trained by Giampaolo Dallara, Loris Bicocchi was trained at Sant'Agata by none other than the legendary Lamborghini test drivers Bob Wallace and Valentino Balboni. Loris was born in 1958, just a few hundred metres from where the Lamborghini factory was destined to be built five years later, and was enchanted by cars from childhood. He applied to be a storekeeper at Lamborghini SpA at the age of 16, much against the wishes of his family. His father was a carpenter, who worked every hour of the day to ensure that the children were

properly tutored, so Loris' decision to leave school early came as a big disappointment to the family. However, his enthusiasm for all things mechanical, and the work ethic that he had clearly absorbed from his father, soon endeared him to the mechanics at Lamborghini, who took him under their collective wings. Too young to hold an Italian car license, he charmed his bosses at Lamborghini into allowing him to drive these supercars from the production line and the repair garages to the car washing station – always taking the long route round the factory, rather than the direct route straight across. Loris soon wrangled his way into the small, but hallowed, test driving team at Lamborghini. He stayed on as a test driver for Lamborghini until 1989.

And herein lies my fascination with Loris Bicocchi. I first met him on September 8, 2001 at the Lamborghini Murcielago launch event at the Sant'Agata factory, and then again a few days later at the nearby Pagani factory.

At the launch party, Loris told me that he had performed the pre-delivery inspection and test-drive of my 88 1/2 Lamborghini Countach 5000 QV chassis number 12399, which carries the United Kingdom registration plate F920OYR. I had bought this one-owner, Rosso Siviglia with tan interior car barely six months previously, after a 28-year wait (the Countach was launched in 1973), so meeting the person who had done the final fettling of the car before it left the Sant'Agata temple was like meeting God's own assistant.

Loris then cemented this fascination, about 48 hours later, by taking me on a never to be forgotten test drive in a Pagani Zonda. Having politely helped me into the passenger seat, and satisfied himself that the seatbelts were securely fastened, we slowly reversed out of the factory, and trundled sedately along the industrial estate ring road for about a minute. Soon a solid brick wall appeared in the medium distance, beyond which travel was quite clearly impossible. Almost as soon as this wall came into sight, Loris went into maximum acceleration mode, aiming straight for the wall. The Zonda gained speed like I had never experienced before, and we were soon travelling rather too fast towards a rendezvous with an immovable object. My primary concern in those last few moments was not with my upcoming meeting with my Maker – after all I was going to be presented to Him by His own personal assistant, so things were looking fairly bright on that front. Rather, I remember thinking that it was such a shame that such a beautifully designed and meticulously built car would soon cease to exist. Very soon we were very close to the wall, but still the acceleration continued unabated. At a point well beyond all hope of a happy outcome, two quite extraordinary things happened. Firstly, Loris braked very heavily, and I experienced deceleration like never before. Secondly, when the wall was almost within touching distance, a very narrow escape road, 90 degrees to the left, suddenly appeared. The Zonda had decelerated massively by now, but it was still obvious that there was no way that it could negotiate the 90-degree turn at this speed. My meeting with my Maker had clearly been temporarily postponed in favour of a rather long hospital stay, and it remained sad that this perfect Zonda was soon going to be reduced to a pile of carbon fibre shards. At the very, very, last moment, the Zonda made an unbelievable, completely controlled, no drama, 90-degree left turn, and I experienced lateral G-force I had never before experienced on a public road. A long straight opened up in front of us, and Loris instantaneously had the Zonda accelerating fiercely once again.

This test drive was a demonstration of perfect car design and suspension engineering, married to extraordinary agility endowed through low mass by extensive use of carbon fibre, espoused to Loris Bicocchis' chassis development and driving talents. And the KTM X-BOW benefits from each and every one of these seven virtues.

Loris left Lamborghini to work with Paolo Stanzani on the four-wheel-drive, quad-turbo, carbon fibre-tubbed Bugatti EB110, which was being developed in Campogalliano. He spent five years working as the chassis engineer and test driver on the EB110, and says that this is where he really began to understand how to set up a car, and, more specifically, learnt "where the tyre ends and the suspension starts." Loris then went to work with the perfectionist Horatio Pagani (who designed the lower sill side strakes on the 881/2 Countach while at Lamborghini) on the Zonda. Pagani's daily goal was "look for 110 per cent, so as to achieve 99 per cent."

Christian von Koenigsegg was next to call on Bicocchi, and they met in Paris. Loris was delighted to take up Koenigsegg's offer of developing his new Swedish supercar. As with the Romano Artioli Bugatti crew and the Pagani squad, Loris likes to work within a small, talented and dedicated team – a family. The CC8, CCR, CCX, and even the One carry some of Loris' fingerprints. It is notable that Christian von Koenigsegg, who does not own a Koenigsegg car, has purchased a KTM X-BOW – surely a testament of the highest order, to both Loris and the X-BOW.

Since 2000, Loris has worked with the Volkswagen conglomerate Bugatti, first on the Veyron, and then on the Chiron. The primary goal at VW-controlled Bugatti has been slightly different: to engineer a very stable car, in which an extremely high top speed can be relatively easily and safely reached by a non-racing driver.

It is telling that when Loris Bicocchi set up the Loris Bicocchi Supercar Driving Academy (through his company, Modena Driving Experience) in 2009, to teach budding chassis engineers how to set up a car, he chose the KTM X-BOW as the course car.

Loris Bicocchi spent a year working on the chassis engineering and suspension set up of the X-BOW, together with Dallara. He is emphatic that the one aspect of the X-BOW that is perfect is that everything on the suspension can be adjusted – the castor, the camber, the ride height and the anti-roll bars. He also says that the X-BOW is very sensitive to small adjustments of its chassis settings.

Loris Bicocchi's intimate involvement in engineering the chassis of some of the world's most highly acclaimed supercars, and his year-long total immersion in setting up and refining the suspension of the X-BOW is an important part of the X-BOW's heritage, and contributes strongly to its pedigree.

The final two people that we should mention in this comparison of the Countach and the X-BOW are Ferruccio Lamborghini and Stefan Pierer. Lamborghini was an established industrialist at the launch of the Countach, with a huge tractor and heating and air-conditioning empire, while Forbes Magazine announced that Pierer's KTM Industries AG had sales of US $1.8billion in 2017. It is also interesting, when drawing parallels between these men, to note that Pierer started off as a sales assistant at the heating and air-conditioning manufacturer Hoval. While Ferruccio Lamborghini did race in the 1948 Mille Miglia, he actively sought to avoid his supercar company becoming involved in motorsports. Pierer, who has been riding motorcycles since his early teens, has not raced, but actively encourages KTM's racing activities – not surprising as racing almost defines KTM. Ferruccio was known as a happy, cheerful and kind man, who, in 1969, was given the honorific title of Cavaliere by the Italian President. Pierer is a generous contributor to Sebastian Kurz and the extreme Austrian People's Party. At the height of their industrial powers, the revenues from car production contributed only a small part to each of these industrialist's wealth. I am of the opinion, completely unsubstantiated, that they were and are respectively, genuine petrolheads, who also saw their super sports cars as very cost-effective and impressive advertising platforms for their other non-car related businesses.

On a superficial level, the KTM X-BOW attracts by the sheer audacity of its external design. Car design appears to have to softened over time – probably driven by the need to be more aerodynamic for environmental and performance reasons, and also by the need to offer car occupants and pedestrians better protection in the event of an accident. These factors have directly led to super sports cars from different manufacturers having more or less the same appearance, and having a more anodyne and 'soap bar' look than their predecessors.

The original Lamborghini Murcielago Roadster of 2005, for instance, is quite simply beautiful. It can effortlessly drop jaws at a hundred paces. But it is clearly an evolution of the dramatic Countach LP 500 prototype that stole the 1971 Geneva Motor Show. The completely new, and almost anarchistic, external design seen at the launch of the Countach was not repeated at the Murcielago's debut.

In the same vein, the 981 Porsche Boxster S is a modern day classic, and carries with it the glamour and heritage of a naturally aspirated flat-six engine. It is a wonderful and genuinely useable sports car that will take you, your passenger, and both your kitchen sinks, in complete comfort, half way across Europe in a day. But again, its external design is plainly a derivation of the radical Porsche 550 Spyder.

The Series 1 Mazda MX 5 of 1989 can now be picked up at a bargain basement price, which belies what a brilliant car it is. With a front mid-engined layout, classic double wishbone suspension at each corner, a precise and slick manual gearbox, and a free revving naturally aspirated petrol engine, it is all the convertible sports car that you could reasonably ask for. To belittle it by calling it a 'hair-dressers car' is not only to disrespect a perfectly honest trade, but also to publicly exhibit total ignorance about what makes a great car. Its sheer ubiquity – actually an indication of its build quality – its reliability, its cheeky appeal and its affordability have worked against it here. In November 2014, the *Guinness Book of Records* certified the MX 5 as the world's bestselling two-seater sports car, and in April 2016, the one-millionth MX 5 rolled off the production line. I totally adore both my Series 1 MX 5s, but the truth is that the external styling of these cars steals many design cues from the lightweight (680kg), Colin Chapman era, Lotus Elan Roadster, which was launched in 1962.

The KTM X-BOW on the other hand steals no one's design ideas, and is breath-taking in its bravery of executing Sebastien Stassin's almost mad (genius very often being a close bed-fellow to madness) concept.

My first sighting of the KTM X-BOW was at the 2008 NEC Autosport International Show in Birmingham. My mother-in-law, Joan Reck, had given me a copy of *Classic and Sports Car* magazine, in which was a voucher for a draw offering free tickets to the Show. I had bought the prototype Brooke 260 RR in September 2007, and as this was the only such car in existence in the world at that point in time, Brooke and I had come to an agreement that the car would stay with them for promotional activities until the following spring, after which it would have a full suspension refurbishment and a body-off repaint. I was therefore keen to see the 260 RR being presented at the NEC, and was also keen to buy suitable helmets, clothing, footwear and eye protection at the show, as the roofless, doorless and windscreen-less Brooke was a completely new type of vehicle to me. I was therefore delighted to win a ticket – the first time I had won anything. Even better, a KTM X-BOW was going to be in attendance at the show.

The Brooke 260 RR is a very, very pretty car, and has exceptional performance, courtesy of its Cosworth fettled 260bhp, 200lb/ft torque Ford Duratec engine, propelling a 593kg vehicle. However, it only took an ungraceful clamber into the KTM X-BOW's cockpit to recognise that the X-BOW was on an entirely different level of component and build quality to my 260 RR prototype. Even in early 2008, the X-BOW was already double the price of my Brooke, so I just enjoyed my 260 RR over the following seven years, although the X-BOW was never far from my thoughts.

KTM's local agent contacted me soon after the Autosport Show, and sent me a full press pack, which included a mini CD. Happily, as the price of the X-BOW rose and the prospects of my ever getting one declined in equal measure, I never totally lost hope, and therefore never threw away this press pack.

In around 2010, I first made direct contact with Michael Woelfling, the long-standing Managing Director of KTM Sportcar GmbH, and Michael invited me to visit the Graz facility to see the X-BOW being brought to life. This was delayed, in chronological order, by a second low-mileage Series 1 MX 5 in 2012, an Arancio Atlas Murcielago Roadster in 2014, and the very last Racing Yellow flat-six, naturally aspirated 981 Boxster S that Porsche imported into the UK in 2016 – all three of which, together with my 88 1/2 Countach Chassis 12399 and KTM X-BOW R Chassis 0642, are now Beaulieu National Motor Museum Photographic Library Reference Examples.

My search for an X-BOW never really stopped, but when funds became available, the search took on renewed vigour. A brand new X-BOW built to my exact specification, with me at the Graz factory to see and photographically record its progress down the production line would have been lovely, but it was too expensive. In my position, a secondhand X-BOW was the only realistic way forward. From late 2016, the used car sales websites were scanned on an almost daily basis, and every likely lead was carefully followed up. But the four-wheeled KTM is a rare beast, and even rarer in the used car market, so I was never over-burdened chasing up potential purchases.

This was very largely because I wanted a pristine, low-mileage, secondhand X-BOW that had only been used as a road car, and had never been subjected to the trauma of the racetrack. Inconsistent and contradictory, I hear you yell, and I entirely agree: the X-BOW was designed for the circuit – its natural stomping ground – but I wanted mine to be immaculate. I choose to take other people's cars (from track-day hire companies) when I go on track, and am prepared to pay for the privilege of not risking my own pride and joy.

An X-BOW turned up for sale in Italy, claiming to be chassis No 1, but it had clearly been used as a driving school track-hack, and so was automatically discounted. Three other half-suitable cars came up over the next 18 months, but none were exactly what I wanted. Then, very late on a Wednesday night, June 14, 2017, an almost unbelievable advertisement suddenly appeared on the web. My co-author retires early, and sleep interruption is not tolerated lightly, but this car was such a close match to my ideal specification that it demanded an immediate response. Equally, the asking price was such that it, too, demanded consultation. Throwing caution aside, and calling upon all my bravery, a late night conversation was initiated, which ended with an email being sent to the vendor well past midnight.

The car in question was chassis 0642, a 2012 KTM X-BOW R carrying the United Kingdom registration plate X80WRS, with a mere 1012 miles, two previous private owners, and said never to have been on track. Unusually, the advertisement claimed that this X-BOW R was absolutely factory standard with no post-factory modifications or additions. This in itself was fairly extraordinary, as just about every other X-BOW that I had come across thus far had been modified, some very heavily indeed. The car did, however, have quite a few factory-fitted options, including: performance pack 1, aerodynamic pack 1, performance suspension with hard sports springs, racing brake discs and pads, adjustable brake balance, racing roll-over hoops, racing headlight covers, a quick shifter and a sports exhaust. Intriguingly, the advertisement ended with the following: "I bought this as part of a major collection of cars, and have not used it due to time pressures. The car is as new, and barely run in."

At precisely 8.00am the following morning, I rang the vendor, and we agreed to meet on Saturday June 17 at his house in the Cotswolds. Remote controlled electric gates greeted us forty-eight hours later, and after skirting around a large lake and passing a series of low buildings, there was KTM X-BOW R Chassis 0642 parked in the courtyard. The low buildings housed a total of 37 cars, some classic and some very modern, but every one of them immaculate, and each stored within a 'carcoon.' The 'R' was exactly as described, except that the spare key was missing, which turned out to be a blessing in disguise, as this later led me to Mr Craig Johnston, an Audi Master Engineer-Technician who has maintained the car ever since.

Upon asking my routine battery of questions, it was reassuring when the vendor said that the only cosmetic imperfection on the car was a single 2mm round paint chip on the lowermost corner of the driver's side body panel. This married well with the claim that the car had never been used on track. The history of the car was that it had been imported by Hangar 111, the UK franchise holder for the X-BOW, as a static display car, and was then sold to the CEO of a large and well-established escalator installation company in the north of England, who used this car for precisely three journeys. The present vendor was the CEO of a renewable energy company based in Wales, and had used the car for just one return journey between the Cotswolds and Cardiff.

The reason I have described the searching and buying process in such detail is that the purchase of any sports car is a major investment for almost every one of us. Depreciation is usually the most expensive aspect of car ownership. Prices of rare and special cars can go up, but this is very much the exception rather than the rule. Each and every time a car is bought and then sold, the owner stands to lose a significant amount of money through depreciation. But depreciation only comes into the equation if and when a car is sold. A buyer who really thinks about why he wants a particular car, and then patiently waits for the right car with the correct specification in the best possible condition to come along, is likely to be happy with that purchase, and is therefore unlikely to want to move on to another car at short notice. The car in question is therefore not sold, depreciation does not kick in, and we end up with a richer and more contented owner. So, be brutally honest with yourself about whether that particular make and model is what you definitely want; do your background research diligently; do not compromise on specification, options or colour; and be prepared to wait for just the right car to come along. I waited three years for the right Countach, and I would never willingly let it go. Only spend your hard-earned money on what you really, really want.

For any car, there are three avenues of purchase (franchised main dealer, independent dealer or private sale) and three avenues of servicing (main dealer, independent or owner servicing) and each carries its own advantages and disadvantages.

Buying from a private individual carries the benefit of meeting the owner, and getting a feel for how he or she might have treated the car during their ownership. I bought my first Ferrari – a 355 GTB – from a gentleman privately, and within a few minutes of meeting this very knowledgeable and straight-talking owner, it was obvious that he cherished the car. He insisted that only he would drive the car during the test drive, and the gentle way in which he warmed up the car beforehand spoke volumes.

The person from whom I bought my KTM X-BOW R was clearly a car enthusiast, with 37 'carcooned' vehicles – all immaculate, and serviced by the book. Meeting and gently interrogating owners can be very revealing. I have huge respect for owners who have the knowledge and ability to service their own cars, but many modern cars require specialist tools even for routine servicing, and this leads me to worry that there might sometimes be corner-cutting when a car is home-serviced.

Factory-franchised main dealers not only have their reputations to maintain, but also those of their associated manufacturers. They should only be selling the very best cars, and each of their cars should have been fully checked by a factory-trained mechanic. Their cars should also come with a water-tight warranty, and you, the buyer, will of course be happy to pay generously for this premium service. Main dealers should have the latest electronic updates and all the manufacturer-recommended tools available, and will, of course, provide the supposedly all-important 'dealer service stamp' in the maintenance book. While some of my cars are main dealer serviced, others are not – and for good reason. Some cars are just too old for main dealers to have much experience with them. I bought my one-owner Lamborghini Countach from what was then the only franchised Lamborghini dealer in the United Kingdom, H R Owen, and they immediately recommended that I have the car serviced by one of two independent technicians who had specific experience of, and expertise in, maintaining a Countach. Another problem with main dealers is that an owner's contact with the technician working on the car has to go through the filter of a service receptionist. I always insist on speaking directly to the technician before any work is started – it at least informs the technician that the owner is genuinely interested and very hands-

on. Sadly, some main dealers are just not interested, as they have enough trade just dealing with corporate customers, and have staff who do not fully appreciate that their jobs rely on providing each and every customer with high quality, timely service.

Independent dealers do not have this luxury, be it in sales or servicing, as their income is directly dependent on their current reputation. Some independents have invested heavily in personnel and garage equipment, including access to bespoke electronic interrogation systems. Independents are particularly great when it is a one-man band, as you are then dealing with a technician who is also the business owner, and these people are often very well trained, extremely knowledgeable and highly motivated.

Maintenance is a major issue that each prospective owner needs to have researched deeply before committing themselves to a purchase. Obviously the cost of routine servicing, as well as the cost of unexpected repairs once outside the warranty period, both need to be within the available budget.

Most challenging of all can be finding a good mechanic. In an era of technicians who replace parts, often in a random sequence, finding an engineer-mechanic is like finding the mother lode. Fellow owners and marque clubs will be able to advise on who has the necessary experience, facilities and tools to service a given model, but I always make a trip to meet and personally appraise the actual mechanic who will be working on my car, well before making a definite service booking. This has, in the past, involved a round trip of more than 400 miles just to see a technician who might, or might not, end up working on my car.

Once you have found a good engineer-mechanic, do not let them go. Like a physician, a specialist mechanic who looks after a car over a long period will develop a deep knowledge of, and a bond with, that car, and will be able to exercise preventative maintenance. My Countach has only been serviced by three different people since it left Sant'Agata more than 30 years ago, and I am hugely grateful to every one of them.

I was hugely fortunate to stumble upon Craig Johnson totally by chance. The only real fault with KTM X-BOW R 0642 when I first came across it was that the spare key was missing. It was also due to have its routine cambelt replacement within six months of my purchase. KTM initially had three service centres in the UK, but by 2017 only one was still operating. My first call was therefore to this franchised dealer, to get a replacement key straight away and also to book a service for six months time. Let us just say that this initial contact was significantly less than perfect.

In despair, I contacted the KTM factory in Graz, and the service was just wonderful. A spare key was sourced, coded, and dispatched to me within a few days. This is very important information for existing and prospective X-BOW owners – the Graz factory is very efficient and very knowledgeable, and will bend over backwards to accommodate its customers. It is very client orientated, and it has been a pleasure dealing with them. I have never owned a Pagani or a Koenigsegg, but the quality of care that I received from the KTM factory mirrors the legendary service that owners of these two very exclusive bespoke supercars apparently enjoy from their respective manufacturers.

With the spare key problem resolved, my remaining issue was the imminent major service involving a cambelt replacement. I considered taking the car to Belgium, Germany, or even back to Austria, where there were, and still are, franchised X-BOW service centres with good reputations.

During my attempts to get a replacement key, I spoke to many, many people, including some rather dubious ones who could clone keys. I also contacted several Audi centres, as the immobiliser system in the X-BOW is from Audi. I left a telephone message with one centre, explaining the problem, and shortly afterwards a gentleman called Craig Johnson called back. Craig was clearly hugely knowledgeable, but much more importantly, was genuinely enthusiastic about the X-BOW – he even offered to come to my house in his free time just to look at the key and immobiliser system.

When I interview junior surgeons for jobs, one of the key things that I look for is genuine enthusiasm – it is vital in any and every job – and Craig had it in spades.

When I discovered that Craig was also one of the most highly trained Audi technicians in the UK, even I recognised that the mother lode was right in front of me, and I placed a limpet-like grip upon him. The real message here is to take your time in finding the best possible person to work on your car, whatever make or model it might be, and then do your best to hang on to them. They are a vital part of your car.

I have had two problems with my X-BOW R thus far. First, a few of the bolts have developed very superficial corrosion, where I suspect a wrench has removed the protective surface coating. Second, an oxygen lambda sensor failed, which turned on a 'check engine' warning light on the dash display. This issue was diagnosed by attaching an Audi-VW OBD 2 hand-held scanner to the car, and reading the fault codes stored within the car's memory. In this case, the scanner identified which of the two lambda sensors was faulty. After the faulty sensor was replaced, the scanner was also able to clear the fault code. Every X-BOW owner would benefit from having one of these Audi-VW compliant scanners – they can be bought for about £30 from various online retailers.

This might also be the right time to introduce the reader to what is known as the 'Mattighofen Shuffle.' This may sound like a dance routine, and, to be honest, that's not so far off the mark. Mattighofen refers to the town in Austria where KTM has its headquarters, and is the 'M' in KTM. The 'shuffle' refers to the way a mechanic has to move about in order to access the many different parts, including the battery and the pedal box, which are located in the passenger and driver footwells. These could, of course, be accessed more comfortably by removing the crashbox that is attached to the front of the monocoque, but that is a time-, labour- and money-intensive process.

Instead, the owner or mechanic can get into the cockpit, then enter the footwell headfirst, before rotating their upper body in whichever direction is necessary for the task at hand. Almost inevitably, you end up lying with your back on the footwell floor, and your feet pointing towards the sky. It's these contortions that make up the Mattighofen Shuffle, and having done it myself a few times, I can tell you that Michael Jackson's moonwalking move is very easy in comparison.

The KTM X-BOW presents an almost unique ownership experience. The Pagani Zonda Cinque Roadster is one of the two cars that I most desire, although it has to take second place to the Countach. The Cinque Roadster – a Loris Bicocchi fettled, lightweight (1210kg dry), bespoke-built, open-topped, carbon fibre (albeit laced with titanium strands) fest, with that all-important snorkel to make it look even more spectacular – is so like the X-BOW, but it costs many times more than the X-BOW when new, and now, on the secondhand market, it's even more expensive. I look upon the KTM X-BOW as the only half-realistic, semi affordable (if you are very lucky) alternative to a Cinque Roadster.

The X-BOW is an eccentric choice of road car, and its idiosyncrasies come to the fore as you try and get into the cockpit. The barge boards that are an extension of the flat underfloor tray mean that the driver and passenger stand further away from the cockpit than they otherwise would. KTM say that the barge boards can be used as mounting platforms for getting into and out of the cockpit, but doing this would soon scratch and disfigure the boards, and so is not the best idea. The next obstacle is the very high cockpit side wall that has to be climbed over. KTM say that it is permissible to stand on the seat base during entry and egress, but again, doing so would soon scratch the seat, so is best avoided if you are in the slightest bit 'car proud.' I can see that racers would not worry about such trivial cosmetic issues, but for some of us it matters. KTM have acknowledged this concern by leaving a U-shaped indent in the seat base to allow occupants to step directly onto the cockpit floor, but this is very difficult to do if one is not unusually tall. What I do is place a small thin piece of plastic on the seat base, then climb across the cockpit side wall without touching the barge board, and stand on this sheet of plastic. I then half sit down, lifting myself using only my arms, supported on the cockpit side wall and the central console. Finally, I feed my feet, one at a time, into the footwell and simultaneously pull away the plastic sheet before lowering down onto the seat base. This method does place quite a strain on the shoulders and the lower back, and I do worry about how I will continue to manage this quite complex manoeuvre as I get older, but it works for me at present. Each owner will find a method of entry and exit that works best for them.

Once ensconced in the cosy cockpit, the X-BOW occupant has to fasten, and then tighten, the four-point, harness-style seatbelt – also tricky if the four belts have not been carefully placed in accessible positions beforehand. I also place a small foam pad between the seatback and my lower back, as I find that this really helps with comfort. That said, belying their appearance, the Recaro seats themselves are unexpectedly comfortable, even over long distances. Once the foam pad is in place and the harness belts are tightened, I put on my quarter balaclava and helmet.

The start-up procedure of the X-BOW is, quite simply, bizarre – and also wonderful. First the key fob has to be placed in its pocket on the central console, which deactivates the immobiliser. Next, the start button is pressed, and the dash lights up in KTM orange, asking the question 'Ready To Race?' The driver answers in the affirmative by pressing the 'mode' button on the steering wheel. Both the brake and clutch pedal are depressed simultaneously, after which the start button is pressed once again. The engine should now burst to life with a moderate roar, which settles down to a loud purr after about 30 seconds.

The centrally mounted digital display has a variety of display parameters, each of which can be scrolled through by repeatedly pressing the steering-wheel-mounted 'mode' button. There is even a footwell heater, but sadly it is not very effective.

The clutch pedal is not heavy, and contrary to press reports, I think that the gearlever moves with both ease and precision. The steering wheel is perfect for me – both the rim thickness and the wheel diameter are ideal, and the high quality leather covering the rim imparts a luxurious yet slightly springy feel, which is wonderfully tactile.

The accelerator pedal has a long travel, which allows acceleration to be precisely metered out. The X-BOW pulls away without fuss or drama. The steering weight is perfect at low speed – an issue that other low-volume manufacturers producing lightweight sports cars with unassisted steering have not yet mastered (Lotus being a notable exception) – and lightens up nicely as the car's speed increases. There is good feedback through the rim – the messages from the steering wheel are filtered of unwanted 'noise,' but not over-filtered to the point that vital information about the road surface and the tyre contact patch are lost.

The brake pedal is firm, and requires strong pressure to achieve maximum deceleration. With a modicum of sensitivity, it can be done without locking the wheels. An in-cockpit brake balance dial allows the front-to-rear braking attitude to be easily and quickly altered.

The control buttons on the steering wheel are a mixed blessing. They do allow the driver to keep both hands on the steering wheel at all times, but pressing the correct button when the steering wheel is not in the straight ahead position can be a problem. In particular, I find that the turn indicator buttons are unnecessarily difficult to use. The other steering wheel mounted buttons are used less frequently, so are not as much of a real-world problem.

My single biggest problem with the X-BOW is the unacceptably large amount of in-cockpit turbulence when driving at or above 70mph. The airstream buffets the driver's helmet and visor, which distorts vision, and is plain uncomfortable. The airstream also causes helmet lift, which, again, degrades the driving experience. Discussing this issue with owners who race their cars, and owners who only use their cars on roads, reveals that this is a common complaint that affects drivers both short and tall, and which happens irrespective of the helmet being worn. There is an optional Racing Windshield available from the factory, but people who have used both the standard curved Makrolon wind deflector, and the straight carbon fibre racing windshield say that there is minimal, if any, reduction in cockpit turbulence when using the latter. At over €1000 extra, the Racing Windshield is not a cheap option, so is of questionable value.

The long-stemmed rear view wing mirrors provide a surprisingly comprehensive view of what is happening behind the X-BOW, but unlike more conventional cars, there is no centrally mounted cockpit rear view mirror. The X-BOW is a small and low car that is easily missed by fellow road-users. This is particularly dangerous on multi-carriage roads, as the X-BOW can accelerate so rapidly that it can quickly move into the blind-spot of another car, unnoticed by its driver. If that driver then suddenly changes lane not having registered that you are already alongside, an accident is almost inevitable. The X-BOW's headlights come on automatically as soon as the ignition is switched on, and cannot be turned off thereafter – this is a very useful in-built safety feature, as it makes the car more visible to other road users.

The Sports Exhaust is a good option, as it provides a lovely aural accompaniment to the car's quite startling acceleration. The standard back box is just too quiet to do justice to a super sports car. Other aftermarket tuners provide even more exciting alternatives, which I have been sorely tempted by, but having seen the care, expertise, and facilities with which KTM develops its components, I have chosen not to indulge in anything outside the factory range. For exactly the same reason, I have not played around with the adjustable bound and rebound damper settings, choosing instead to follow the factory recommendations.

The X-BOW is quite a fuel-efficient car, bearing in mind that its performance potential

Tulks expedition plaque, bearing the authors' names from chassis number 0642. You can go to all sorts of places in an X-BOW!

Above left: Path pictured with Paolo Stanzani – chief technical officer for Lamborghini, who also assisted Romano Artioli with the relaunch of Bugatti. Above right: with Loris Bicocchi, chassis guru/test engineer with Lamborghini, Bugatti, Zonda, KTM and Konigsegg.

is comparable to many supercars. Filling the fuel tank is, however, a slightly tedious process, at least in the United Kingdom. Here, the angle at which the petrol pump nozzle enters the X-BOW leads to fuel splash-back, which then automatically and instantly stops the petrol pump from delivering any more fuel. The petrol therefore has to be trickled in at a slow and gentle pace, which can be frustrating. Checking the car's engine oil and coolant levels are also more difficult than in most cars, as the floating rear body panels need to be unscrewed and removed to gain access to the engine oil dipstick and to see the coolant tank.

The KTM X-BOW is a completely open car, and adequate protective clothing and headgear are essential. Eye protection is particularly vital: I wear spectacles, and I find a full face helmet difficult to use as the spectacle stems get trapped and moved by the interior walls of the helmet. When this happens, the spectacle lenses rotate, distorting vision. I have managed to get some lightweight helmets that leave the ears completely uncovered, thus allowing the spectacle stems to sit undisturbed in their natural position over the tops of the ears. Some people choose to use protective goggles only, but my fear here is that a stray stone could do untold damage to the rest of the occupant's head and face. Without a helmet, driving in even a gentle drizzle is an exquisite torture, as each raindrop is like a burning needle piercing through unprotected skin. An unexpected benefit of using a helmet that doesn't cover the ears is that the exhaust music can be more readily heard. Choosing the right helmet, and using it, will make your life much more comfortable, entertaining and safer.

Lightweight, flexible, water- and wind-proof jackets and trousers are essential if the X-BOW is to be used regularly in the non-summer months. Likewise gloves and a scarf. I have also bought electrically heated vests (made by Exo 2) for driver and passenger, and electrically heated gloves for the passenger, which plug into the 12-volt power outlet socket in the passenger footwell. These items of heated clothing are really great, and make the X-BOW much more usable during the colder months of the year. When the car is garaged, I attach a battery tender to the 12-volt power outlet socket to maintain the battery in the best possible condition.

The KTM X-BOW is a rare and expensive hand-built car. Only about 1300 units currently exist. This means that every temporary custodian of every X-BOW has a responsibility to drive, garage, service and repair these cars with due respect. I always allow the car's engine oil to reach its full operating temperature (the coolant temperature climbs much more quickly, but is less relevant) before using all the available revs, and always allow the engine plenty of time to idle after a hard run before turning off the engine, so as to prevent heat soak from damaging the turbocharger bearings. These cars need a regular exercise schedule, even in the winter, though not on salt-laden roads. Leaving an X-BOW sitting idle on a battery tender for long periods risks drying out the seals, and seizure of mechanical components. I exercise my cars every

six weeks, all year round. Each time a car is woken up part way through its winter slumber, it needs to be fully warmed up (at the least, I wait until the radiator fans start up, which in the winter can take up to twenty minutes). This is necessary because for every litre of petrol used in a car's engine, one litre of water is produced, which will stay within the car's system until it evaporates. Once a car is started up, it is therefore highly desirable that sufficient heat is generated within its drive-train to evaporate away this water. There is probably nothing worse for a car than just starting it up, and allowing it to idle for five minutes half way through its hibernation. I keep my cars in a dehumidified garage to avoid the elements. During long-term winter storage, I use a battery tender and I hyperinflate the tyres to avoid, or at least minimise, flat spots. Every week, I also hand roll the car forwards or backwards a few inches within the garage, so that the same wheel bearings and the same tyre contact patch do not have to support the weight of the car for an extended period. I do this without starting the car's engine, so that unwanted water is not produced.

What is most striking about living with, and driving, the KTM X-BOW is its sheer Herculean solidity. It looks robust, and it is. Much criticism was levelled at KTM when the X-BOW's specification details were first released, because the press and potential owners felt that such an expensive road-racer, with a carbon fibre chassis, should be a lot lighter. But in terms of build quality, the X-BOW exists on a totally different plane to its competitor track-day rivals. I have been privileged to drive a variety of sports cars and lightweight track-biased road-racers, but the first time I drove an X-BOW, I was blown away by its absolute composure. The X-BOW felt like a roofless version of the W124 Mercedes saloons of the 1980s. I have driven hundreds of thousands of miles in W124s over the last two decades, and this comparison is the biggest compliment that I can give the X-BOW, with regards to its build quality.

Mr Toad of *The Wind in the Willows* fame, was almost certainly referring to the KTM X-BOW when he uttered his celebrated quote: "A most unusual car."

The pertinent and pressing question is whether it is really just a car. Yes, it is a car, but it is also so much more than just a car. It can, and should, be appreciated on many different levels to fully understand and enjoy it. It is a racing car for the road, and a road car that can excel on track. It is a byword for carbon fibre and aerodynamics. It was the world's first production car with a full carbon composite monocoque. It is an aesthetic masterpiece, created by a near genius working in an almost mythical land, where 'designing desire' is not only allowed, but positively encouraged. It was brought to life by the virtually unlimited monetary resources of an industrial giant steeped in motorsport, who demanded that it be technologically cutting-edge. It was honed to perfection by, arguably, the finest racing car engineers in the world, for whom 'best in class' was a minimum requirement. It is an objet d'art that can race in anger, or can transport in style: it startles, it fascinates, it wins. We are lucky that this most unusual car, the KTM X-BOW, exists in our lifetime.

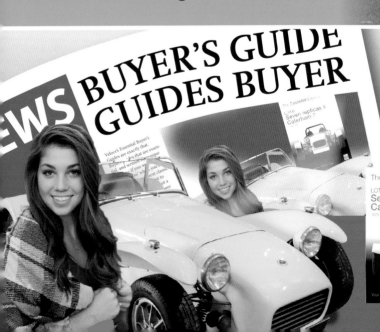